HANDS-ON
PHONICS
ACTIVITIES
FOR
Elementary
Children

KAREN MEYERS STANGL

Illustrations by Deborah C. Wright

JOSSEY-BASS
A Wiley Imprint
www.josseybass.com

5050301086002

Published by Jossey-Bass
A Wiley Imprint
989 Market Street, San Francisco, CA 94103-1741   www.josseybass.com

Jossey-Bass books and products are available through most bookstores. To contact Jossey-Bass directly call our Customer Care Department within the U.S. at (800) 956-7739, outside the U.S. at (317) 572-3986 or fax (317) 572-4002.

Jossey-Bass also publishes its books in a variety of electronic formats. Some content that appears in print may not be available in electronic books.

Library of Congress Cataloging-in-Publication Data

Stangl, Karen Meyers
Hands-on Phonics Activities for Elementary Children / Karen Meyers Stangl; illustrations by Deborah C. Wright.
    p. cm.
    Includes bibliographical references.
    ISBN 0-87628-490-X
    1. Reading—Phonetic method. 2. Education, Elementary—Activity programs. I. Title.
LB1573.3.S72 2000
372.46'5—dc21   99-36920
                                          CIP

Acknowledgments

I would like to thank my mother, Laura Meyers, for her hours of proofreading, as well as the many dinners she provided so that I could keep working without stopping for the mundane chore of cooking!

I would also like to acknowledge Charlie Sinche and Julie Perkin for their patient help and encouragement with all of my computer trials and tribulations!

I would especially like to acknowledge the illustrator, Deborah Wright, for all of her hard work in helping me put this book together!

About the Author

Karen Meyers Stangl received her B.A. in Education from the State University of New York at Oneonta. As a classroom teacher for the last 22 years, she has taught grades 1 through 6. She has been active on many committees, involved in writing and editing a variety of curriculum materials, and has taught staff-development seminars. She has participated in activities for the gifted and has been lead teacher for a program designed for at-risk students. She is currently working as a first-grade teacher at the Anne E. Moncure Elementary School in Stafford, Virginia.

About This Book

Children must use a variety of tools to understand written language. Reading can be divided into two major components: decoding and comprehension. The decoding process can be subdivided into phonics, structural analysis, sight words, and context clues. Decoding skills are necessary tools to help readers identify unfamiliar words; however, just teaching students word-attack skills in isolation does not make a reader. As the end result we seek success in comprehension, we do not want the children to become bogged down with the task of decoding. We need to be sure that while we are providing instruction in these skills, the students are also developing a positive self image so that they see themselves as readers! The best way to do this is to teach the decoding skills in the context of meaningful learning experiences. Letter-sound knowledge should be tied to the child's experiential background. Children should be immersed in language and surrounded by books. They should be provided with a wide variety of materials.

This book provides hands-on phonics activities to take your students through the developmental steps toward becoming good readers. The ideas are instructional, enjoyable, and rich in children's literature.

The book is divided into four sections:

- **Hands-on Phonics Activities for Pre-Readers (Grades K–1)**—Activities are provided to develop knowledge of the alphabet and phonemic awareness. These activities are interwoven in all areas of the curriculum. Tactile activities support the visual skills needed to identify the letters. Additional activities, such as sound sorting, cooking, mini-field trips, and interviews support beginning sound knowledge. Exciting ideas are provided for the classroom teacher, or specialist, to reinforce decoding skills in the context of meaningful learning.

- **Hands-on Phonics Activities for Emerging Readers (Grades 1–2)**—Ideas are provided for individual, small group, or whole class instruction. These activities can be used to introduce, supplement, and reinforce specific phonics skills. There are sorting and manipulative activities, puzzles, and games. Many ideas are presented for simple activity cards that can be done independently.

- **Hands-on Phonics Activities for Developing Readers (Grades 2–5)**—Activities are presented to continue the teaching of phonics to developing readers. Many sorting activities, puzzles and games are provided that can be used as presented, or modified to meet the specific needs of the students. Task cards are provided for independent work.

- **Lists for Developing Hands-on Phonics Activities**—Book lists are provided to assist the teacher in choosing authentic literature to reinforce sound awareness. The word lists enable the instructional activities to be modified to meet the specific needs of the students.

These activities are described in detail on the opening page of each section. Also included in this book are reproducible forms, patterns, gameboards, and phonics rules in the Appendix.

Enjoy the delightful activities and illustrations to introduce your students to the wonderful world of letters and their sounds!

Karen Meyers Stangl

Contents

Section Three:
Hands on Phonics Activities for Developing Readers (Grades 2-5)

Section Four:
Lists for Developing Hands-on Phonics Activities

Section Five:
Appendix

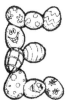

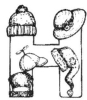

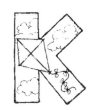

Section One

Hands-on Phonics Activities for Pre-Readers

(Grades K–1)

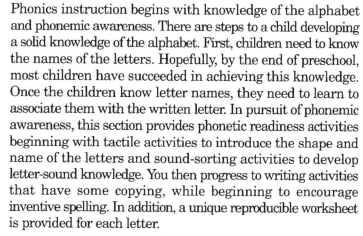

Phonics instruction begins with knowledge of the alphabet and phonemic awareness. There are steps to a child developing a solid knowledge of the alphabet. First, children need to know the names of the letters. Hopefully, by the end of preschool, most children have succeeded in achieving this knowledge. Once the children know letter names, they need to learn to associate them with the written letter. In pursuit of phonemic awareness, this section provides phonetic readiness activities beginning with tactile activities to introduce the shape and name of the letters and sound-sorting activities to develop letter-sound knowledge. You then progress to writing activities that have some copying, while beginning to encourage inventive spelling. In addition, a unique reproducible worksheet is provided for each letter.

The activities provided are interwoven in all areas of the curriculum. They are meant to enhance and supplement the present early childhood curriculum. They are not meant to be used in sequence or in total. You should evaluate the needs of the students and utilize the appropriate activities.

Following is the organization for each of the alphabet units covered in this section:

Tactile Introduction of Letter

The letter activities begin with a tactile experience to introduce the letter shape and name to children who do not have this knowledge. Have letter patterns available for the children to trace and cut, or the letters can be pre-cut on a die-cutter. After introducing the letter shape and its corresponding name and sound, the children can then cover the letter in one of the materials suggested. The letters can then be mounted on tagboard and taken home to share, or used as a focal point for a bulletin board or a sound table. After placing their letters on the sound table, the children are then encouraged to bring in items from home that begin with that particular sound.

Letters can also be provided in other textures—sandpaper, textured fabrics, and sponge letters. Children can also be encouraged to trace these letters with their fingers. They may want to dip the sponge letters in paint for printing. Pipe cleaners can be provided to bend into the correct shape. You may also want to provide a small box lid filled with sand in which the children write letters. Templates to trace the letters provide yet another tactile experience. When several letters have been introduced, a partner game can be played where one child keeps both eyes closed, feels a letter picked out by the partner, and attempts to identify it correctly.

Alphabet puzzles provide another tactile experience to introduce the sound of the letter. Some suggestions are given for you to prepare cards for each letter of the alphabet by thinking of an object that begins with each letter. Draw the outline of each object on a piece of posterboard and cut it out. Cut the outline into puzzle pieces and write the appropriate letter on each. Put all the puzzle pieces into a manila envelope and write the letter on the outside. Children can then put the puzzle together as an individual activity.

All of these tactile activities support the visual skills of identifying the letters, which is a prerequisite to all phonic development.

Sound Sorting

Both group and individual sound-sorting activities are presented to reinforce beginning sound knowledge. In addition, room labels are suggested. It is important to create a print-rich environment in the classroom. After introducing the letter sound, you may ask the children what they see in the classroom that begins with that particular letter. With the children watching, write the word on a 3 x 5 index card and label the appropriate object. These labels can be left in place all year and used for a quick reading activity whenever there are a few extra minutes during the day.

Oral Language

Oral language is an extremely important part of internalizing letter-sound knowledge. Suggested oral sharing activities are provided to help children develop good listening and speaking skills.

Cooking and Tasting

Cooking is an enjoyable and educational experience for children. Not only does it offer a way to introduce or reinforce letter sounds, but when a recipe is written in chart form, it can be used to teach the skill of sequencing. When you label ingredients and provide picture directions, children can "read" the recipe with a minimum of assistance. As an added bonus, math measurement skills can be interwoven.

Mini Field Trips

Field trips are an excellent motivational and learning tool. As the number of field trips is usually limited, many of the trips suggested can be taken in the school building itself, in other county schools, or to local businesses. In preparation for the trips, you should elicit questions the children would like answered. Post these on a chart and read before leaving for the trip. After returning, the questions should be answered orally. The responses may then be written under the questions on the chart. A field trip form is provided in the Appendix for use as a possible follow-up activity. Classroom stories and appropriate thank-you notes may also be written.

Interviews

Classroom interviews are an excellent way of forming a learning partnership with area businesses as well as with parents. Interviews can be an interesting way of introducing or reinforcing the initial consonant sounds. Many reading skills can be developed during preparation for classroom interviews. Have the children develop questions they would like to ask the visitor and post these questions on a chart. After the visit, write a classroom story about what the children learned. Don't forget to have the children send a group thank-you note as a literacy extension activity.

Literature and Writing

Any meaningful phonics instruction should be presented in an environment rich in children's literature. Many ideas are suggested for individual writing activities based on authentic children's literature, including books and poems. Additional writing activities are included for appropriate classroom or individual books. You may develop additional activities using the book lists provided in the last section of the book.

Sight Vocabulary

Sight vocabulary is an important part of word-attack skills. Pre-primer and primer words are provided that can be introduced as appropriate. These words can be displayed on a chart in the room, sent home on word cards, and reviewed as needed.

Another strategy for vocabulary development is to display the selected words on a wall in the classroom. The *Word Wall* not only keeps words visible throughout the year, but it provides many opportunities for listening, speaking, reading, and writing activities. By cutting out the cards around the shape of the letters, the children are encouraged to focus on word structure.

There are many activities that can be done with the *Word Wall*.

1. **Rhyming Games:** Ask the students to find a word on the wall that rhymes with a given word.

2. **Reading the Room:** Provide the children with pointers. Have them work in pairs to go around the room and read the labels and the words on the *Word Wall*.

3. **Sentence Making:** Have the children develop sentences using the words on the *Word Wall*.

4. **Mystery Word:** You (or a student) select a Mystery Word and give clues for the children to guess the correct word. For example: (1.) It has four letters. (2.) It starts with *wh*. (3.) It is a question word. (4.) It has the *at* chunk in it.

5. **Cloze Sentences:** This is a variation of Mystery Word. You (or a student) give a sentence and leave out a word. The children must find a word on the *Word Wall* that makes sense in the sentence.

6. **Related Groups of Words:** As the children progress, suggest that the children find all the color words; plurals; contractions; words ending in *-ed* or *-ing*; pronouns, nouns, action words, adjectives; one-, two-, or three-syllable words; all compound words; words that can be put together to form compound words; words that have short or long *a, e, i, o,* or *u*; words that use the *at, ake, ed, ell, ot* chunks, etc.; words that have two vowels together; words with prefixes or suffixes.

7. **Classifying the Words on the *Word Wall:*** Have the children categorize the words on the wall: color words, number words, weather words, science words, happy words, sad words, things in a school, things in a store, things outside, things inside, things that make you laugh, action words, things that can move, etc.

8. **Writing Extension Activities:** The children can draw a picture and write a sentence using the words on the wall, write a riddle about a word on the wall, make up nonsense sentences, find words that can be changed to form new words by changing one letter, draw a picture and write down all the words on the wall that can describe it. Use your imagination!

Math

Many math activities lend themselves to reinforcing beginning sound knowledge. After the math activity, a group experience chart story may be written about the children's discoveries. In this way children have additional exposure to letter sounds and words.

Science and Social Studies

The more connections that are made across the curriculum, the quicker the students will begin to internalize the letter-sound associations. Social studies and science lend themselves well to activities that reinforce these concepts. A list of animals is provided at the beginning of this section. Children love animals! Investigating some of the animals listed is a great way to integrate science with the study of letter-sound correspondence. *K-W-L* charts are a great way to get started. First, list what the children think they know about a particular animal. Next, have them tell you what they would like to learn about the animal. Finally, after stories have been read and research has been done, go back and write down what the class has learned. There are many other extension activities you can do with this list, such as making animal puppets, working on the sounds the animals make, and their movements, etc. (Refer to the list of art activities and sorting games.) A variety of activities are provided so that you can choose activities that fit your specific curriculum requirements.

Art, Physical Education, and Music

More connections can be made through exciting special activities. These may be done by the classroom teacher or in coordination with the specialists in these areas. Chanting, singing, and physical activity all provide natural language experiences. Interaction with one another will strengthen the children's listening, speaking, and reading skills.

Activities for the Letter A

Tactile Introduction of the Letter

Letter Shape: Alphabits® (cereal); Animal Crackers®

Alphabet Puzzle: apple

Sound Sorting

Apple Basket: (Group Activity)

Gather the children in a circle around an apple basket. Discuss the uses of the basket and the first sound of the word *apple*. Let each child pull one item from the Mystery Box and tell what it is. If it begins with *a*, the child then places it in the apple basket. If it does not begin with *a*, it is placed back in the Mystery Box. After each child has had a turn, review each item in the apple basket with the group.

Apple Cutout: (Individual Activity)

Give each child a large apple cut from red construction paper. (See Apple Cutout Template provided.) Provide magazines for the children to use to find pictures beginning with the a sound. The children can paste the pictures they find on the apple cutout. If they can think of something for which they cannot find a picture, encourage them to draw the picture on their apple. When they have completed the pasting and drawing, let them add a stem and leaves to their apple with scraps of green and brown construction paper. These should be displayed around the room. Some can be displayed on a large classroom apple tree that you have made.

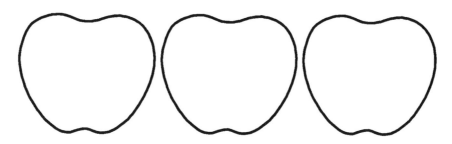

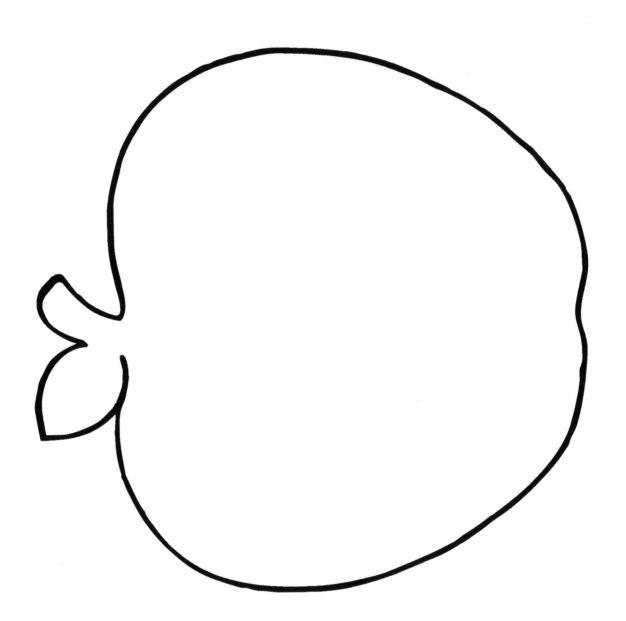

Apple Cutout Template

Adding Machine Tape: (Individual Activity or Pairs)

Each child (or pair) gets a long piece of adding machine tape. Show the children how to fold it into many boxes. In each box the children draw something that starts with the letter *a*. This can be done as a contest with an apple as the prize for the person who can think of the most *a* words.

Room Labels: alphabet; art supplies

Oral Language

Sharing:

The children can share their favorite kind of animal, or answer the question, "If you could be any kind of animal, what would you like to be? Why?"

Cooking and Tasting

Slow Cooker Applesauce:

Peel and slice 8–10 apples. Place in a slow cooker with 1/2 cup water, 1 teaspoon cinnamon, and 1/2 to 1 cup sugar. Cook on low overnight. If this is done as the last activity of the day, the children will have a tasty snack in the morning. If you would rather do it early in the morning, it can be eaten by late afternoon. It will be just as good, although a little bit chunkier, if it cooks less than eight hours.

Ants on a Log:

Each child spreads peanut butter on a small piece of celery (the log) and then places some raisins (the ants) on the peanut butter.

Alphabet Soup:

You will need several cans of alphabet soup. Give each child a piece of waxed paper. Open a can of soup and put a scoop of the condensed soup on each child's waxed paper. Provide plastic spoons for the children to separate the letters. See how many they can name. After that activity, water may be added to the rest of the cans of soup and the class can make Alphabet Soup for snack.

Other Possible A Foods: apple butter; apples; apricots; avocados; artichokes; asparagus; almonds

Mini Field Trips

athletic department of the local high school; apple orchard

Interviews

athlete; attorney; actor; actress

Literature & Writing

Authentic Literature & Related Writing Activity:

Read *Antarctica* by Helen Cowcher or *A Tale of Antarctica* by Ulco Glimmerveen. Make a classroom chart of how that continent is being destroyed. Elicit a list of ideas from the children on how to preserve Antarctica.

Poetry:

1. Read *The Alligator* by Mary MacDonald. Elicit a classroom sentence about alligators. The students copy the sentence and illustrate it. See "Art" for how to make clay alligators.

2. Read *Antarctic Antics: A Book of Penguin Poems* by Judy Sierra.

Additional Writing Activities:

1. Begin making individual booklets entitled *My ABC Book*. Each day the children can write the letter they are learning on the left side of the booklet and draw a picture of an appropriate object on the facing page. "A is for..."

2. *My Apple Book* is a great way to review adjectives, including the color words *red, green,* and *yellow*. Start by putting a big apple cut from construction paper in the front of the room. Give each child an apple and elicit as many adjectives as they can think of to describe the apples (hard, sweet, red, yellow, juicy, crunchy, etc.). Write these adjectives on the paper apple. Hand out blank booklets. The children draw an apple on each page and describe their apple in a complete sentence. "My apple is..." is written on the board and the children try to find the adjective they need on the classroom "Adjective Apple." (Example: *My apple is red. My apple is juicy.*)

3. See the "A Book List" for further appropriate literature ideas.

Sight Vocabulary

- **Pre-primer:** a; am; and; are; at; away
- **Primer:** about; across; afraid; again; all; an; apple; around; ask; ate

Math

Patterning:

1. This is a great time to introduce patterning. After a discussion on the different colors of apples, take a bag of each color apple and have the children make some patterns using the three colors. When they understand the concept, give each child some one-inch squares of construction paper cut from red, green, and yellow. Let the children work individually or in pairs to come up with some patterns. After they have checked their pattern with you, they can paste their squares on a strip of tagboard.

2. An enjoyable follow-up activity is to let each child paint a paper plate in one of the three colors. The children set their plate to dry with similar colors. When the plates are dry, the children can add leaves and a stem with scraps of green and brown paper. When everyone has an apple ready, the class decides on a pattern and the paper plate apples are displayed in that order either around the wall or on a bulletin board.

Classifying:

Apples lend themselves to classifying, comparing, and grouping by color, size, circumference, weight, and number of seeds.

Graphing:

Pictograph

Give each child a slice of each color apple to taste and a small apple cut out of drawing paper. The children then color their paper apple to match the color of the apple slice they liked best. These apples are then placed on the pictograph to determine which color apple was the classroom favorite. Other discoveries the children make can be written on chart paper to provide additional exposure to letter sounds and words.

Bar Graph

Ask the parents to send in a variety of apple desserts. Have a tasting party! Graph the children's favorite apple snack.

Measurement:

When you are making the applesauce, lots of opportunities present themselves to do some measuring. Obviously, the children are getting some experience with a variety of measuring devices, such as teaspoons, cups, etc. In addition, when you are peeling the apples, try to peel them in long pieces.

It is fun to have a contest with a couple of parents or teachers to see who can get the longest peel. To find the winner, of course, the peel must be measured!

Numerals:

Usually the words and numerals for the numbers are being taught at about the same time as the sound of the letter *a*. To correlate this instruction with your study of *a*, you can make several large apple halves. Draw a specific number of seeds in the apple (correlated to the numbers you are introducing) and make cards with the number words and the numerals. The children can match the cards to the correct apples. A smaller set can be made for an individual game.

Addition:

Do some hands-on addition with real apples. You can state the problem and pick a child to illustrate it concretely with the apples. If the children are ready, have individuals make up oral word problems about apples and choose a classmate to solve.

Subtraction:

Read *Mr. Brown's Apple Tree*, by Yvonne Winer. In this book someone steals one of Mr. Brown's apples every night. If you have prepared the apples as described in "Numerals," they can be used to have the children act out the story and learn the concept of subtraction at the same time.

Science & Social Studies

Living Things:

Animals: alligator; ant; antelope

Ant Farm

Provide an ant farm for the children to observe. Keep a chart of ant information.

Apples

Investigating apples is a great way to begin a study of plants. "How do we get an apple from a seed?" A diagram of an apple tree can be provided and the children can label the parts of the tree.

Alfalfa seeds

Alfalfa seeds can be grown on a moistened sponge. Place the sponge on a Styrofoam meat tray. (Most grocery stores will donate these to schools, if asked.) Water will need to be added to the meat tray daily.

Simple Machines:

The word *attraction* can be used to introduce a study of magnets. Provide a variety of magnets as well as various objects. Have the children experiment with the magnets. Keep a class chart of which objects the magnet attracts. See if the children discover a similarity in the objects attracted to the magnet.

Seasons:

After reading *The Seasons of Arnold's Apple Tree* by Gail Gibbons, give each child a long strip of light blue construction paper. Have them fold the paper in fourths. In each box an apple tree is drawn to represent one of the four seasons. For more fun, let the children sponge paint the trees in the appropriate colors for each season!

Art

Apple Prints:

Put out three meat trays of paint (red, yellow, green) and cut some apples in half. The children will dip the apple halves into the paint and make some prints. You can ask them to make a specific pattern if you wish. When these are dry, details can be added. Provide a green ink pad for the children to press their thumb on and add leaves to their apples. An old-fashioned clip clothespin (*not* the spring kind) can be dipped in black paint to make two seeds!

American Flags:

Give each child a 12" x 18" piece of white paper. They will paste 1" x 18" strips of red paper on the white. Add a 6" x 9" blue field. Let the children add self-sticking stars.

Clay Alligators:

Give each child a ball of green clay. Have the children roll the clay into a log. Show them how to pinch the surface with their thumb and pointer finger to make scales. Have them flatten out a head and "pull" out a tail. They can make eyes and texture by poking with a pencil.

Physical Education & Music

Games:

Pass the Apple

The children form two lines. The apple is passed under the chin from one child to the next. The first team to pass the apple to the last person wins!

Alphabet Bounce

A my name is *Alice* and

My husband's name is *Alex.*

We come from *Alabama*

To sell you *apples.*

Continue the rhyme for each letter. This game is played with the child bouncing a ball in rhythm. If the child is developmentally ready, the leg may be passed over the ball on the italic words. This continues through the alphabet!

Movement:

Alligator Walk

Have the children move across the room in a front-lying position with their weight on the lower arms. They will need to drag their feet behind them.

Music:

"The Ants Go Marching…"

All children love to sing "The Ants Go Marching…" to the tune of "When Johnny Comes Marching Home." Teach this song on the same day the children make Ants on a Log!

The ants go marching one by one, hurrah, hurrah!

The ants go marching one by one, hurrah, hurrah!

The ants go marching one by one—

The little one stops to suck his thumb

And they all go marching down into the ground.

(Repeat nine times with necessary changes listed below or have children make up their own rhymes!)

two:	the little one stops to tie his shoe
three:	the little one stops to see the tree
four:	the little one stops to shut the door
five:	the little one stops to see the hive
six:	the little one stops to pick up sticks
seven:	the little one stops to point to heaven
eight:	the little one stops to shut the gate
nine:	the little one stops to pick up a dime
ten:	the little one stops to pet the hen

Name:_____

Andy's room is a mess!

1. Circle the objects with a short "a" sound.
2. Color the objects with a long "a" sound.

USE YOUR NOODLE: Draw 5 things that begin with "A" on the back of this page.

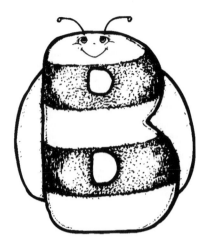

Activities for the Letter B

Tactile Introduction of the Letter

Letter Shape: beans; buttons; blue glitter

Alphabet Puzzle: bat; bus

Sound Sorting

Big Brown Bag: (Group Activity)

Gather the children in a circle on the floor. Show the children a big brown grocery bag. Elicit from the children what this object is. With a brown marker write "BIG BROWN BAG" on the outside of the bag, emphasizing the sound of the letter *b*. Place the Mystery Box on the floor. Let each child pull one item from the box and tell the class what it is. If it begins with a *b*, then the child places that item in the "BIG BROWN BAG." If it does not begin with a *b*, it is placed back in the Mystery Box. After each child has had a turn, review each item in the "BIG BROWN BAG" with the group.

Little Brown Bag: (Individual Activity)

Give each child a brown lunch bag and a magazine. Each child writes his or her name on the bag with a brown crayon. They also write a capital letter *B* on the bag. The children then cut out pictures that begin with the letter *b* and put them in the bag. This bag can be taken home and shared with parents and/or siblings that evening.

Room Labels: blackboard; bulletin board; blocks; books; bookcase; blue; black and brown brushes

Oral Language

Sharing:

The children can share stuffed bears, "Beanie® Babies," baby pictures, or their favorite book in a Show & Tell format.

Cooking and Tasting

Bread and Butter:

Pour heavy cream into a Tupperware™ container and seal tightly. Have the children sit in a circle and take turns shaking the container. When the cream turns to butter, give each child a slice of party bread. Have plastic knives available to spread the butter.

Other Possible B Foods: bananas; biscuits; berries; butterscotch candy; bologna

Mini Field Trips

bakery; school cafeteria on baking day; local bank

Interviews

baker; banker; builder; body builder; beautician; businessperson; bus driver

This is a great time to have the school bus driver come in and talk about bus safety!

Literature & Writing

Big Books:

This is a great time to introduce kids to Big Books! Hopefully this will be the beginning of a daily use of Big Books to reinforce the phonetic concepts being taught.

Authentic Literature & Related Writing Activity:

Read *Brown Bear, Brown Bear What Do You See?* by Bill Martin, Jr. Read once through for enjoyment. (This can be done on the day *b* is introduced or just prior to the writing activity.) When the story is reread, emphasize the *b* sound. When the children are ready for the writing activity, ask them if they would like to make their own class Brown Bear Book! Give each child a sheet of white paper on which to draw whatever imaginary animal they would like. Tell them to make the illustration big and colorful like the ones they have seen in Bill Martin's book. When they are done, have each child tell you what they "saw" (a purple kangaroo, a green cat, etc.). You then write the story on their papers using the same format as the original book. Choose one child to illustrate a cover on construction paper. If individual photos are available, it is fun to use actual pictures of you and the children for the last few pages of the book. After the book is laminated and bound, the children will enjoy reading it together or using it individually during sustained silent reading time.

Poetry: Read "Banananananananana" by William Cole. Serve bananas as a snack!

Additional Writing Activities:

1. Continue the individual *My ABC Book*, "B is for…"
2. The children might like to make a *Beautiful Babies Book*. Each child has an individual page with his or her baby picture pasted in the middle of a page. Underneath they carefully print their name. It is fun to include your baby picture! (Photostat photos that may need

to be returned.) When this is laminated and bound, the children can use it over and over.

3. See the "B Book List" for further appropriate literature ideas.

Sight Vocabulary

- **Pre-primer:** baby; be; big; boy
- **Primer:** back; ball; barn; bird; black; blue; box; bread; brown; but; by

Math

Patterning:

Attribute Blocks (Group Activity)

Divide the class into small groups and give each group a set of attribute blocks. The children will try to copy the patterns you make on the overhead projector. (Pattern cards can be made by tracing the attribute blocks on the correct colored construction paper and gluing them on strips of tagboard. These can be laminated and then used over and over again for individual activities.)

Stringing Beads (Individual Activity)

Give each child two colors of beads. Tell the children to string the beads into a pattern. They should be able to tell you the pattern they have chosen (for example red blue red blue = abab pattern; red blue blue = abb pattern, etc.).

Classifying:

Buttons: Buttons can be classified by size, shape, color, number of holes, etc.

Graphing:

Pictograph

An early opportunity to introduce graphing presents itself during the study of the letter *b*. Display the Class Birthday Pictograph. Explain that it will be used all year. On his or her birthday, each child will have an opportunity to put a candle next to the correct month. (The back of a piece of wallpaper is great to make this graph! Laminate it and you can use it for several years.)

Bar Graph

To make a graph of the children's favorite breakfast foods, place a blank bar graph on the overhead projector. Ask the children to name some breakfast foods. Label the columns with the food names. Call each child to fill in the next box above his or her favorite breakfast food with a marker. When the graph is completed, ask appropriate questions. (Example: "Which food did most children prefer?" "How many children liked pancakes the best?" etc.) This is a good opportunity to discuss proper nutrition.

Measurement:

Demonstrate how to use a balance. Have a variety of objects available to weigh. Hold up two objects and ask the children to predict which will be heavier. Use the balance to see if they were correct. Have the children place an object, such as a pencil, on one side of the balance and guess how many Unifix™ cubes it will take to balance. Let them test their predictions.

Addition:

You will need a bag of brown pinto beans and a black marker. Color one side of the beans with the marker. Divide the children into groups of two. Give each pair a small paper cup containing five or six beans. One child shakes the cup and dumps out the beans. The other child writes the appropriate addition problem on a sheet of paper (for example: 3 black beans + 2 brown beans = 5 beans.) Let the children see how many different combinations they can come up with. As the children advance in their math skill, other beans can be added to do three and four addend problems, while reviewing the related consonants and consonant blends.

Geometry: See *Beautiful Blobs* under "Art."

Science & Social Studies

Air and Water:

Blowing Bubbles

Make each child a bubble blower by cutting out the bottom of a paper cup. In shallow pans, such as pie tins, mix liquid detergent with a little bit of water. The children then dip the bottom of the cup into the mixture and blow gently. They'll get some *big bubbles!* This can be used as a springboard into a science unit on air.

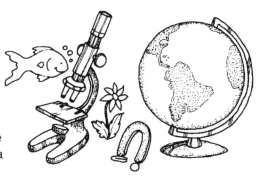

Living Things:

Animals: bear; beaver; bee

Bird Feeder

After taking a "bird walk," let the children make these simple bird feeders. Give each child a paper plate, a pine cone with a piece of yarn attached, a small cup of peanut butter, and a plastic bag of birdseed. The children spread peanut butter (using their fingers or a plastic knife) on the pine cone and sprinkle it with seed. The pine cones will be tied to a tree in the school yard where the children can observe birds coming to feed.

Bug Boxes

Each child will need a shoe box for this activity. Before distributing the shoe boxes, cut a large window in the lid and cover from the inside with clear plastic wrap and tape. Help each child fit the bottom of the box with aluminum foil. Let the children fill their boxes halfway with dirt or potting soil. When the boxes are ready, the children go on a "bug hunt." Each child looks around the designated area outside and finds ants, rolly pollys, etc. When each child has carefully placed some bugs in his or her box, it is time to go inside and discuss what else the bugs need for survival. Using jar lids the children can add water to the bug habitat and later some leaves, pieces of potato, etc. Let the children observe the bugs over the next few days and then release them back into their natural habitat.

Nutrition: See *Bar Graph* under "Math"

Art

Brown Bear:

Give each child a 9" x 12" piece of brown construction paper. Make a bear pattern for the children to share. After the children trace and cut out their bear, let them add *b* details, such as a blue bow, black hair or eyebrows, button eyes, etc.

Beautiful Blobs:

Give each child a sheet of white paper and have them fold the paper in half. Set out three or four margarine tubs of watered-down tempera paints of various bright colors. Put an eye dropper or a straw in each tub. Let the children drop "blobs" of paint on one side of the paper only. Quickly have them fold the paper and rub their hand across the top. When they open their papers, they will have beautiful (symmetrical) blobs! (This can also be used as a math activity when introducing symmetry in the geometry strand.)

Physical Education & Music

Games:

Beanbag Toss: Children take turns tossing beanbags into a wastebasket.

Beanbag Balance Relay Race

Divide the children into teams. The object is to run a relay race while balancing a beanbag on a body part. For example, the children might balance the beanbag on their head during one race, forearm the next, top of the foot, etc. If the beanbag falls off the designated body part, the child must go back and start over.

Balloon Blow

Divide children into teams for a relay race. Everyone is given a drinking straw. The lead children get on their knees and are given balloons. They must blow through a straw to move the balloon to a designated point. Then they run back with the balloon and give it to the next person in line. The first team to complete the race is the winner. (This is another good activity for a science unit on air.)

Button, Button, Who Has the Button?

The children sit in a circle. One child is "It" and sits in the middle of the circle with his or her eyes closed. The children then pass the button until time is called. The child who is "It" has three chances to guess who has the button. If he or she guesses correctly, the child with the button becomes "It." If he or she does not guess correctly, you pick a new child to be "It."

Movement:

B Animal Movement Game

Pick a child who has thought of an animal that begins with the letter *b*. The child whispers it in your ear. If the child is correct, you then tell the child to pantomime the animal's movement.

When someone guesses correctly, the whole class mimics the movement. Another child is then chosen and the game continues. (Examples: butterfly; bumblebee; bear; buffalo; bird; bunny; etc.)

Creative Movement

The children can do some shadow boxing! Try having them pretend to be a balloon slowly being blown up and getting bigger and bigger. Next—let them go! How about blowing them up until they burst? How about moving like a baby?

Bending

Explore with the children different ways the body can bend. Bend individual parts of the body separately, several parts at a time, bend forward, backward, sideways, etc.

Music:

"Boa Constrictor Song"

This song is sung by Peter, Paul and Mary on their *Peter, Paul and Mommy* album. Children love to sing this song about a boa constrictor swallowing more and more of the singer! In addition to reinforcing the *b* sound in boa constrictor, this song also mentions various body parts, which lends itself to movement activities, as well as a science/anatomy lesson.

Chants & Rhymes

"Blue Bird, Blue Bird"

Blue bird, blue bird, in and out my window,

Blue bird, blue bird, in and out my window,

Blue bird, blue bird, in and out my window,

Oh, Johnny, I am tired.

Take a little bird and tap him (her) on the shoulder,

Take a little bird and tap him (her) on the shoulder,

Take a little bird and tap him (her) on the shoulder,

Oh, Johnny, I am tired.

The children form a circle, join hands, and raise arms to form arches. The "blue bird" stands outside the circle. As the children sing, the "blue bird" weaves in and out of the arches. On "Take a little bird and tap him (her) on the shoulder," the "blue bird" taps another child on the shoulders. When the first verse begins again, both children weave in and out. Play continues until all the children have been tapped.

Additional B Songs

- "Baa Baa Black Sheep"
- "Baby Beluga" by Raffi

Name:_____

Which path should Betsy Bear follow to find her basket?

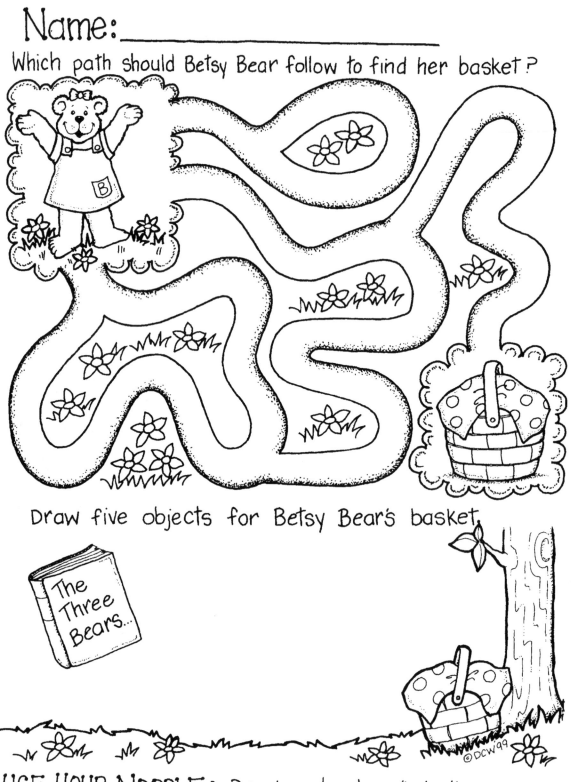

Draw five objects for Betsy Bear's basket.

The Three Bears...

© DCW 99

USE YOUR NOODLE: Draw and color 4 balloons on the back of this page.

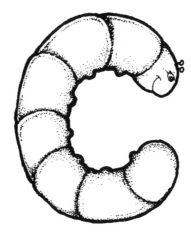

Activities for the Letter C

Tactile Introduction of the Letter

Letter Shape: cotton; cornmeal; corduroy; clay

Alphabet Puzzle: cat; car

Sound Sorting

Cafeteria Can: (Group Activity)

Gather the children in a circle on the floor. Show the children an industrial-sized can (from the school cafeteria). Elicit from the children what this object is and what sound it starts with. Write *can* on the outside of the can before you continue. Place the Mystery Box on the floor. Let each child pull one item from the box and tell the class what it is. If it begins with a *c*, then the child places that item in the "Cafeteria Can." If it does not begin with a *c*, it is placed back in the Mystery Box. After each child has had a turn, review each item in the "Cafeteria Can" with the group.

Campbell's® Soup Can: (Individual Activity)

Give each child an empty, clean, Campbell's® soup can and a magazine. Instruct the children to circle the letter *C* in *Campbell's®*. The children then cut out pictures that begin with the letter *c* and put them in the can. This can may then be taken home and shared with parents and/or siblings that evening.

Room Labels: clock; crayons; calendar; computer; color chart

Oral Language

Sharing:

The children can draw a picture of something in their favorite color and share with the class.

Cooking and Tasting

Cookies:

Provide a different kind of cookie each day that the class is studying *c*. At the end of the week, graph the children's favorite kind of cookie.

Other Possible C Foods: carrots; crackers; cupcakes; corn muffins; carrot salad; cole slaw; cocoa

Mini Field Trips

cafeteria; computer lab; custodian's office

Interviews

college student; computer programmer; school computer technician; custodian; cook; carpenter; contractor; clerk

Literature & Writing

Authentic Literature & Related Writing Activity:

Read *The Very Hungry Caterpillar* by Eric Carle. Read once through for enjoyment. (This can be done on the day *c* is introduced or just prior to the writing activity.) When the story is reread, emphasize the *c* sound. To make a classroom caterpillar, give each child a circle cut from construction paper. Let the children draw a picture of something that starts with *c* (or find magazine pictures) and have them write the word under the picture. You may need to write the word for those children who are not developmentally ready to do this. Attach the finished circles and add a head to form a classroom caterpillar.

Poetry

Read "The Caterpillar" by Christina Rossetti. (See *Sing a Song of Popcorn*, by De Regniers) Have the children make caterpillars out of brown pompons—and add squiggly eyes! Paste onto a small branch.

Additional Writing Activities

1. Continue the individual *My ABC Book*, "C is for…"
2. After reading *Hi, Cat!* by Ezra Jack Keats, have each child dictate what he or she thinks would happen the next day. After writing what they dictate, let the children illustrate their page and bind into a classroom book.
3. Making a class cookbook can be fun. Ask each parent to send in his or her child's favorite recipe. Let each child decorate the recipe from home. Make enough copies to make a cookbook for each child to bring home. (This makes a great Christmas present.)
4. See the "C Book List" for further appropriate literature ideas.

Caterpillar Head

Sight Vocabulary

- **Pre-primer:** can; car; come; cat; cap
- **Primer:** cake; call; came; chair; children; clock; could; cover

Math

Graphing:

Pictograph

Prepare a floor graph with the types of cookies that were served during the study of *c*. Give each child a small circle to decorate as the cookie he or she liked the best. Let each child come up and place the circle in the corresponding column on the graph. Discuss the results and write the discoveries on a chart.

Bar Graph: Graphs can be made for favorite colors, cars, etc.

Telling Time:

This might be a good time to introduce clocks. Let the children make clocks out of paper plates. Attach hands with a brass fastener and let the children work on telling time to the hour.

Counting:

Many counting activities can be done. Depending on the readiness of the children, you may want to have them practice counting forwards, backwards, by two's, by five's, or by ten's.

Addition:

Ask the parents to send in old decks of cards. (These need not be complete decks!) Remove any face cards and jokers. The children can work individually or in pairs to pick two cards, write an addition problem, and solve it by counting.

Science & Social Studies

Living Things:

Animals: cat; crabs; crickets; crocodile

Crystals:

Rock Candy

Boil two cups of sugar with one cup of water until the sugar dissolves. Tie a string to a pencil and suspend it over a glass. Pour the cooled syrup into the glass. Crystals will form on the string. (This should be observed for several weeks.)

Health:

To reinforce the idea of covering your mouth when you cough, give each child a paper plate to make into a face. Provide crayons, yarn for hair, etc. Give each child a tissue to glue over the mouth.

Community: Now is a good time to introduce the concept of community and community helpers.

Character Education:

Cooperation

Courage

Art

C Collage:

Explain what a collage is. Provide catalogs, old workbooks, magazines, scraps of material and ribbon, scissors, and glue. Have the children make a class collage of things that begin with *c*.

Sand Castles:

Mix 6 cups of sand with one cup of wallpaper paste. Add water until it forms a doughy consistency. Give each child a paper cup to pack with this mixture. Turn out onto waxed paper and let the children decorate with flags, etc. This will harden overnight.

Physical Education & Music

Games:

Concentration

Prepare a series of cards with pictures of objects that start with *c*. Make matching cards with the word for the object. Divide the children into pairs. Have them place their cards face down on the floor. The first child turns over two cards. If they match, the child puts the cards in his or her pile. If

they do not match, the cards are turned face down again. Play continues until all cards are paired. The winner is the child with the most cards in his or her pile.

Movement:

Creative Movement

Have the children be crazy cats! They can stretch, crawl, pounce, scratch, creep, and curl up and sleep!

Crab Walk

The children squat down and take their weight on their hands and feet without letting their bottom touch the floor. Have them walk forward and backward.

Music

Chants & Rhymes

Who Stole the Cookie from the Cookie Jar?

ALL:	Who stole the cookie from the cookie jar?
STUDENT #1:	Mary stole the cookie from the cookie jar.
MARY:	Who me?
ALL:	Yes, you!
MARY:	Couldn't be!
ALL:	Then who?
MARY:	Billy stole the cookie from the cookie jar.

Students sit in a circle and one student begins by naming someone else in the class. The game is repeated until everyone has had a turn.

Name: _____

Say each picture name. Write the beginning
sound. Color each picture. On the back draw
3 colorful and crazy cats.

Activities for the Letter D

Tactile Introduction of the Letter

Letter Shape: dish detergent

Alphabet Puzzle: dog; duck

Sound Sorting

Duffel Bag: (Group Activity)

Gather the children in a circle around a duffel bag. Discuss the uses of a duffel bag and the first sound of the word *duffel*. Let each child pull one item from the Mystery Box and tell what it is. If it begins with *d*, the child then places it in the duffel bag. If it does not begin with *d*, it is placed back in the Mystery Box. After each child has had a turn, review each item in the duffel bag with the group.

Beware of the Dog: (Individual Activity)

Give each child a sheet of drawing paper and a smaller rectangle cut from brown construction paper. Show the children how to fold along one of the long edges of the brown paper and paste that edge on the drawing paper to make a door. They can add a doorknob to complete the door. Have the children write *Beware of the Dog* on the outside of the door. They then "open" the door and draw a scary dog behind it!

Room Labels: desk; dictionary; door; drawer

Oral Language

Sharing:

Have a "dog day" when children who have dogs can bring in a picture of their dog (or the actual dog, if possible) and tell about their pet. (If the actual pet is brought to class, be sure there is adult supervision.)

Cooking and Tasting

Decorated Doughnut Deckers: Split doughnuts. Top each half with cream cheese and decorate with sprinkles!

Other Possible D Foods: dates; Devil's food cake; deviled eggs; dill pickles; divinity drops; drop cookies; dumplings; dunks for veggies or fruit

Mini Field Trips

dairy; dairy department at the supermarket; dinosaur exhibit

Interviews

dads; dentist; doctor; dog trainer; police K-9 officer

Literature & Writing

Authentic Literature & Related Writing Activity:

1. Read *Doctor DeSoto* by William Steig. Make a chart on dental care.
2. Read *The Doorbell Rang* by Pat Hutchins. Using packages of chocolate chip cookie dough, demonstrate the steps in making cookies. Make a chart of the directions. Work in small groups to prepare the cookies.

Poetry: Read "December" from *Chicken Soup With Rice* by Maurice Sendak.

Additional Writing Activities:

1. Continue the individual *My ABC Book*, "D is for…"
2. After reading some books about dogs, such as *Harry the Dirty Dog* by Gene Zion, have each student draw a dog and dictate a story about it. Bind into a classroom *Dogs* book.
3. Children love dinosaurs! After reading some appropriate books to the class, divide the children into groups and let each group pick a favorite dinosaur to write about. Give the children large sheets of tagboard to draw the dinosaur or you may wish to copy the Dinosaur Templates pages that are provided here. Make sure they draw it in an appropriate habitat. These can be labeled, or you can add text about the specific dinosaur chosen. Bind into a classroom Big Book.
4. See the "D Book List" for further appropriate literature ideas.

Sight Vocabulary

- **Pre-primer:** did; dog; down
- **Primer:** day; dinner; do; doll; door

Dinosaur Template

Dinosaur Template

Math

Patterning: Let the children make patterns with picture dominoes.

Classifying: Plastic dinosaurs are available that can be sorted by size, color, etc.

Measurement: Introduce the concept of *dozen* by giving each child an egg carton and letting the children fill the depressions with twelve objects.

Money: This is a great time to introduce dimes and counting by ten's. If the children are ready, they can be taught that ten *dimes* equal one *dollar!*

Addition: Besides using dominoes to match and count numbers, the children can use them to make up addition problems.

Science & Social Studies

Living Things:

Animals: deer; dinosaur; dog; donkey; duck

Dinosaur Dioramas

After reading several books on dinosaurs (see "D Book List"), give each child a shoe box. Have the children cover the bottom with sand or dirt and decorate the inner sides of the box with trees, volcanoes, etc. They can make dinosaurs out of clay to add to their box.

Safety:

Danger!

This is a perfect time to discuss safety. Not only can you discuss various dangers (poisons, strangers, etc.), it is also a perfect opportunity to teach children about how to use the phone to obtain help by dialing 911. Use phones to role-play situations in which it might be necessary for a young child to dial 911. Make sure you discuss *inappropriate* times as well!

Character Education:

Dependability

Art

Dot-to-Dot Designs:

Using a little bit of paint on a brush, have the children run a finger across the brush to spray dots onto their paper. Show them how to connect the dots and color in the spaces formed to create unique designs.

Dragons:

Cut cardboard egg cartons in half lengthwise. Give each child a strip to be used as the body of the dragon. These can be painted and decorated to be made into Chinese dragons!

Doodles:

Give the children white paper and let them "doodle" with colored crayons. Doodling to different styles of music is fun!

Physical Education & Music

Games:

Duck, Duck, Goose: The traditional "Duck, Duck, Goose" game can be played or it can be adjusted to add other *d* words, such as *Dinosaur, Dinosaur, Lizard.*

Dizzy Relay

Divide the class into two groups. One half of the class become racers and the other half are the spotters. Racers are blindfolded and lined up along the starting line with their spotter behind them. On the signal, the spotters turn the racers around five times and point them in the direction of the finish line. The spotters do not tell the racers in which direction to run, but they do run "interference" for them so they don't run into trees or rocks! After someone wins by crossing the finish line, the spotters switch places with the racers.

Following Directions

A game can be made up of three- or four-step directions. Pair the children and let them tell each other "what to do." For example, "Walk to the blackboard, pick up the eraser, balance it on your head, and walk back to your seat."

Movement:

Dancing: Let the children dance to different types of music or move to different drum beats.

Music:

Suggested Songs
- "Darling Clementine"
- "Puff the Magic Dragon"

Name:_____

Draw 4 more ducks in the pond.

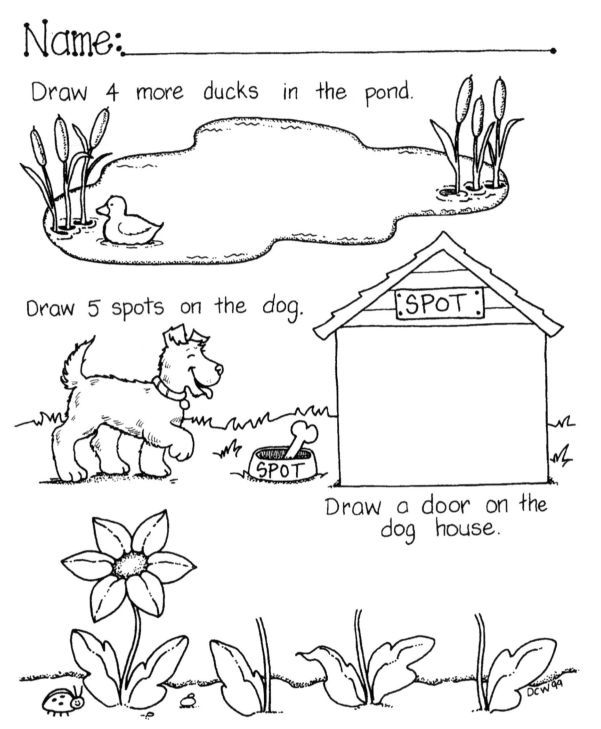

Draw 5 spots on the dog.

SPOT

SPOT

Draw a door on the dog house.

Draw 3 more daisies and 2 more bugs.

USE YOUR NOODLE: Danger! Beware of the dog! Draw a scary dog on the back of this paper.

Activities for the Letter E

Tactile Introduction of the Letter

Letter Shape: eggs shells (dyed and crushed); elbow macaroni

Alphabet Puzzle: egg

Sound Sorting

Ee Envelope: (Group Activity)

Gather the children in a circle around two large manila envelopes. One envelope is filled with a variety of pictures, including many that begin with the letter *e*. The other envelope is empty. Discuss the uses of envelopes and the first sound of the words *envelope* and *empty*. With a marker, draw a capital and a lower-case *e* on the empty envelope. Let each child pull one item from the picture envelope and tell what it is. If it begins with *e*, the child then places it in the *Ee* envelope. If it does not begin with *e*, it is put aside. After each child has had a turn, review each item in the *Ee* envelope with the group.

Ee Envelope: (Individual Activity)

Give each child a business envelope. Provide magazines for the children to use to find pictures beginning with the *e* sound. The children can place the pictures they find in their envelope. This envelope is then checked by you and sent home with the children.

Room Labels: easel; exit

Oral Language

Sharing:

Ask the children to bring in a photo of an exciting event in their lives. Tell them that the photo should be kept secret in an envelope until sharing time.

Cooking and Tasting

Egg Salad

Boil several eggs. Mix with mayonnaise and chopped celery. Serve on crackers. Make a sequence chart as you go along.

Eggs in a Nest

Give each child a slice of bread and let the children pinch out a circle in the middle. The bread is then buttered and placed on an electric griddle. Crack an egg into the hole and cook until firm.

Both recipes are great for a science lesson on changing physical characteristics with heat. Just be sure the recipes are done under adult supervision.

Other Possible E Foods: egg rolls; eclairs; eggnog; eggplant

Mini Field Trips

exhibit (school art show, art gallery, museum, historical society, etc.)

Interviews

engineer; exercise leader; electrician; energy specialist

Literature & Writing

Authentic Literature & Related Writing Activity:

Read *The Enormous Egg* by Brenda Parkes. Give each child an empty L'Eggs® container. Let them draw a picture of whatever they want to hatch from their egg and put it inside! A story about what is in the egg can then be dictated or written, depending on the ability level of the child.

Poetry: Read "Eletelephony" by Laura Richards. (See *Sing a Song of Popcorn* by De Regniers, edited by Eve Moore et al.)

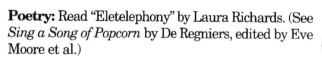

Additional Writing Activities:

1. Continue the individual *My ABC Book*, "E is for…"

2. Read *The Enormous Watermelon* by Brenda Parkes. Have the children make pictures and label other *enormous* objects.

3. Give each child a piece of elastic about 45 inches long. Let them stretch it and play with it for a while to create different shapes. Ask them to form their elastic into something and add a page to the class book *Exciting Elastic!* The children can draw their shape and complete the sentence *I made an elastic…*

4. See the "E Book List" for further appropriate literature ideas.

Sight Vocabulary

- **Pre-primer:** eat; every
- **Primer:** egg

Math

Patterning:

Cut egg shapes out of 1-inch graph paper. Let the children decorate the shapes by coloring in the squares in a pattern.

Classifying: Plastic eggs can be sorted by color.

Estimating:

Fill a L'Eggs® container with small eggs (jelly beans or maltball eggs) and have the children estimate the number. The winner gives every child in the class one of the candies and keeps the rest as a prize.

Symmetry: "Exactly Half!"

Give each child a symmetrical magazine picture that has been cut in half. Have them glue it on a piece of drawing paper and try to draw the other half *exactly* the same.

Eleven:

Have the children count out groups of eleven. Use crayons, pencils, chalk, students, stuffed animals, pieces of paper, Unifix™ cubes, paper clips, etc.

Science & Social Studies

Living Things:

Animals: elephant; elk

Endangered and Extinct Animals

Now is a great time to introduce the concept of *endangered* and *extinct* animals. Invite an upper-grade class to share its reports on various endangered or extinct animals. Afterward, have the class write a thank-you note to the upper graders.

Echolocation

If a study of bats has been part of your science activities, echolocation can be introduced. Give several children in your class small film canisters filled with rice; give several others empty canisters. Have some small flashlights available for the remaining children. Take the children to a darkened room. Have those with the canisters scatter and stop when you instruct them to and then shake their canisters. The object is for the children with the flashlights to shine their light on the children with rice-filled canisters.

Physical Science

Exciting Egg Experiments

There are several fascinating experiments that can be done with eggs. If you soak a raw egg in vinegar, the calcium is removed and the shell becomes rubbery. This allows you to see inside the egg. Another exciting egg experiment is to hard boil and peel an egg and place it in the top of an old-fashioned type milk bottle (or any similar bottle that will not allow the egg to pass through). Burn paper in the bottom of the bottle and the egg will slip in. Blow into the bottle and the egg will pop out!

Patriotism:

Emblems

Quite often patriotism is part of the curriculum at the elementary level. Introduce such emblems as the Great Seal of the United States, the eagle, and Uncle Sam.

Art

Hatching Eggs:

After reading *Chickens Aren't the Only Ones* by Ruth Heller, give each child a L'Eggs® container and some modeling dough. Let them construct an animal they think hatches from an egg. Sentence strips can be written about their animals for a classroom display.

Physical Education & Music

Exercises: Pick a child to lead exercises for that day.

Games:

Eraser Tag

Divide the class into two teams. The object of the relay race is for the players to balance an eraser on their heads while walking as quickly as they can to the finish line and back, and passing the eraser to the next person in line. The first team to have all players complete the race is the winner.

Music:

Chants & Rhymes

Engine, Engine Number Nine

Engine, engine, number nine
    Going down Chicago Line.

If the train falls off the track,
    Do you want your money back?

"No" N–O spells no and out you go!

or

"Yes" Y–E–S spells yes and out you go!

The children form a circle and "It" points to each child in turn. The child pointed to on "back" answers either "yes" or "no" and the rhyme continues by spelling that word. The person pointed to on "go" leaves the circle. Play continues until a winner remains.

Name:_____

Color each picture. Carefully cut along the solid black lines. The Teacher will staple your book together when you are finished.

MY E BOOK !
Name: _____ 1

egg 2

elephant 3

elbow 4

elf 5

envelope 6

USE YOUR NOODLE:
On a piece of paper draw six eggs. Decorate each one differently.

Activities for the Letter F

Tactile Introduction of the Letter

Letter Shape: fake fur fabric; craft feathers; foam craft sheet

Alphabet Puzzle: fish

Sound Sorting

Fill the Fishbowl: (Group Activity)

Gather the children in a circle around a fishbowl. Discuss the uses of the bowl and the first sound of the word *fish*. Let each child pull one item from the Mystery Box and tell what it is. If it begins with *f*, the child then places it in the fishbowl. If it does not begin with *f*, it is placed back in the Mystery Box. After each child has had a turn, review each item in the fishbowl with the group.

Fan Fold: (Individual Activity)

Give each child a large sheet of construction paper. Show the children how to fold the paper to make a fan. Provide magazines for the children to use to find pictures beginning with the *f* sound. The children can paste one *f* picture on each fold of the fan. If they can think of something for which they cannot find a picture, encourage them to draw the picture on their fan. When they have completed the pasting and drawing, display the fans around the room.

Room Labels: fish; flag; floor

Oral Language

Sharing: The children can share their favorite kind of food, or tell about their family.

Cooking and Tasting

Fantastic Fudge:

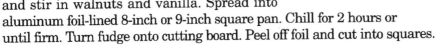

You need 3 cups semisweet chocolate chips, 1 can sweetened condensed milk, dash of salt, 1 cup chopped walnuts, and 1-1/2 tsp. vanilla. In saucepan, over low heat, melt chips with condensed milk and salt. Remove from heat and stir in walnuts and vanilla. Spread into aluminum foil-lined 8-inch or 9-inch square pan. Chill for 2 hours or until firm. Turn fudge onto cutting board. Peel off foil and cut into squares.

Frozen Fruit Salad:

You need 1 cup mayonnaise, 1 3-ounce package cream cheese, 24 large marshmallows, 2 tablespoons pineapple juice, 2 cups crushed pineapple (drained), and 1 cup whipped whipping cream. Blend mayonnaise and cream cheese together. Melt marshmallows in pineapple juice over low heat. Beat until smooth. Cool. Add mayonnaise and cream cheese mixture. Add pineapple and fold in whipped cream. Freeze in trays.

Other Possible F Foods: fortune cookies; French fries; fruit; Fig Newtons™

Mini Field Trips

farm; firehouse; a fourth-grade classroom; another first-grade classroom; florist shop

Interviews

farmer; father; firefighter; florist; forest ranger

Literature & Writing

Authentic Literature & Related Writing Activity:

Read *Clifford's Family* by Norman Bridwell. Give each child a large piece of experience paper. Have the children draw their family in the blank space at the top and write a story about their family. If children have difficulty with drawing, provide them with magazines and newspapers to cut out and paste family members on the paper.

Poetry: Read "Firefly" by Elizabeth Maddox Roberts. (See *Sing a Song of Popcorn*, by De Regniers edited by Eve Moore et al.)

Additional Writing Activities:

1. Continue the individual *My ABC Book,* "F is for..."

2. Read *What Neat Feet* by Hana Machotka. Give each child a piece of experience paper. Have the children take off their shoes and trace their feet on the blank space at the top. Give them the story starter *My feet take me to...*

3. Give each student a paper plate. Have some scraps available for the children to draw and decorate a "funny face." Each child then writes a story about his or her "funny face" that will be attached to the bottom of the plate for display.

4. See the "F Book List" for further appropriate literature ideas.

Sight Vocabulary

- **Pre-primer:** fall; father; find; for; friend; funny
- **Primer:** farm; fast; five; four; found

Math

Graphing:

Bar Graph

Ask several parents to send in a different flavor of Pepperidge Farm® Goldfish crackers. Let the children sample each variety and decide which flavor is their personal favorite. Make a classroom bar graph with the results.

Measurement:

Feet

Read *The Foot Book* by Dr. Seuss. Have each child trace one foot on a piece of paper and measure it using different manipulatives, such as Unifix™ cubes, paper clips, etc.

Fractions:

Fourths

Explain the concept of fourths. Have the children fold a piece of drawing paper into fourths and draw a picture of something beginning with *f* in each box.

Science & Social Studies

Living Things:

Animals: fish; fox

Fish: Set up a classroom aquarium. Discuss the special characteristics of fish.

Farm Animals

Make a classroom book of farm animals. Have each child draw a picture of a different animal that lives on a farm. Depending on the readiness of the children, stories may be written or dictated.

Seasons:

Discuss the characteristics of the season of fall. Have the children draw a fall picture. Ask them to draw themselves in the picture, making sure they are wearing appropriate clothing for the weather.

Nutrition:

Have the children cut out pictures of food and classify them into two categories: *Junk Food* and *Nutritious Food.* This may also be used as a math activity.

Fossils:

After showing some real fossils, have the children make their own fossils! Pour plaster of Paris into small aluminum containers, such as pot pie tins. While still soft, gently press in shells, marbles, chicken bones, twigs, etc. Pull these out just before hardening.

Float or Sink:

Divide the class into small groups. Provide a dishpan of water for each group and several small objects. Have the children divide a piece of paper in half and label the columns *Float* and *Sink*. As they test each object, the children can draw a picture of the object in the correct column.

Senses:

Fragrances

Put cotton balls at the bottom of baby food jars that have been covered with self-stick vinyl so the children cannot see inside. Add a "fragrance" to each. Some suggestions are: cinnamon, coffee, bubble bath, lemon juice, cologne, etc. Have the children smell and try to identify the fragrance.

Families:

Discuss what a family is and what the needs of a family are. Have each child draw his or her family or display photos of each family.

Fire Prevention:

Invite someone from the local fire department to visit the classroom to discuss fire safety. Ask the firefighter to drive a fire truck—if possible—to show the children!

American Flags:

Give the children a 12" x 18" piece of white paper. They will paste 1" x 18" strips of red paper on the white. Add a 6" x 9" blue field. Let the children add self-sticking stars.

Character Education:

Fairness
Forgiveness

Art

Fall Leaf Rubbings:

Take the children on a nature walk to find some fall leaves. Have the children make leaf rubbings in fall colors. If you are unable to do this in the area in which you live, reproduce the Leaf Patterns page for the children to color. Discuss fall colors with them before the activity. (You may also want to visit a craft shop to purchase silk leaves to serve as models for children.)

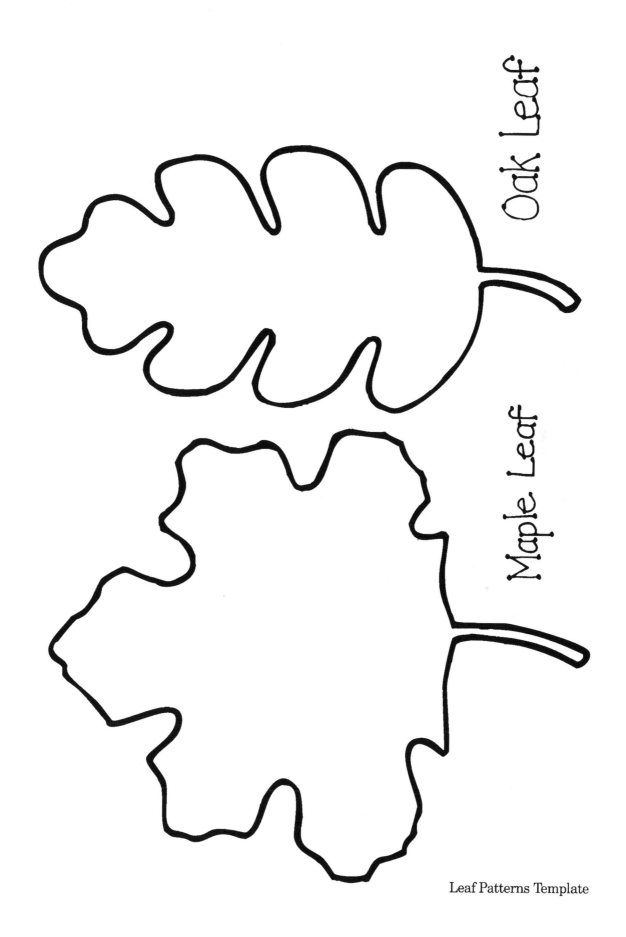

Oak Leaf

Maple Leaf

Leaf Patterns Template

Fragrant Flowers:

Have the children draw a vase or a garden on a piece of paper. Use colored tissue paper to add flowers to the stems. Put a drop of perfume on each flower.

Fingerprint Fun:

Show the children one of Ed Emberley's books on fingerprints, such as *Ed Emerley's Great Thumbprint Drawing Book* and *Ed Emberler's Thumbprint Drawing Box*. Demonstrate making these creations on the overhead projector. Provide ink pads for each table and let the students make their own fingerprint creations.

Finger-painting: Let the children fingerpaint to fast music and then to slow music.

Physical Education & Music

Games:

"The Farmer in the Dell"

Frisbee™!

Small children like to throw and catch a Frisbee™! Teach them to place the edge of the Frisbee™ into the space between the thumb and first finger. Show them how to keep the thumb on top and fan the other fingers out beneath the Frisbee™. Tell them to stand sideways with the throwing arm facing the target. Have them bring their arm towards the chest and whip it outward, snapping the wrist, as they release the disc. To catch the Frisbee™ illustrate a thumbs-up or thumbs-down technique.

After they have had some practice throwing and catching you can develop a simple game. Mark goal lines on the playing field and divide the class into two teams. The object of the game is to throw the Frisbee™ over the opposing team's goal line for a point. Toss a coin to determine which team will make the first throw. The throwing team positions themselves about five feet in front of their goal line and makes the first throw. The throw is returned from wherever it lands. Running with the Frisbee™ is not allowed. The winning team is the one to score the most points in the allotted time.

Freeze Tag

On the signal, "It" players try to tag "free" players before they get to the "safe" spot. When players are tagged, they must immediately "freeze." Play continues until all "free" players are frozen. New "it" players are chosen.

"A-Hunting We Will Go"

A-hunting we will go,

A-hunting we will go.

We'll catch a little fox

And put him in a box

And then we'll let him go.

The children form a circle with hands joined. The "fox" stands outside the circle. As the children circle left, the fox skips right. When the verse reaches "We'll catch a little fox," the two children nearest the fox lift their arms and force the "fox" into the circle by bringing their linked arms behind him. On "let him go," the children raise their arms and let the fox escape. The fox then chooses another fox and the game continues.

Movement:

Fast vs. Slow: Have the children move to varied beats.

Creative Movement

Have the children pretend to be fairies. They can move lightly on tippy-toes. Classical music can be added!

Music:

Suggested Songs: Sesame Street albums have lots of *f* songs, such as "Five People in My Family," "Let a Frown Be Your Umbrella," and "Four Furry Friends."

Name: _____

Circle the 2 fish that are exactly the same. Color them the same color.

☆ Find these hidden objects and circle them:
feather   foot   fork   fan   'F'
football   '5'   fence   face

Color the picture when you are finished.

USE YOUR NOODLE:

Draw a picture of your family on the back of this paper. Write their names if you can!

Activities for the Letter G

Tactile Introduction of the Letter G

Letter Shape: gold glitter

Alphabet Puzzle: ghost

Sound Sorting

Garbage Bag Grab: (Group Activity)

Gather the children in a circle around a paper grocery bag. Discuss the uses of the bag (to carry groceries, to use as a garbage bag, etc.) and then emphasize the first sound of the word *garbage*. Let each child pull one item from the Mystery Box and tell what it is. If it begins with *g*, the child then places it in the garbage bag. If it does not begin with *g*, it is placed back in the Mystery Box. After each child has had a turn, review each item in the garbage bag with the group.

G Garden: (Individual Activity)

Give each child a large sheet of construction paper. Tell the children to draw a garden on the paper. Provide magazines for the children to use to find pictures beginning with the *g* sound. The children can have the garden *grow g* objects by pasting appropriate pictures on their drawing. When they have completed the pasting, display the garden pictures around the room.

Room Labels: green; graph; green tags to label *guys* and *gals*

Oral Language

Sharing:

1. Each child brings in something green to talk about.
2. Have a Grandparents Day when the children tell about their grandparents or actually bring in a grandparent to introduce to the class.

Cooking and Tasting

Green Glass: Make green gelatin according to package directions. Cut into small squares and serve as "green glass"!

Other Possible G Foods: graham crackers; green beans; gumdrops; grapes; grapefruit; granola

Mini Field Trips

greenhouse; grocery store; guidance counseling office

Interviews

garbage collector; gardener; grandfather; grandmother; grocer; guidance counselor; guitarist

Literature & Writing

Authentic Literature & Related Writing Activity:

1. Read *Good as New!* by Barbara Douglas. Emphasize the *g* words such as Grady, grandfather, good. Have the children draw a picture of their grandfather and tell how he helps them. (Be sensitive to those students who do not have a grandfather or whose grandfather is in poor health.)

2. Read *Three Billy Goats Gruff* and then give the children a piece of drawing paper and a paper cut-out of a bridge (Use Template provided.). Have them paste the bridge on their paper and draw something that starts with *g* under the bridge. They can describe what is under their bridge orally or in written form.

Poetry: Read "Quack! Said the Billy Goat" by Charles Causley. (See *Animals Animals* by Eric Carle.)

Additional Writing Activities

1. Continue the individual *My ABC Book,* "G is for…"
2. Have the children make *The Green Book.* Each child prepares one page: "See the green…" (an object beginning with a *g*) and illustrates. Prepare a cover, laminate, and bind.
3. See the "G Book List" for further appropriate literature ideas.

Sight Vocabulary

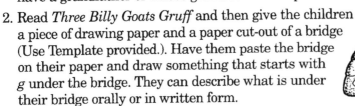

- **Pre-primer:** go; good; green
- **Primer:** game; gave; get; give; going; good-bye; guess

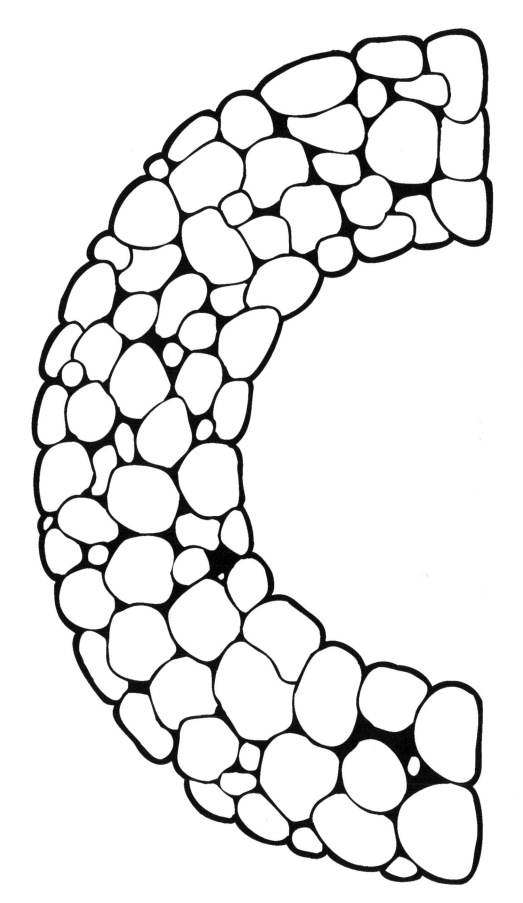

Bridge Template

Math

Classifying:

Give the children a large sheet of paper folded in three columns. Have them label the columns *Gray*, *Green*, and *Gold*. Let them look for pictures in magazines to paste under the appropriate headings.

Graphing:

Bar Graph

1. (Use this activity if you have not used it for *f.*) Ask several parents to send in a different flavor of Pepperidge Farm® Goldfish crackers. Let the children sample each variety and decide which flavor is their personal favorite. Make a classroom bar graph with the results.

2. A Grocery Graph can be made while setting up a classroom store. Each child brings in an empty food container to use in the store. The graph is labeled with general food groups such as *Cereal, Soup, Cookies,* etc. As each child shares the container he or she has brought, the graph is marked in the appropriate category.

Guessing (Estimation):

Fill a jar with gumdrops or gumballs and have the children guess how many green ones there are in the jar and how many in total.

Science & Social Studies

Living Things:

Animals: goat; gorilla; groundhog

Gardens:

This is a good time to start some gardening activities. If space is available outside, the class can start a small garden. If this is not possible, each child can grow an individual grass garden. Give each child a Styrofoam meat tray and a small clean sponge. Have them dampen the sponge and sprinkle with grass seed. If you keep water in the tray, the sponge will absorb the water gradually and the grass will begin to grow.

Families:

As part of a study of the concept of family, have the children make a *Grandparents Book*. Begin by reading several books about grandparents, such as *When I Go Visiting* by Anne and Harlow Rockwell; *Big Boy, Little Boy* by Betty Jo Stanovich; *Happy Birthday Sam* by Pat Hutchins; *Just Grandpa and Me* by Mercer Mayer; *If I Could Be My Grandmother* by Vera Williams; and *Grandparents Around the World* by Dorka Raynor. Give each child several sheets of newsprint folded into a booklet. Each child draws a picture of each grandparent he or she is going to tell about. Stories can be dictated or written depending on the capability of each student.

Map Skills:

Divide the class into small groups. Each group is given a World Map or a globe and a piece of paper. The object of the game is to find as many places on the map that start with the letter *G*. One child in each group records the answers. When time is called, the winning team is the one with the most *G* places recorded!

Art

Glitter-and-Glue Ghost Pictures:

Children love to make glittery pictures. Provide drawing paper, crayons, glue, and various colors of glitter! Their glittery ghosts will reinforce the sound of *g*.

Physical Education & Music

Games:

Goal-line Beanbag Toss

Divide the class into two teams. The object is to toss the beanbags to teammates and try to get the beanbags over the opposing team's goal line for a point. The first team to get a certain number of points is the winner.

Movement:

Galloping: Introduce the galloping movement. Have the children gallop to various rhythms.

Music:

Suggested Songs: Sesame Street albums have lots of *g* songs, such as "Garbage," "Being Green," "Giggles," and "The Garden."

Guitars:

Make shoe box guitars! Each child will need a shoe box and five rubber bands. You should cut a 4-inch hole in the lid. Each child completes his or her own instrument by wrapping the five rubber bands around the box and over the hole. Play a record to which the children can strum.

Name:_____

"G" GARDEN

Color each picture. Cut out the pictures beginning with the 'G' sound. Glue the circles to the flowers.

USE YOUR NOODLE: Draw 5 things that are green on another piece of paper.

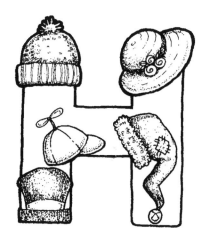

Activities for the Letter H

Tactile Introduction of the Letter

Letter Shape: punched holes from different colors of construction paper

Alphabet Puzzle: heart

Sound Sorting

Hatbox: (Group Activity)

Gather the children in a circle around an old-fashioned hatbox. Discuss the uses of the hatbox and then emphasize the first sound of the word *hatbox*. Let each child pull one item from the Mystery Box and tell what it is. If it begins with *h*, the child then places it in the hatbox. If it does not begin with *h*, it is placed back in the Mystery Box. After each child has had a turn, review each item in the hatbox with the group.

Hat Hunt: (Individual Activity)

Let each child bring in a hat of some sort. Provide magazines for the children to use to find pictures with the beginning *h* sound. The children can cut out pictures that begin with *h* and place them in their hats. When they have filled their hats, the results can be shared orally.

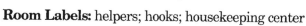
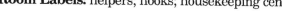

Room Labels: helpers; hooks; housekeeping center

Oral Language

Sharing:

1. Each child wears a crazy hat to school and shares it with the class.
2. Each child can tell what makes him or her happy!

Cooking and Tasting

Heavenly Hash

You need 2 cans Mandarin oranges, 1 large can crushed pineapple, (drained) 1/2 package of flaked coconut, 2/3 package mini-marshmallows, and 1/2 pint sour cream.

Mix all ingredients together and refrigerate.

Other Possible H Foods: ham; hot dogs; hamburgers; Hawaiian Punch®; Heavenly Hash ice cream

Mini Field Trips

hardware store; health club; hospital

Interviews

harpist; hospital worker

Literature & Writing

Authentic Literature & Related Writing Activity:

Read *A House Is a House for Me* by Mary Ann Hoberman. Have each child make up his or her own sentence to illustrate. (Example: A *box* is a house for a *crayon.*)

Poetry: Read "Hug O' War" by Shel Silverstein. (See *Where the Sidewalk Ends.*)

Additional Writing Activities

1. Continue the individual *My ABC Books,* "H is for…"

2. Give each child a sheet of white paper in which a large hole has been cut out in the middle of the page. (Make sure the holes are cut in the same place so that they match up when the classroom book is made!) Each child decides what to make from his or her hole and completes a picture around it. Stories can be dictated or written by the student.

3. Provide a large chart with various hats drawn on it. (Examples: cowboy hat, firefighter hat, police hat, bonnet, wizard hat, etc.) Each child traces the hat he or she likes best and draws his or her own face underneath. A story is written that is appropriate for the hat chosen.

4. See the "H Book List" for further appropriate literature ideas

Sight Vocabulary

- **Pre-primer:** has; have; he; help; here; house
- **Primer:** had; happy; head; her; him; his; home; how

Math

Graphing:

Bar Graph: Graph the children's hair color!

Geometry:

Hexagon

As part of an introduction to Geometry, present the hexagon. Give each child a piece of red paper and a hexagon pattern to trace. Have the children make stop signs.

Fractions:

Half

Now is a good time to introduce the concept of one half. Divide the class into pairs. Give each pair one granola bar and ask the children how they can divide it fairly.

Numbers:

Hundred

The children should practice their counting! Use flash cards with the numerals 1–100 to reinforce number recognition.

Science & Social Studies

Living Things:

Animals: hamster; hippopotamus; horse

Hibernation

Read *Buzz Bear Goes South* by Dorothy Marino. Discuss the various animals that hibernate for the winter.

Habitats

1. Make a huge classroom chart. Elicit and label various habitats along the top of the chart, (such as above ground, below ground, forest, underwater, desert, etc.). Divide the class into groups and assign each group a habitat to investigate. The group then draws pictures of the correct animals under the appropriate habitat heading.

2. As part of a study on habitats, the children can do their own "habitat" by making a classroom *House Book*. Each child can draw a picture of his or her home and write the address on the paper. These can be bound into a classroom book.

Health:

Body Parts

Identify parts of the body that begin with h. (Examples: hair, hands, head, heart, heel, hips.) Play a game similar to "Simon Says" called "Harry Says." The children can only touch the parts of the body that begin with *h*. (For example, if Harry says, "Touch you toes," anyone who does it is out!)

Senses: Hearing

Discuss the sense of hearing. Have the children shut their eyes and let one child make a noise. The students guess how the child made the noise. Continue until all children have had a turn.

Map Skills:

Have the children find Hawaii on the map. Invite a parent with slides of Hawaii to make a presentation.

Character Education:

Honesty

Art

Hats:

Read *Jennie's Hat* by Ezra Jack Keats. Provide a paper plate for each child. Have available assorted materials, such as ribbons, beads, sequins, pompons, pasta, glitter, feathers, etc.; for the children to use in creating their unique hats! Have a Hat Parade in the hall when they are completed.

Physical Education & Music

Games:

Play "Hula Hoop Relay." Divide the class into two teams. The children must run to the hula hoop, step into it, pull it over their head, and then run back to their team. The first team to finish is the winner!

Movement:

Hopping

Hula Hoops: Hula hoops can be used to provide movement activities that reinforce the concept of inside, outside, under, over, and through.

"Hokey Pokey": Children love to do the "Hokey Pokey"!

Creative Movement

Have the children pretend to be helicopters! They can twirl their blades, spin around, go up and down, and hover!

"A-Hunting We Will Go"

A-hunting we will go,

A-hunting we will go.

We'll catch a little fox

And put him in a box

And then we'll let him go.

The children form a circle with hands joined. The "fox" stands outside the circle. As the children circle left, the fox skips right. When the verse reaches "We'll catch a little fox," the two children nearest the fox lift their arms and force the "fox" into the circle by bringing their linked arms behind him. On "let him go," the children raise their arms and let the fox escape. The fox then chooses another fox and the game continues.

Music

Suggested Songs: Sesame Street albums have lots of *h* songs, such as "Hello," "High, Middle, Low," "Ha Ha," and "Hard, Hard, Hard."

Instruments: Form a horn and harmonica band!

Name:_____

Say each picture name. Write the beginning sound.
Color each picture.

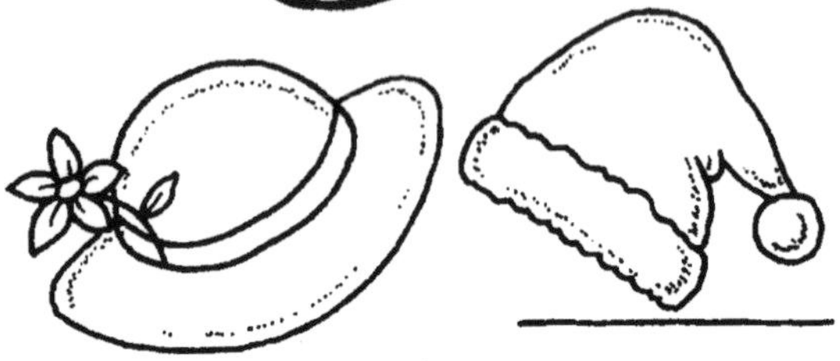

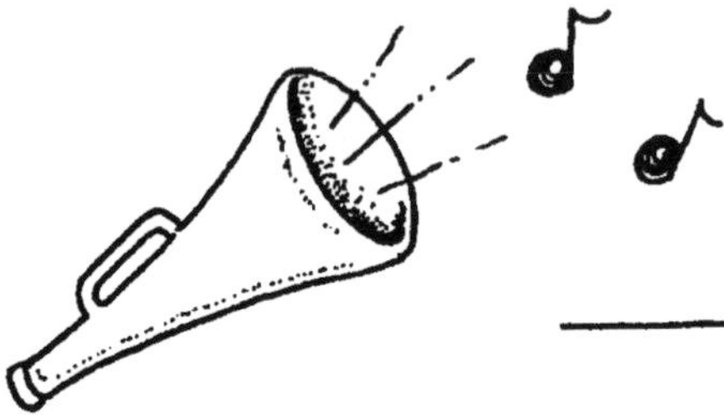

HOME   HAPPY   HAND
HOT   HEN   HAT
HOW

H	A	T	S	B	D
A	M	O	H	E	N
P	C	H	O	W	A
P	F	R	M	Q	H
Y	D	Z	E	G	J

Circle
the hidden
words!

USE YOUR NOODLE: Draw a picture of
your house on the back of this page.
Write your address if you can!

DCW 99

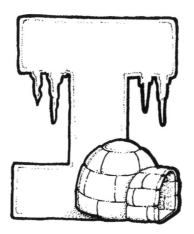

Activities for the Letter I

Tactile Introduction of the Letter

Letter Shape: thumbprints made with ink pads

Alphabet Puzzle: igloo

Sound Sorting

I Box Sort: (Group Activity)

Gather the children in a circle on the floor. Place an empty box in the middle of the circle. Have the children decorate the box by having each one write an upper- or lower-case *i* on it with an assortment of colored markers. Tell the children the only objects that will be placed inside the *I* Box will be those that begin with the short sound of *i*. Place the Mystery Box on the floor. Let each child pull one item from the box and tell the class what it is. If it begins with an *i*, then the child places that item inside the *I* Box. If it does not begin with an *i*, it is placed back in the box. After each child has had a turn, review each item in the *I* Box with the group.

Inside the I Envelope: (Individual Activity)

As an individual activity, each child is given an envelope to decorate with *i*'s. Provide magazines for the children to look for pictures or words that begin with *i*. The children then cut out the pictures and place them inside the envelope to be taken home and shared with parents.

Room Labels: ink pads, inch

Oral Language

Sharing: Ask each child to bring in something interesting to share that can fit inside a margarine tub.

Cooking and Tasting

Indian Fry Bread:

You need 3 cups all-purpose flour, 1 tablespoon baking powder, 1/2 teaspoon salt, 1/4 cup milk, and 1-1/2 cups warm water.

Combine flour, baking powder, and salt in a large mixing bowl. Add milk; blend thoroughly. Add warm water in small amounts. Knead dough until soft but not sticky. Cover bowl and let stand 15 minutes. Pull off balls of dough about the size of an egg, roll in rounds about 1/8-inch thick, and punch hole in center.

Fry in a heavy skillet that has 1 inch of hot oil until bubbles appear on top of bread. Turn over and fry until golden. Drain on paper towels. Serve with butter or jam. (CAUTION: This activity must be done only under adult supervision.)

Other Possible I Foods: Italian bread; Italian ice

Mini Field Trips

instrument store

Interviews

illustrator; instrument maker; insurance adjuster; inventor; investigator

Literature & Writing

Authentic Literature & Related Writing Activity:

Read *It Didn't Frighten Me* by Janet Gross and Jerome Harste. Give each child a blank piece of white paper on which to draw a scary animal. Give the children strips of brown paper to paste around the edges to make the paper look like a window. Have each child name the animal and dictate a story about it.

Poetry: Read "One Inch Tall" by Shel Silverstein. (See *Where the Sidewalk Ends.*)

Additional Writing Activities:

1. Continue the individual *My ABC Books*, "I is for…"
2. Read *The Big Pets* by Lane Smith. Ask each child to write about an imaginary pet he or she might like to have. What would the pet help the child do?
3. See the "I Book List" for further appropriate literature ideas.

Sight Vocabulary

- **Pre-primer:** I; in; is; it
- **Primer:** into

Math

Geometry:

Intersecting Lines: Have the children play Tic-Tac-Toe. Explain intersecting lines.

Measurement:

Introduce the use of the inch ruler. Give each child a gummy "inchworm" and have him or her measure it. Divide the class into pairs and have the children measure the lengths of various small objects in the room, such as pencils, crayons, chalk, etc.

Science & Social Studies

Living Things:

Animals: iguana; inchworms; insects

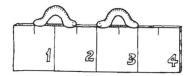

Inspecting Insects

Take the children on an insect walk. Carefully collect some insects in margarine tubs that have lids with holes. When you get back to the room, inspect the insects with magnifying glasses and make a classroom chart of the characteristics they have in common. Then return the insects to their habitats.

Patriotism:

Independence Day: Explain the importance of freedom. Sing some patriotic songs!

Art

Indian Vests and Headbands:

Give each child a large brown grocery bag. Help each child cut a hole for their head in the bottom of the bag and holes for their arms. Cut the vest open in the front. Show some examples of traditional Indian designs. Let the children paint their vests using some of these symbols. Each child can make a matching headband from a folded 4" by 24" strip of construction paper. Real feathers can be added for decoration.

Indian Beads:

Have the children string a variety of materials into necklaces. (Examples: beads, macaroni, cut-up straws, Styrofoam packing material, etc.)

Inkblot Designs:

Give each child a piece of paper and have the children fold it in half. Let each child put a dropper full of ink on the fold and then press the sides together. Have them incorporate the inkblot into a picture.

Physical Education & Music

Games:

Imagine

Have the class scatter on a field outside (or in the room on a rainy day) and have a leader tell others what to pretend. For example: "Your left foot is a balloon." "You are made out of clay."

Movement:

Creative Movement

Divide the class into groups. Let each group think of an invention or an instrument. Have the groups act out the motion of their invention or how to play their instrument, and let their classmates guess!

Music:

Suggested Songs: "The Itsy Bitsy Spider"

Instruments

Read *What Instrument Is This?* by Rosmarie Hausherr. Have a variety of instruments to show the children. If possible, have some demonstrations by musicians.

Name:_____

If the inchworm is next to an object that begins with "I," color it green. If the inchworm is next to an object that begins with a different letter, color it yellow.

USE YOUR NOODLE: Draw 4 icky insects on the back of this paper.

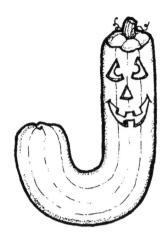

Activities for the Letter J

Tactile Introduction of the Letter

Letter Shape: powdered Jell-o®; mini jelly beans

Alphabet Puzzle: jar

Sound Sorting

Jar Sort: (Group Activity)

Gather the children in a circle around a big jar that you get from the cafeteria. Discuss the uses of the jar. Emphasize the beginning sound of the word *jar*. Let each child pull one item (or picture) from the Mystery Box and tell what it is. If it begins with *j*, the child then places it in the jar. If it does not begin with *j*, it is placed back in the box. After each child has had a turn, review each item in the jar with the group.

Room Labels: jars of paint; jar of paste

Oral Language

Sharing:

1. If they wish, children can share their journal writing for the day.
2. Each child can tell a joke. (you may want to preview the jokes before they are told to the class.)

Cooking and Tasting

Jell-o® & Juice: The children can make Jell-o® and juice according to package directions. Decorate each Jell-o® serving with a jelly bean!

Other Possible J Foods: jelly; Cracker Jacks®; jelly; jam

Mini Field Trips

janitor's office; Japanese garden; jewelry store

Interviews

janitor; jeweler; journalist; juggler

Literature & Writing

Authentic Literature & Related Writing Activity:

Read *Jack and the Beanstalk* by Paul Galdone and *Jim and the Beanstalk* by Raymond Briggs. Give each child a long, skinny piece of paper and have the children draw a beanstalk. They will then write about what they find at the top of their beanstalk.

Poetry: Read "January" by Maurice Sendak. (See *Chicken Soup With Rice.*)

Additional Writing Activities:

1. Continue the individual *My ABC Book,* "J is for…"
2. Read *Jump, Frog, Jump* by Robert Kalon. Discuss verbs. Each child can draw a frog doing something and complete the sentence *My frog is…* with a verb. These can be bound into a classroom book.
3. See the "J Book List" for further appropriate literature ideas.

Sight Vocabulary

- **Pre-primer:** jump
- **Primer:** join, just

Math

Classifying & Graphing:

Jelly Bean Sort

Give each child a small bag of jelly beans. Elicit the fact that the jelly beans can be sorted by color. Give each child an individual "Jelly Bean Graph" sheet and let the children color in the columns with the appropriate color and amount. When everyone is done, make a classroom graph and write a math story using the results. For example, how many more green than red? How many less…? Which color has the greatest (least) number? etc.

Junk Food vs. Nutritious Food: Graph the children's snacks and discuss the benefits of nutritious foods!

Jack-o'-Lantern Faces

Show the children the categories they will be using for the floor graph (Happy, Sad, Mad, Scary). Give each child a small paper plate to be used to make into a jack-o'-lantern face. The children decide which type of face they want to make and use the assorted materials provided to decorate their jack-o'-lantern. When all are completed put a word card for each category on the

Jelly Bean Graph

number of jelly beans	pink ⬭	white ⬭	purple ⬭	black ⬭	orange ⬭	green ⬭	red ⬭	yellow ⬭

floor (or at the bottom of a free wall) and call each child individually to come and place their jack-o'-lantern above the correct category. Write a math story with the results.

Estimation and Counting by Tens:

1. Fill a jar with jelly beans and have the children guess how many of each color there are and how many in total.

2. Cut out a jack-o'-lantern from a real pumpkin. Ask the children to estimate how many seeds were in the pumpkin. Have them put their guesses on a folded piece of paper, which you collect. After the seeds are separated, dry them in the microwave. Give each child a long thin strip of paper (usually available from your local printer for free) and have them put ten dots of glue on the strip. They then place one seed on each dot. Continue to do this until all seeds are used. As you have the children count by ten's, staple the strips onto the wall to form one long strip. After they arrive at the total, check the guesses collected and find out who came the closest!

Science & Social Studies

Living Things:

Animals: jaguar; Japanese beetle

Jungle Habitat

Let each child create a jungle diorama out of a shoe box. The children first draw in the background. Have some green tissue paper and crepe paper available to make leaves and vines. Next the children will make animals out of clay (or find pictures in magazines) and add them to their dioramas.

Nutrition:

Have the children make a classroom chart of *Junk Food vs. Nutritious Food.* Use the math graphing activity to graph the snacks the children have brought that day.

Map Skills:

Have the class find Japan on the map. Invite a guest who has visited or lived in Japan to make a presentation.

The J Months:

Discuss January, June, and July. Have the children make pictures showing the difference in seasons.

Art

Jumbled J's:

Give each child a sheet of white paper. Tell the children to draw several *J*'s in different directions all over the paper, leaving space between each one. The child now is instructed to make each *j* into something different.

Physical Education & Music

Physical Activities:

Jogging: The children can start a jogging program and keep track of laps on a room chart.

Jumping Rope: This is a good time to introduce jumping rope. Teach the children the meaning of *jingle* and have them jump rope to some familiar ones.

Movement:

Rhythmic Movement: The children can do jumping jacks to various rhythms.

Creative Movement

The children can have fun pretending to move like a jack-in-the-box! How about being jet planes? They can travel down the runway, getting faster and faster. They can fly straight, zoom around, turn, glide, and come in for a landing!

Music:

Suggested Songs: Sesame Street albums have lots of *j* songs, such as "J Friends," "J Jump," and "J Poem."

Jazz

Have the children listen to some jazz!

Chants & Rhymes

Who Stole the Cookie from the Cookie Jar?

ALL:	Who stole the cookie from the cookie jar?
STUDENT #1:	Mary stole the cookie from the cookie jar.
MARY:	Who me?
ALL:	Yes, you!
MARY:	Couldn't be!
ALL:	Then who?
MARY:	Billy stole the cookie from the cookie jar.

Students sit in a circle and one student begins by naming someone else in the class. The game is repeated until everyone has had a turn.

Name: _____

Juggling Jack

Color each picture. Cut out the pictures beginning with the j sound. Glue the circles for Jack to juggle.
☆ Draw 3 different jack-o-lanterns on a new piece of paper.

Activities for the Letter K

Tactile Introduction of the Letter

Letter Shape: Kellogg's™ Special K® cereal; Kix® cereal

Alphabet Puzzle: kangaroo; key

Sound Sorting

Kitchen Container Grab: (Group Activity)

Gather the children in a circle around a kitchen trash container. Emphasize the first sound of the word *kitchen*. Let each child pull one item (or picture) from the Mystery Box and tell what it is. If it begins with *k*, the child then places it in the trash container. If it does not begin with *k*, it is placed back in the box. After each child has had a turn, review each item that begins with *k* with the group.

Room Labels: kitchen center

Oral Language

Sharing: Read *One Kitten for Kim* by Adelaide Holl. Have each child draw a kitten. Each child can tell about his or her kitten.

Cooking and Tasting

Kiwi: Cut up some kiwi. Many children have never tasted this exotic fruit.

Other Possible K Foods: Kix® cereal, Kool-Aid®, chocolate Kisses™, kabobs, kumquats.

Mini Field Trips

kittens at a pet store; school kitchen; hardware store to see keys made; art room to see kiln; a kindergarten class; kennel

Interviews

kennel keeper; kitchen remodeler

Literature & Writing

Authentic Literature & Related Writing Activity:

Read *Katy No-Pocket* by Emmy Payne. Discuss *random acts of kindness.* Have each child write about how they were kind to someone else or how someone else was kind to them.

Poetry: Read "Travel Plans" by Bobbie Katz. (See *Animals Animals* by Eric Carle.)

Additional Writing Activities:

1. Continue the individual *My ABC Books,* "K is for…"
2. Read any of the *kitten* books listed in the "K Book List" and let each child draw a kitten, name it, and write a story about it.
3. See the "K Book List" for further appropriate literature ideas

Sight Vocabulary

- **Pre-primer:** keep, kick
- **Primer:** kitten, know

Math

Geometry:

Kites: To introduce the diamond shape, have the children design kites.

Science & Social Studies

Living Things:

Animals: kangaroo; kittens; koala

Endangered Environment

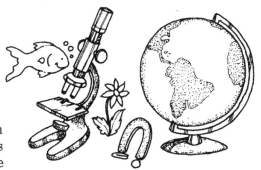

Read *The Great Kapok Tree* by Lynne Cherry. On a huge cut-out tree have the children paste pictures of the species that are being endangered by the destruction of the rain forest.

Map Skills:

Have the class find Australia on the map. Invite a guest who has visited or lived in Australia to make a presentation on koalas and kangaroos.

Character Education:

Kindness

Art

Kites and Kindness:

Give each child a large brown grocery bag. Fold a 1-inch cuff around the top of the bag. Provide a variety of materials (fabric scraps, sequins, ribbon, glitter, etc.) to decorate the bag. Attach streamers of crepe paper to the bottom of the bag. Attach a 40-inch piece of string to the cuff. To fly the kite, the children run to fill it with air. When everyone has gotten a chance to fly his or her kite, turn it right side up and cleanup the school yard by filling the bag with litter.

Physical Education & Music

Games: Introduce the children to kickball.

Music:

Suggested Songs

- "Kum Ba Ya"
- "Let's Go Fly a Kite" from *Mary Poppins*

Instruments: Form a kazoo band!

Name:_____

Say each picture name. Write the beginning sound.
Color the picture.

USE YOUR NOODLE: Draw a kite on the
back of this paper. Decorate it however you like.

Activities for the Letter L

Tactile Introduction of the Letter

Letter Shape: letters (buy the small macaroni letters used to make alphabet soup)

Alphabet Puzzle: lemon; lunch box

Sound Sorting

Lunch Box Sort: (Group Activity)

Gather the children in a circle around a lunch box. Discuss the uses of the lunch box and then emphasize the first sound of the word. Let each child pull one item from the Mystery Box and tell what it is. If it begins with *l*, the child then places it in the lunch box. If it does not begin with *l*, it is placed back in the Mystery Box. After each child has had a turn, review each item in the lunch box with the group.

Room Labels: (chalk) ledge; letters

Oral Language

Sharing: The children share something *little*.

Cooking and Tasting

Luscious Lemon Mousse:

You need 2 cups boiling water, 1 6-ounce package lemon Jell-o®, 2 7-oz bottles lemon lime soda, grated rind and juice of 1 lemon, and 2 cups heavy cream, whipped.

Pour boiling water over Jell-o® and stir until dissolved.

Add soda, lemon rind, and juice. Chill until slightly thickened (about 2 hours.) Beat until foamy. Fold in whipped heavy cream. Put into 2-quart soufflé dish and chill until firm.

Other Possible L Foods: lemonade; lettuce; licorice; lemonade; limeade; lollipops

Mini Field Trips

library (school or local); loading dock at the school to see how deliveries are made

Interviews

landscaper; lawyer; librarian; locksmith

Literature & Writing

Authentic Literature & Related Writing Activity:

Read *The Lorax* by Dr. Seuss. Discuss the problems of the environment. Have the children make posters about saving the environment. The children might also like to write letters telling how they help to save the environment.

Poetry: Read "The Lion" by Jack Prelutsky. (See *Animals Animals* by Eric Carle.)

Additional Writing Activities:

1. Continue the individual *My ABC Books,* "L is for…"
2. Give each child a lollipop. Have the children draw their lollipop and write a description of it. Put these together in a booklet to help reinforce the color words.
3. Make a classroom *I Like* book. Have each child fill in the missing word in the sentence and illustrate.
4. See the "L Book List" for further appropriate literature ideas.

Sight Vocabulary

- **Pre-primer:** let; like; little; look
- **Primer:** laugh; live

Math

Estimating, Sorting, and Graphing:

Show the children a bag of lollipops and have them estimate the number of each color in the bag. Count the lollipops with the class and sort by color. Give each child a copy of a prepared classroom lollipop graph. Fill in the graph correctly and write a math story using the results.

Telling Time:

Read *The Very Grouchy Ladybug* by Eric Carle. After an introductory lesson on clocks, give each child a large paper plate. Have the children write the numerals in the correct place. Give them paper hands and help them attach with a brad. Have the children demonstrate times you write on the board.

Less Than...:

This is an appropriate time to introduce the concept of "less than". Give each child an index card on which to draw a number of lollipops. The children must then go around the room and find a buddy who has "less than" the number of lollipops on his or her card.

Measurement:

Explain the concept of length. First, do a length comparison with several objects, reinforcing the "less than" concept already taught. The children can then work in small groups to measure objects first with lollipops and then with a ruler.

Science & Social Studies

Living Things:

Animals: ladybug; lamb; lion; lizard

Living vs. Nonliving

Have the children name some living things and discuss the characteristics and needs of living things. Discuss nonliving things and how they differ from living things. Make two classroom books, *Living* and *Nonliving*. Have each child do a page for each book using either pictures cut from magazines or personal drawings.

Leaves

Have the children bring in an assortment of leaves. After pressing the leaves for several days, give each child one leaf. The children can glue the leaf to the blank space on a sheet of experience paper. The lines below it are then used to complete three sentences written on the board: *My leaf looks like...; My leaf feels...; My leaf smells....* These pages can be laminated and bound into a classroom book.

Physical Science:

Liquids, Gases, and Solids

When making the Luscious Lemon Mousse, the children can observe the various states of matter: liquid (water you are heating), gas (the steam rising from the pot when the water is boiling), and solid (the firm Jell-o®).

Abraham Lincoln and His Log Cabin:

After reading some books on Abe Lincoln, have each child save a milk container at lunch. These can be covered with stick pretzels to make log cabins. Finish with a folded brown construction paper roof.

Character Education:

Loyalty

Art

Leaf Rubbings:

Provide an assortment of leaves and a variety of colored chalks or crayons. Show the children how to make leaf rubbings. Mount and display.

Lion and Lamb Puppets:

After reading *Lazy Lions, Lucky Lambs* by Patricia R. Giff, give each child a large paper plate. Distribute copies of "Lion and Lamb Faces" reproducible for children to cut out and glue on plates. On one side the children make a lion using crayons and curled strips of yellow and brown construction paper for a mane. They then turn the plate over and use cotton balls to make a lamb face. The plates can be attached to tongue depressors so the children can use them to act out their favorite part of the book.

Physical Education & Music

Games:

"Looby Loo"

Children form a circle and skip around while singing the Looby Loo chorus:

Here we go Looby Loo

Here we go Looby Light

Here we go Looby Loo

All on a Saturday Night.

Children drop hands and act out the next verse:

I put my right hand in

I put my right hand out

I give my hand a shake, shake, shake

And turn myself about.

Repeat chorus. Additional verses: left hand; right foot; left foot; whole self; etc.

Three-Legged Race: Pair the children and have a three-legged race!

Movement:

Leaping

Locomotion Commotion

Have the children explore different ways of locomotion. You might try flying, zooming, leaping, swooping, gliding, crawling, creeping, skating, and whatever else the children can suggest!

Lame Dog Walk

Have the children walk on their hands and one foot. They have to keep the "injured" foot off the floor while making "lame dog" noises.

Lion and Lamb Faces

Music

Chants & Rhymes

London Bridge

London bridge is falling down,
    falling down, falling down,

London bridge is falling down,
    My fair lady.

Chorus: Take the key and lock her up...

              Build it up with iron bars...

              Iron bars will bend and break...

Two children join hands and form an arch. The other children pass through the arch in single file. On "My fair lady," the bridge falls and captures a prisoner. At the end of the "iron bars" verse, the prisoner takes the place of one of the children in the bridge and play continues.

Name:_____

Circle these hidden "L" objects:
lollipop, ladder, lamp, letter, lizard,
light-bulb, lock, lady, lemon, "L"
* When you are finished, color the picture!

USE YOUR NOODLE: Draw a tree with lots of
colorful Fall leaves on the back of this paper.

Activities for the Letter M

Tactile Introduction of the Letter

Letter Shape: macaroni; markers; mini marshmallows; M & M's®

Alphabet Puzzle: moon; mouse

Sound Sorting

Mailbox Sort: (Group Activity)

Gather the children in a circle around a rural mailbox. Discuss the uses of the mailbox and then emphasize the first sound of the word. Let each child pull one item from the Mystery Box and tell what it is. If it begins with *m*, the child then places it in the mailbox. If it does not begin with *m*, it is placed back in the Mystery Box. After each child has had a turn, review each item in the mailbox with the group.

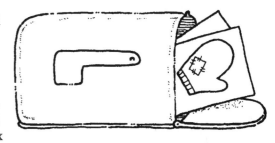

Room Labels: markers; math center; music

Oral Language

Sharing:

The children tell the class about their moms! You can have a Mom's Day at school to introduce everyone's mom. (Be sensitive to those students who do not have a mother. Perhaps these children could talk about their grandmother, aunt, guardian, etc.)

Cooking and Tasting

Marvelous Marshmallow Treats:

You need 1/4 cup of margarine, 4 cups mini marshmallows, and 6 cups Kellogg's™ Rice Krispies® cereal. Melt margarine in large pan over low heat. Add marshmallows and stir until melted. Remove from heat. Add Rice Krispies®. Stir until well coated. Using buttered spatula or waxed paper, press mixture evenly into buttered 13 x 9 x 2 pan and cut into squares when cooled.

Other Possible M Foods: M & M's®; muffins; marshmallows; macaroni; mints; macaroons; melon; marmalade; milk shakes

Mini Field Trips

mail room; local mall (make a list of *m* things at the mall!); music room; school office to have secretary show how the mail is sorted

Interviews

mailcarrier; mother; model; model builder; magician

Literature & Writing

Authentic Literature & Related Writing Activity:

Read *The Mitten* by Jan Brett. Have each child make up his or her own page with a unique animal coming into the "class mitten." Bind into a classroom book and share with another class.

Poetry: Read "March" by Maurice Sendak. (See *Chicken Soup With Rice.*)

Additional Writing Activities:

1. Continue the individual *My ABC Book*, "M is for..."
2. Several suggestions for classroom books include: *What Makes Me Mad! Monsters, Monsters, Monsters! My Mom,* and *My Favorite Month.*
3. Read *If You Give a Moose a Muffin* by Laura J. Numeroff. Have the class make a book about giving a moose things that begin with *m*.
4. See the "M Book List" for further appropriate literature ideas.

Sight Vocabulary

- **Pre-primer:** may; me; mother; my
- **Primer:** made; make; milk; must

Math

Sorting, Estimating, and Graphing:

Mittens: Have each child bring in an old mitten. Sort and graph the mittens by color.

M & M's®

Give each child a small bag of M & M's®. Have them estimate the number of each color and the total number in the bag and record. Provide individual graphs to graph by color.

More Than…:

This is an appropriate time to introduce the concept of "more than". Give each child a handful of mini marshmallows. Have the children compare the number they receive with that of a buddy before they eat the treat!

Measurement:

Explain the concept of length. First, do a length comparison with several objects, reinforcing the "more than" concept already taught. The children can then work in small groups to measure objects with marshmallows, then mini marshmallows, and—finally—a ruler.

Science & Social Studies

Living Things:

Animals: moose; mouse

Physical Science:

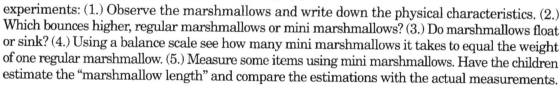

Marshmallow Madness

Divide the class into small groups. Set up several stations around the room with marshmallow experiments: (1.) Observe the marshmallows and write down the physical characteristics. (2.) Which bounces higher, regular marshmallows or mini marshmallows? (3.) Do marshmallows float or sink? (4.) Using a balance scale see how many mini marshmallows it takes to equal the weight of one regular marshmallow. (5.) Measure some items using mini marshmallows. Have the children estimate the "marshmallow length" and compare the estimations with the actual measurements.

Simple Machines

This would be an ideal time to introduce simple machines. Make a classroom *Machines Mural* with pictures the children find in magazines or catalogs.

Magnets

Read *Mickey's Magnet* by Franklyn M. Branley. Provide a variety of magnets and let the children explore the room to make a list of what *is* and *is not* attracted to the magnet.

Map Skills:

Moon Maps

Give each child a square of cardboard. Have the children paint the cardboard black and let dry. While the squares are drying, read some books about the moon. Mix up a batch of salt dough. (*Basic Recipe:* 1 cup salt, 1 cup flour, enough water to make pliable. Mix with hands.) Give each child a lump of dough to flatten onto the cardboard. Let the children make craters using their thumb to make the indentations.

Art

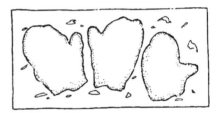

Marshmallow Prints:

Give each child a black sheet of paper. Provide trays of white paint and marshmallows. The children dip the marshmallows in the paint and make prints with them.

Marble Painting:

Provide several shallow box tops from shoe boxes. Tape paper to the bottom of the box tops. Using plastic spoons, let each child dip a marble into a container of paint and drop the marble on the paper. As the child tilts the box, the marble leaves a design on the paper. Continue with a variety of colors.

Mitten Paintings:

Provide several shallow trays of a variety of colors of paints. Instead of putting a brush in each, use a mitten! The children slip their hand in the mitten and make prints on their paper. This is messy, but lots of fun!

Physical Education & Music

Games:

Musical Chairs

Mousetrap

This game is played with a parachute. Have the children spaced evenly around the parachute, holding it waist high. Select six children to be the "mice". On the signal, the children "inflate" the parachute and the "mice" try to run across and out the other side before the signal is given and the chute falls and traps them. Trapped "mice" join the chute holders until only one "mouse" is left. Then six new "mice" are chosen.

Movement:

Creative Movement

1. Have the children explore as many different kinds of movements as they can think of! (running, jumping, galloping, hopping, twisting, rolling, etc.)
2. Divide the class into groups. Let each group think of a machine and act out its motion. Have their classmates guess what they are.

Marching: Have the children march to different beats.

Music:

Marches: Introduce John Philip Sousa and his marches.

Sheet Music: Introduce the children to sheet music. Explain the staff, lines, spaces, etc.

Chants & Rhymes

Muffin Man

Oh, do you know the Muffin Man,
the Muffin Man, the Muffin Man.
Oh, do you know the Muffin Man,
Who lives on Drury Lane?

2. Oh yes, I know the Muffin Man.
3. Now two of us know the Muffin Man.
4. Now four of us know the Muffin Man.
5. Now all of us know the Muffin Man.

Children form a circle with one child in the center. At the end of the verse, the child takes a partner into the center and they form a smaller inner circle. At the end of each verse, each child in the center picks a partner. Change the numbers in the verse each time until all are in the center.

Miss Mary Mack (traditional clapping song)

Miss Mary Mack, Mack, Mack,
All dressed in black, black, black,
With silver buttons, buttons, buttons,
All down her back, back, back.

She asked her mother, mother, mother,
For fifty cents, cents, cents,
To see the elephant, elephant, elephant,
Jump over the fence, fence, fence.

He jumped so high, high, high,
That he reached the sky, sky, sky,
And he never came back, back, back,
Till the Fourth of July, 'ly, 'ly.

Name:_____

Which path should Matilda Mouse follow to the cheese?

Say the picture name. Write the beginning sound.
Color each picture.

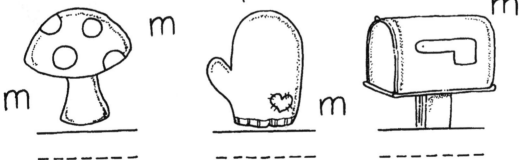

m

m

m

m

m

_____

_ _ _ _ _ _

_____

_ _ _ _ _ _

_____

_ _ _ _ _ _

USE YOUR NOODLE: Draw a mad monster
on the back of this paper.

Activities for the Letter N

Tactile Introduction of the Letter

Letter Shape: newspaper

Alphabet Puzzle: nail; nut

Sound Sorting

Fishing Net Sort: (Group Activity)

Gather the children in a circle around a fishing net. Discuss the uses of the net and then emphasize the first sound of the word. Let each child pull one item from the Mystery Box and tell what it is. If it begins with *n*, the child then places it in the net. If it does not begin with *n*, it is placed back in the Mystery Box. After each child has had a turn, review each item in the net with the group.

Newspaper Fun: (Individual Activity)

Give each child a square cut from a newspaper. Have the children circle all the *n*'s they can find. Who can find the most?

Room Labels: nametags; numbers

Oral Language

Sharing: The children tell the class about their favorite next-door neighbor!

Cooking and Tasting

Nests:

You need 1 cup honey, 1 cup peanut butter, 2 cups powdered milk, and shredded coconut.

Mix ingredients into a dough. Each child gets a dough ball to roll in coconut. Shape into a nest using thumb. Add some jelly bean eggs!

Other Possible N Foods: noodles; nectarines; nuts

Mini Field Trips

local newspaper; nurse's office; nursery; nature walk; neighborhood

Interviews

newspaper reporter; nail technician; nurse

Literature & Writing

Authentic Literature & Related Writing Activity:

Read *There's a Nightmare in My Closet* by Mercer Mayer. Give the children a piece of brown construction paper to fold in half and make a door. On the outside, the children can draw a doorknob; on the inside, they can draw something that starts with an *n*. The children can dictate a story about what's in their closet.

Poetry: Read "November" by Maurice Sendak. (See *Chicken Soup with Rice.*)

Additional Writing Activities:

1. Continue the individual *My ABC Book,* "N is for..."
2. Have children find animal pictures in magazines and cut out just their noses. Make a classroom *Noses Book,* telling about each animal.
3. Make a *Names Book.* Each child writes the letters of his or her name vertically down a side of a sheet of paper and draws an object that begins with that letter.
4. See the "N Book List" for further appropriate literature ideas.

Sight Vocabulary

- **Pre-primer:** no; not
- **Primer:** name; new; night; now

Math

Sorting, Estimating, and Graphing:

Nuts

Show the children a bag of nuts. Have them estimate the number of each variety and the total number in the bag. Record the numbers. Provide individual graphs to graph by type.

Numbers: This is a great time to do a review of counting, recognition of numerals, and writing of numerals.

The Nine Family: Give the children nine nuts. Have them record as many addition possibilities as they can figure out.

Money:

Nickels

Provide nickels and pennies for comparison. Ask the children how many pennies make a nickel. Have them count out nickels and pennies up to ten cents.

Science & Social Studies

Living Things:

Animals: newt; nuthatch

Solar System:

Near and Far

To explain to the children why the sun and moon do not appear large in the sky, have them look at an object up close and draw what they see. Next, have them step to the far side of the room as they watch the object grow small. Have the children draw the *far picture* on the back of the *near picture*.

Nutrition:

This is a good time to teach the children about the food pyramid. After you have discussed good nutrition, give each child a magazine and a paper plate. Have the children cut out pictures of nutritious foods and glue them on the plate. Take turns having children explain their nutritious selections!

Community Helpers:

Nurse: Invite the school nurse to tell about her job. Have children brainstorm a list of questions for the nurse before the visit.

Art

Nifty Noodle Necklaces:

Provide an assortment of types of noodles (macaroni) that can be strung to make necklaces. Other materials, such as beads, cut-up straws, etc., can also be added.

Physical Education & Music

Games:

Nose Tag

During this version of tag, the "safe" position is kneeling down, hooking one arm under the leg, and grabbing the nose with the hand that is under the leg!

Music:

The Nutcracker: The children can listen to a recording of *The Nutcracker* or watch the video *Storyteller's Classics: The Nutcracker* by Orion Home Videos.

Name:_____

Color each picture. Cut out the pictures beginning with the 'N' sound. Glue the eggs in the nest.

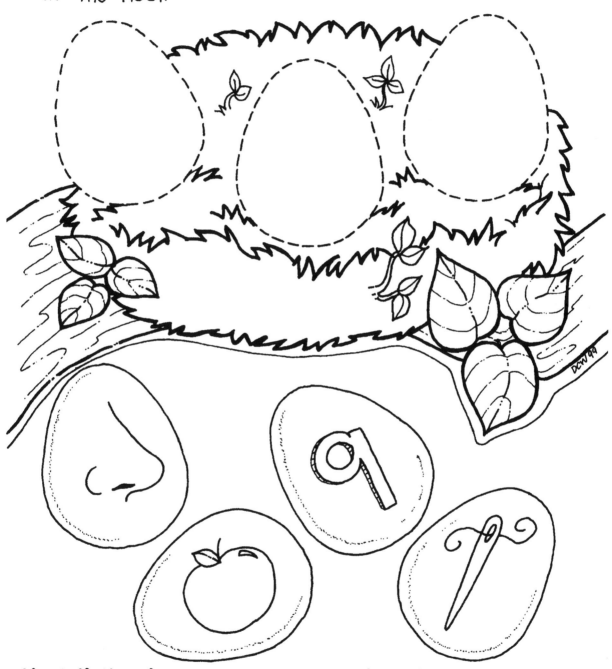

USE YOUR NOODLE: Draw a night picture on a piece of paper.

Activities for the Letter O

Tactile Introduction of the Letter

Letter Shape: General Mills™ Cheerios® cereal; dry oatmeal

Alphabet Puzzle: octopus

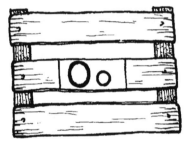

Sound Sorting

Orange Crate Sort: (Group Activity)

Gather the children in a circle around an orange crate. Discuss the uses of the crate. Elicit other words that begin with the short *o* sound. Let each child pull one item from the Mystery Box and tell what it is. If it begins with *o*, the child then places it in the orange crate. If it does not begin with *o*, it is placed back in the Mystery Box. After each child has had a turn, review each item in the orange crate with the group.

Room Labels: orange; overhead projector

Oral Language

Sharing: The children bring something orange to share.

Cooking and Tasting

Olive Eyes:

Give each child a slice of party bread spread with cream cheese, an olive, and a triangle of pineapple (cut from canned slices.) Have the children take out the pimento and make a mouth on the bread. Slice the olive in half and let the children place them on the bread to make eyes. The pineapple forms the nose.

Other Possible O Foods: Oreo® cookies; oranges

Mini Field Trips

observatory; ophthalmologist, optometrist, or optician's office; school office; children's opera

Interviews

ophthalmologist; optometrist; optician; opera singer

Literature & Writing

Authentic Literature & Related Writing Activity:

Read *Oscar the Grouch's Alphabet of Trash* by the Sesame Street Staff. Have the children draw a trash can on their paper or use the template provided. Provide magazines to find *o* words. Have the children "throw away" the *o* words by pasting them on the trash can. Help the children write a list of the objects in the can.

Poetry: Read "Octopus" by Ogden Nash.

Additional Writing Activities:

1. Continue the individual *My ABC Book,* "O is for…"
2. Make an *Occupations* book. The children tell what they would like to be when they grow up. Bind into a classroom book and share with another class.
3. Divide the class into pairs to develop an *Opposites Book.* Each pair decides the opposites it wants to draw; each child will then draw a picture for one of the words and write the word below it.
4. See the "O Book List" for further appropriate literature ideas.

Sight Vocabulary

- **Pre-primer:** oh; on; one
- **Primer:** of; old; open; or; our; out; over

Math

Numbers:

One: Reinforce the concept of one and more than one.

Odd and Even

Discuss the concept of odd and even numbers. Provide some sheets that have boxed missing numbers to be filled in. Have the children color the odd-numbered boxes.

Trash Can Template

Science & Social Studies

Living Things:

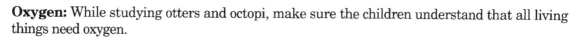

Animals: ocelot; octopus; opossum; ostrich; otter; oxen

Observing Otters and Octopi

Read some books on these animals or watch a video. Make a classroom story about their characteristics.

Oxygen: While studying otters and octopi, make sure the children understand that all living things need oxygen.

Occupations: As part of the study of community helpers, invite some parents to tell about their occupations.

Art

Balloon Octopus:

(This is a bit difficult, so it would be helpful to have parent helpers.) Blow up a balloon. Mix flour and water to form a smooth paste. Dip strips of newspaper into paste and slide through fingers to remove excess. Apply the strips to the balloon. Do two or three layers. Let dry for 24 hours. Paint the octopus's body and add some matching tentacles! Paint a face on the octopus. Then poke a hole through the octopus to break the balloon.

Physical Education & Music

Games

Obstacle Course: Set up an obstacle course for the children to run through!

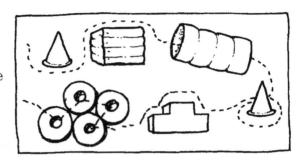

Music:

Orchestra: Take the children to see the high school orchestra play. Teach the names of the instruments to the children.

Opera: Take the children to an opera or show them the video of the opera *Where the Wild Things Are* by Orion Home Videos.

Name:_____

Color each picture. Cut out the boxes. If the picture begins with 'O', glue it on the table. If it begins with another letter, glue it under the table.

OLIVES

OCTOBER

Carefully cut out each box.

USE YOUR NOODLE: On another piece of paper, draw a holiday that is in October.

Activities for the Letter P

Tactile Introduction of the Letter

Letter Shape: paint; pompons; pipe cleaners

Alphabet Puzzle: pig; Popsicle®

Sound Sorting

Pocket Sort: (Group Activity)

Gather the children in a circle around a carpenter's apron with lots of pockets. Discuss the uses of the pockets and emphasize the sound of the letter *p*. Let each child pull one item from the Mystery Box and tell what it is. If it begins with *p*, the child then places it in one of the pockets. If it does not begin with *p*, it is placed back in the Mystery Box.
After each child has had a turn, review all the items in the pockets with the group.

Room Labels: paints; pencil sharpener; pencils; pink; plants; pointer; poster; purple

Oral Language

Sharing: Tell the children they must bring in something to share that can fit in their pocket.

Cooking and Tasting

Party Punch:

You need 1 quart orange or lime sherbet, 46 ounces cold pineapple juice, 2 2-liter bottles ginger ale, 1 pint vanilla ice cream, and 1 6-ounce can frozen concentrated orange juice.

Place all ingredients except ginger ale in a punch bowl. Add ginger ale just prior to serving.

Other Possible P Foods: peanut butter; pumpkin pie; pumpkin seeds; popcorn; potato chips; pickles

Mini Field Trips

park, pizza parlor, paint store,

Interviews

painter; paleontologist; pilot; plumber; police officer; printer

Literature & Writing

Authentic Literature & Related Writing Activity:

Read *The Big Pets* by Lane Smith. Have each child draw a big pet and tell about it. Another good story starter for this book is "(The child's name) is little. The (type of pet) is big."

Poetry: Read "The Purple Cow" by Gelett Burgess. (See *Favorite Poems for Children* by Susan Gaber.)

Additional Writing Activities:

1. Continue the individual *My ABC Book,* "P is for…"
2. Read *Piggybook* by Anthony Browne. Have the children write down ways in which they can help their mothers at home.
3. See the "P Book List" for further appropriate literature ideas.

Sight Vocabulary

- **Pre-primer:** play; pet; put
- **Primer:** party; picture; pie; please; pretty

Math

Sorting: Paper clips can be sorted by color, size, and shape.

Graphing:

Pockets

Provide a classroom graph on the number of pockets the children have on any particular day. Have each child stand up individually and count the number of pockets he or she has. Mark in the appropriate square on the graph. This is a good time to introduce using the overhead projection calculator. When the graph is completed, show the children how to add the pockets to get a grand total for the class.

Popcorn

Ask parents to supply several types of popcorn (buttered, plain, caramel, cheddar, etc.) and have a tasting party. Each child records his or her favorite type; the classroom results are tabulated on a graph.

Pairs:

Discuss the meaning of a pair. Divide the class into pairs and give each child a mitten pattern. The two children working together must design identical mittens so that they have a pair. When completed, attach the mittens with a piece of yarn and display on the bulletin board.

Fractions: Have a pizza party! Before serving, discuss the fractional parts of the pizza.

Science & Social Studies

Living Things:

Animals: penguin; pig; pigeon; porcupine

Physical Science:

Pulleys: As part of a unit on Simple Machines, this is a good time to have some pulleys available with which the children can experiment.

Environmental Science:

Pollution

Read *The Lorax* by Dr. Seuss. Discuss how the environment was being destroyed by the onceler. If it is winter, collect some snow and let it melt in a clear plastic glass so the children can see the pollution that is in the air. If no snow is available, place a coffee filter on the windowsill and observe the dirt that is collected in it.

Air (Puff Painting)

To show the children that air can move, have them do puff painting. Provide each child with a sheet of glossy white paper and a straw. Make available several colors of watered-down tempera paint with small spoons in the containers. The children drop a spoonful of paint on the paper and then blow it around the paper with the straw. By mixing some colors before they are dry, some interesting effects are seen.

Character Education:

Patriotism

Perseverance

Art

Puzzle Piece Frames:

Take an action photo of each child. Give each child a "frame" cut from cardboard. Have available lots of old puzzle pieces. The children glue the pieces on the cardboard, covering all so that no cardboard is visible. This may take 2 or 3 layers. When completed, glue the picture to a backing and put together. Have the children sign their name, date the back, and add a magnetic strip so Mom and Dad can display it on the refrigerator.

Physical Education & Music

Games:

Hot Potato

Have the children form a circle and play the old-fashioned game of Hot Potato! The children must quickly pass the potato to the next person in the circle while music is playing. When the music stops, whoever has the potato is *out*. Play continues until there is a winner, that is, one remaining player.

Parachute

Children love to play games with the parachute. Ask your physical education teacher to play some parachute games this week!

"Pop Goes the Weasel"

All around the cobbler's bench,

The monkey chased the weasel.

The monkey thought

'Twas all in fun,

Pop! goes the weasel!

This can be played with two or more children. One child bounces the ball in rhythm as the others sing. On "Pop!" the child passes the ball to another child.

Alphabet Popcorn

Give each child a card with one letter of the alphabet on it. Have the children form a circle. You call out a letter and the child with that letter must "pop up." This is a good time to practice some of the sight words with the children.

Movement:

Creative Movement: Have the children pretend to be popping corn, plants growing, or pigs playing in the mud!

Music:

Piano: Explain how a piano works. Let the children see the inside of the piano while someone is playing. Invite a pianist to give a short concert.

Chants & Rhymes

Hot Potato

One potato, two potato,

Three potato, four,

Five potato, six potato,

Seven potato, MORE!

The children stand in a circle with fists held out in front of them. As the children chant the rhythm, "It" pounds each fist in turn. The fist pounded on "MORE" is placed behind that child's back. Play continues until only one fist remains. That child is the winner and becomes the next "It."

Name:_____

Say each picture name. Write the beginning sound. Color each picture.

USE YOUR NOODLE: Turn this paper over. Draw a big "P" in the middle of the paper. Use your crayons and imagination to make it part of your picture.

Activities for the Letter Q

Tactile Introduction of the Letter

Letter Shape: scraps of fabric to make a "quilt"

Alphabet Puzzle: queen

Sound Sorting

Quilt Sort: (Group Activity)

Gather the children in a circle around an old quilt. Read the book *The Quilt* by Ann Jonas. Emphasize the first sound of the word *quilt*. Let each child pull one item (or picture) from the Mystery Box and tell what it is. If it begins with *q,* it is placed on the quilt. If it does not begin with the letter *q,* it is placed back in the box. After each child has had a turn, review each item on the quilt with the group.

Room Labels: label the sample quilt brought in

Oral Language

Sharing:

Make a classroom quilt that represents all of the children. Give each child a 5-inch square of paper and let the children draw a picture representative of them (their family, themselves participating in a favorite activity, etc.). Have each child explain his or her individual square and then attach it to the bulletin board. When it is completed, there will be a colorful and interesting classroom quilt on display.

Cooking and Tasting

Spinach Quiche

You need 1/4 cup oil, 1 large onion (chopped), 2 10-ounce packages frozen spinach (cooked), 1/2 lb. mozzarella cheese (grated), 3/4 cup Parmesan cheese (grated), 5 eggs (beaten), and salt, pepper and nutmeg to taste.

Sauté onions in oil and then mix with rest of ingredients. Place in a deep-dish pie shell. Bake at 400 degrees for 35 minutes.

Other Possible Q Foods: quince jelly; quinine water (tonic); quick-cooking oats

Mini Field Trips

quilt shop, walk *quietly* to the library for a *quiet* story

Interviews

quilter

Literature & Writing

Authentic Literature & Related Writing Activity:

Read *The Josefina Quilt Story* by Eleanor Coerr and *The Quilt Story* by Tony Johnston. Make a classroom chart depicting the difference between our present-day life and pioneer life.

Poetry: Read "Quack!" Said the Billy Goat" by Charles Causley. (See *Animals Animals* by Eric Carle.)

Additional Writing Activities:

1. Continue the individual *My ABC Book,* "Qu is for…"

2. Read *Quick as a Cricket* by Audrey Wood. Have the children make up their own similes.

3. Now is a great time to introduce quotation marks. Explain their use and then let each child make up his or her own "quote" for a classroom book. For example: *Michael says, "I love science!"*

4. See the "Q Book List" for further appropriate literature ideas.

Math

Money:

Introduce the quarter. Make crayon rubbings of George Washington and the Eagle and discuss the significance of both.

Measurement:

With the children, develop a chart of measurement questions, such as: "How long is my desk? pencil? crayon? How wide is my book? desk?" etc. Have the children work in pairs to answer the questions.

Science & Social Studies

Living Things:

Animals: queen bee

Queen Bee

Discuss the role of the queen bee in the colony of bees. "What are her jobs? Why is she so important?" This might be a good topic to research as an introduction to the uses of the computer.

Quills

As part of the previous discussion on pioneer days, you might show the children a quill from an animal and explain how it was used for writing.

Art

Q-tip® Painting:

Give each child a piece of paper and some Q-tips®. Let the children dip the Q-tips® in paint and use them instead of brushes to create a masterpiece!

Physical Education & Music

Games:

Quiet Ball

This is a great activity for a rainy day. The children stand near their desks. The object of the game is to throw and catch the ball without making any noises. A player has to sit down if he or she makes any noise, drops the ball, throws it so it is impossible for another to catch it, or throws it back to the person who threw it to him or her.

Music:

"Q" Music Terms: Some topics to be introduced are quarter notes, quarter rests, and quartet.

Name:_____

The Queen's Quilt

Color the Queen's quilt. Draw an X on the squares that begin with a Q.

USE YOUR NOODLE: Draw a big question mark on the back of this paper. Use your crayons and imagination to make it part of your picture.

Activities for the Letter R

Tactile Introduction of the Letter

Letter Shape: rainbow glitter; red glitter; rice

Alphabet Puzzle: rabbit; rainbow

Sound Sorting

Rainbow Bag: (Group Activity)

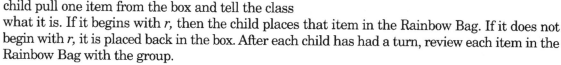

Gather the children in a circle on the floor. Show the children a big brown bag that you have decorated with a rainbow. Elicit from the children what a rainbow is. (You might want to use a prism.) Emphasize the sound of the letter *r*. Place the Mystery Box on the floor. Let each child pull one item from the box and tell the class what it is. If it begins with *r,* then the child places that item in the Rainbow Bag. If it does not begin with *r,* it is placed back in the box. After each child has had a turn, review each item in the Rainbow Bag with the group.

Room Labels: red; reading center; round, ruler

Oral Language

Sharing:

1. The children might share something red.
2. Each child might tell a riddle.

Cooking and Tasting

Rainbow Cupcakes:

Give each child a plain cupcake to frost with white canned frosting. Pass around a shaker of rainbow sprinkles to decorate with!

Other Possible R Foods: Ritz® crackers; Kellogg's™ Rice Krispies® treats; rock candy; raisins; radishes; raspberries; root beer

Mini Field Trips

railroad station; radio station

Interviews

real estate salesperson; railroad conductor and/or engineer; radio announcer

Literature & Writing

Authentic Literature & Related Writing Activity:

Read *Rosie's Walk* by Pat Hutchins. Give each child a large sheet of paper and let the children make a map of where else they would like Rosie to walk. Help the children label their drawings.

Poetry: Read "Rhinoceros" by Mary Ann Hoberman. (Also see *Animals Animals* by Eric Carle.)

Additional Writing Activities:

1. Continue the individual *My ABC Book,* "R is for…"
2. Each child can make a page for the *Red Book* by completing the sentence *My ___ is red.*
3. Divide the children into pairs. Have each pair think of two words that rhyme and illustrate those words. Make a book of the rhyming words.
4. Read *The Wild Christmas Reindeer* by Jan Brett. With a light shining on the children, draw his or her silhouette with chalk on black paper. Have each child cut out their silhouette and glue a big red circle on the end of the nose. Have the children complete the sentence *If I had been born with a shiny red nose…*
5. See the "R Book List" for further appropriate literature ideas.

Sight Vocabulary

- **Pre-primer:** ran; red; rest; ride; run
- **Primer:** rabbit; read; ready; right

Math

Measurement:

Ruler

Read *Inch by Inch* by Leo Lionni as an introduction to using rulers. After instruction, provide lots of objects for the children to practice measuring.

Geometry:

Rectangle

Give each child a paper with a rectangle drawn on it. After discussing what type of shape it is and its characteristics, have the children use their imaginations to incorporate the rectangle into a picture.

Science & Social Studies

Living Things:

Animals: rabbit; rat; reindeer; robin; rooster

Reindeer

Read *The Wild Christmas Reindeer* by Jan Brett. Demonstrate how to find information on the computer about reindeer. Make a classroom list of the characteristics of reindeer.

Reptiles: This is an ideal time to begin a study of reptiles!

Plants: Roots

Give each child a clear plastic tumbler. Help the children line it with paper toweling and dampen. Place a lima bean seed between the outer wall of the tumbler and the paper towel. If you keep the paper towel damp, in a few days roots will sprout and be visible to the children.

Physical Science:

Rocks

Have the children take a rock walk to collect specimens to examine with magnifying glasses. When the observation is complete, the children may pick a rock to paint and use as a paperweight.

Rainbows

Read *Planting a Rainbow* by Lois Ehlert. Have prisms available for the children to "make" rainbows. Teach the children the name *Roy G. Biv* to help them remember the colors of the rainbow in order: red, orange, yellow, green, blue, indigo, violet. Have the children draw a rainbow on white paper.

Environmental Science:

Recycling

Take some of the garbage out of the trashcan in your room and have the children incorporate it into an art project. Have an upper-grade class demonstrate how to make paper by recycling used paper. Make sure students wear disposable latex gloves when handling trash.

Character Education:

Responsibility

Respect

Art

Rock Pets:

Give each child a big rock to decorate as a pet. A follow-up writing activity about their pet could be done in the classroom.

Physical Education & Music

Games:

"Red Rover"

The children line up against the school building. The leader calls "Red Rover, Red Rover, anyone wearing (pick a color) come over." As those children dash for the wall, the leader tries to tag them. Those tagged have to sit out. The game continues until only one person remains.

Jumping Rope

Ring Toss

Movement:

Dancing: Let the children dance to rock-and-roll music!

Creative Movement

The children can have fun with creative movement by having them explore body actions to imitate being a rag doll, a robot, a rocking chair, and a rocket ship blasting off! Can the children think of other movements?

Music:

Suggested Songs: "Home on the Range"

Rock-and-Roll: Introduce the children to rock-and-roll.

Ragtime: Have the children listen to Ragtime.

Rhythm Band: Form a rhythm band with the children in conjunction with listening to rock-and-roll or Ragtime!

Name:_____

Randy Rabbit loves carrots! Say each picture name. Color each picture and cut it out. Glue each carrot for Randy.

USE YOUR NOODLE: Draw 3 rectangles on a piece of paper. Make each rectangle into a different object.

Activities for the Letter S

Tactile Introduction of the Letter

Letter Shape: sand; sequins

Alphabet Puzzle: snake; star

Sound Sorting

Suitcase Sort: (Group Activity)

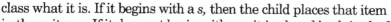

Gather the children in a circle on the floor. Show the children a suitcase. Discuss the uses of a suitcase and emphasize the sound of the letter *s*. Place the Mystery Box on the floor. Let each child pull one item from the box and tell the class what it is. If it begins with a *s,* then the child places that item in the suitcase. If it does not begin with a *s*, it is placed back in the Mystery Box. After each child has had a turn, review each item in the suitcase with the group.

Room Labels: scissors; sink; science center; scale; seat

Oral Language

Sharing: The children might share their favorite *stuffed* animal or bring in *something secret* in a *sack!*

Cooking and Tasting

Stone Soup:

After reading *Stone Soup* by Ann McGovern, make stone soup! Have the children bring in the necessary vegetables. Place a sterilized stone into the pot and fill with water and vegetables. Add some bouillon cubes and cook!

Other Possible S Foods: salad; sandwiches; sausage; strawberries

Mini Field Trips

nearby store (look for items that begin with *s*); school safe; second-grade classroom

Interviews

sailor; secretary; airline steward or stewardess; school social worker

Literature & Writing

Authentic Literature & Related Writing Activity:

Read *The Sneetches* by Dr. Seuss. Have the children write the moral of the story.

Poetry: Read "September" by Maurice Sendak. (See *Chicken Soup With Rice.*)

Additional Writing Activities:

1. Continue the individual *My ABC Book*, "S is for…"
2. Read *The Very Busy Spider* by Eric Carle. Use sentence strips to retell the story in the correct sequence.
3. See the "S Book List" for further appropriate literature ideas.

Sight Vocabulary

- **Pre-primer:** said; sat; saw; see; she; sleep; sun
- **Primer:** say; school; so; some; something; soon; stop; story; surprise

Math

Sorting & Graphing:

Seeds: Mix several types of seeds in a small bag for each child. Have the children sort the seeds by type and graph on an individual graph provided.

Numbers:

The Six and Seven Families: Give each child six (or seven) lima bean seeds with which to work. Have the children record as many number facts as they can with the number of beans they have.

Seed Subtraction: Give each child ten lima bean seeds with which to work. Brainstorm some subtraction problems with the children using their beans.

Geometry:

Square

Give each child a paper with a square drawn on it. After discussing what type of shape it is and its characteristics, have the children use their imaginations to incorporate the square into a picture.

Science & Social Studies

Living Things:

Animals: sand dollar; seal; snake; spider; squirrel

Skeleton

Read *Skeleton Parade* by Jack Prelutsky. Discuss the purpose of skeletons. Put a copy of the skeleton on the overhead projector and help the children identify the bones. When they are done, give them a small black piece of paper. Show them how to make skeletons by dipping their thumb in the white paint provided to make a skull and drawing the rest with Q-tips® dipped in white.

Plants: Seeds

1. Read *Seeds and More Seeds* by Millicent E. Selsam. This is an ideal time for the children to begin a seed collection!

2. Grow seeds in a variety of soils (potting soil, sand, clay) and observe which plants grow the best.

Nutrition:

Super Salad: Have the children bring in nutritious items from home to add to the super salad! Discuss the necessity of vitamins available in fresh vegetables.

Physical Science:

Sink or Float?: Provide several dish tubs filled with water. Have the children experiment with various objects and record which ones *sink* and which ones *float*.

Art

Sponge Painting: Make seasonal sponge paintings. Label each season.

Sand Painting:

Paint a design on the paper with liquid starch. Sprinkle with sand and then powdered tempera. Add glitter for "sparkle"!

Silhouettes:

If possible, have a silhouette artist come for a visit and cut silhouettes of the children. Make silhouettes of each child by attaching black paper to the board and having each child stand in front of the overhead projector light. Trace the silhouette with chalk, let the children cut them out, and paste them on a piece of paper. Then let the children write stories about themselves to be displayed with the silhouettes.

Physical Education & Music

Games:

Snowman Relay Race

The children line up in two teams at a starting point. They race to the end where they have to don the "snowman suit." (Have a bag containing a hat, scarf, and mittens for each team.) The children must dress in everything in the bag, and stick their arms straight out (like a snowman). Next, they must remove the items, place them back in the bag, and run to tag the next player. Play continues until everyone in one of the rows has completed the race.

Movement:

Skipping: Have the children skip to a variety of rhythms.

Stretching: How many different ways can the children stretch? Stretch with a partner.

Creative Movement: Have the children explore different body actions as they imitate being a spinning top, a pair of scissors, a sword fighter, a swimmer, etc.

Seal Walk: The children must move using only their hands for support. They must drag their feet behind them. Encourage them to make seal sounds!

Music:

Symphony: Introduce a symphony. The *Simple Symphony* by Britten would be great to listen to during the study of *S!*

<u>Swan Lake:</u> Have the class listen to Tchaikovsky's famous symphony or watch *Storyteller's Classics: Swan Lake* by Orion Home Videos.

Storm Sounds: Let the children create storm sounds with cymbals, whistles, splashing water, etc.

Chants & Rhymes

A Sailor Went to Sea

A sailor went to sea, sea, sea

To see what he could see, see, see

But all that he could see, see, see

Was the bottom of the deep blue sea, sea, sea!

This is a clapping game done with partners facing each other.

A—clap own hands

sai—clap right hand with partner

lor—clap own hands

went—clap left hand with partner

to—clap own hands

sea, sea, sea—clap partner's hands three times.

Repeat in rhythm until the end of the song.

Name:_____

Circle the objects that begin with "S". Color the Picture.

USE YOUR NOODLE: Draw a picture of your favorite season on the back of this paper.

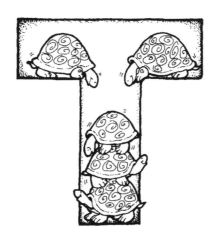

Activities for the Letter T

Tactile Introduction of the Letter

Letter Shape: tissue paper twists; macaroni twists; toothpicks; twine

Alphabet Puzzle: table; turtle

Sound Sorting

Totebag Sort: (Group Activity)

Gather the children in a circle on the floor. Show the children a totebag, explain its uses, and emphasize the sound of the letter *t*. Place the Mystery Box on the floor. Let each child pull one item from the box and tell the class what it is. If it begins with a *t*, then the child places that item in the totebag. If it does not begin with a *t,* it is placed back in the Mystery Box. After each child has had a turn, review each item in the totebag with the group.

Room Labels: table; television; toys; tagboard paper; telephone; three

Oral Language

Sharing: The children can tell about their teddy bears.

Cooking and Tasting

Tapioca Pudding: Make according to package directions.

Other Possible T Foods: tea; toast; Trix® cereal; taffy; tangerines; tuna

Mini Field Trips

television station (many high schools now have small studios)

Interviews

teacher; tree surgeon

Literature & Writing

Authentic Literature & Related Writing Activity:

Read *Town Mouse, Country Mouse* by Jan Brett. Have the children write about where they would rather live and why.

Poetry: Read "The Tiger" by Valerie Worth. (See *Animals Animals* by Eric Carle.)

Additional Writing Activities:

1. Continue the individual *My ABC Book,* "T is for..."
2. Read *Two Tiny Mice* by Alan Baker or *Teeny Tiny* by Jill Bennett. Have the children make a classroom book entitled *Teeny Tiny T Things.* They can write about tiny imaginary people or things!
3. See the "T Book List" for further appropriate literature ideas.

Sight Vocabulary

- **Pre-primer:** the; they; this; to; too; toy; train
- **Primer:** tail; take; tell; thank; that; them; then; thing; three; took; tree; truck; turn; two

Math

Numbers:

Counting by Ten's: Have the children practice counting by ten's.

Geometry:

Triangle

Give each child a paper with a triangle drawn on it. After discussing what type of shape it is and its characteristics, have the children use their imaginations to incorporate the triangle into a picture.

Telling Time: Give each child an individual clock and have the class practice telling time to the hour and the half hour.

Science & Social Studies

Living Things:

Animals: tiger; toad; tuna; turkey; turtle

Turtles

Research turtles on the computer. Make a classroom chart about them. Give each child one half of a walnut shell (these are easily separated if you freeze the nut first). Lay two strips of green construction paper in the shell for legs and a third strip for the neck and head. Press a marble-sized bit of clay in the shell. Now the children have a turtle to take home.

Senses:

Touch: Have the children reach into a bag and touch an object that you have placed there. Can they tell what it is just by touching it?

Taste: Prepare two different flavors of Jell-o®. Blindfold the children and give them a spoonful of one of the types of Jell-o®. See if they can taste the difference!

Physical Science:

Temperature: Show the children a thermometer and explain what it does. Keep a record of the daily temperature on the classroom calendar.

Health:

Teeth: Invite a dentist (or dental hygienist) to the class to talk about dental health.

Transportation:

Trucks and Trains

Read several of the books about trucks and trains listed in the "T Book List." Have the children make a transportation mural divided into three sections: LAND, SEA, and AIR. Display in the room.

Character Education:

Trust

Art

Truck Track Designs:

Provide several trays of paint of varying colors. Let the children dip Matchbox™ type trucks in the paint and roll them across white paper to make some interesting designs.

Tissue Paper Overlay:

Have the children paint a design on paper using liquid starch. Layer on pieces of colored tissue paper. Discuss the results when two or more colors overlap.

Tear a Picture:

Provide the scrap box and glue. Have the children make pictures by tearing the scraps. Do not allow scissors.

Physical Education & Music

Games:

Tag

"A-Tisket, A-Tasket"

A-tisket, a-tasket, a green and yellow basket,

I wrote a letter to my love and on the way I lost it.

I lost it, I lost it, and on the way I lost it,

A little boy (girl) picked it up and put it in his (her) pocket.

The children stand in a circle. "It" stands outside the circle holding a piece of paper. As the children sing, "It" skips around the outside of the circle. When the children sing "I dropped it," "It" drops the paper behind one of the children. "It" then races around the circle back to the empty space; at the same time, the chosen child picks up the paper and runs in the opposite direction, racing to the same space. After the race, the new child is "It."

Movement:

Toe Touches: Have the children do toe touches to various rhythms.

Twisting and Turning

Have the children explore twisting and turning while their feet are "glued to the floor." Have them twist individual parts of the body, two or three body parts together, twist while turning, twist while jumping or running, etc.

Jump Rope Rhymes

Teddy Bear

Teddy Bear, Teddy Bear,
   turn around.

Teddy Bear, Teddy Bear,
   touch the ground.

Teddy Bear, Teddy Bear,
   show your shoe.

Teddy Bear, Teddy Bear,
   that will do!

Creative Movement: Let the children pretend to be tightrope walkers! Move to music on tippy-toes.

Music:

Suggested Songs: "The More We Get Together" by Raffi. (Available on the video *A Young Child's Concert with Raffi* by the ABM Group.)

The Toy Symphony: This is available on the *Storyteller's Classics: The Toy Symphony* by Orion Home Videos.

Triangles: Form a triangle band and have the children play in time to different recordings.

Tom-Toms: Have the children make tom-toms out of coffee cans or oatmeal or salt containers. When completed, add these to the triangle band!

Name:_____

Color each picture. Cut out the pictures beginning with "T." Glue the circles to Tommy Turtle's shell.

DCW99

USE YOUR NOODLE: On a new piece of paper, trace your hand. Use your crayons to make it look like a turkey.

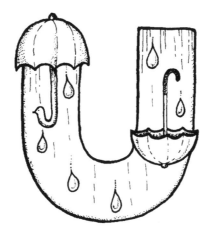

Activities for the Letter U

Tactile Introduction of the Letter

Letter Shape: bu*tt*ons

Alphabet Puzzle: umbrella

Sound Sorting

Umbrella Sort: (Group Activity)

Gather the children in a circle on the floor around an open umbrella. Discuss its uses and emphasize the sound of the letter *u*. Place the Mystery Box on the floor. Let each child pull one item from the box and tell the class what it is. If it begins with a *u*, then the child places that item in the umbrella. If it does not begin with a *u*, it is placed back in the box. After each child has had a turn, review each item in the umbrella with the group.

Room Labels: under; umbrella; U.S.A.

Oral Language

Sharing:

1. See the "under activity" explained in "Literature & Writing." Have the children share their stories and drawings orally.

2. Let the children bring in their umbrellas to share.

Cooking and Tasting

Pineapple Upside-Down Cake:

You need 1/4 cup melted margarine, 1/2 cup firmly packed brown sugar, 1-1/2 cups canned crushed pineapple in natural juices, 1 cup sifted cake flour, 3/4 cup sugar, 1/4 cup vegetable oil,

1/4 cup milk, 1-1/2 teaspoons baking powder, 1/4 cup milk, 2 egg whites, unbeaten, 1/2 teaspoon vanilla extract.

Preheat oven to 350° F. Pour melted margarine into an 8-inch baking pan. Sprinkle with brown sugar. Spread crushed pineapple on bottom of pan. In mixing bowl, sift together flour and white sugar. Add oil and 1/4 cup milk. Stir until flour is dampened. Beat 1 minute. Stir in baking powder, remaining milk, egg whites and vanilla. Beat 2 minutes. Pour batter over pineapple in cake pan. Bake 35 to 40 minutes until toothpick inserted in center comes out clean. Remove from oven, cool slightly and invert onto a plate.

Mini Field Trips

umbrella department of a local store

Interviews

umpire; someone's uncle

Literature & Writing

Authentic Literature & Related Writing Activity:

Read *There's a Monster Under the Bed* by James Howe. Give each child a cut-out of a bed to paste on his or her paper. Have the children draw a creature under it and share the stories orally. (See "Bed Cutout" template.)

Poetry:

Read "Until I Saw the Sea" by Lillian Moore. (See *Sing a Song of Popcorn*, edited by De Regiers.) Have the children write a story about under the water and illustrate.

Additional Writing Activities:

1. Continue the individual *My ABC Book*, "U is for…"
2. Read *My Three Uncles* by Yossi Abolafia. Have the children write a story about their favorite uncle.
3. The children will enjoy making a classroom book entitled *Ugly, Ugly Monsters!*
4. See the "U Book List" for further appropriate literature ideas.

Sight Vocabulary

- **Pre-primer:** up
- **Primer:** us

Math

Numerals:

Up the Beanstalk

Use this activity to practice oral counting. Make a beanstalk with numerals on the leaves. Cut

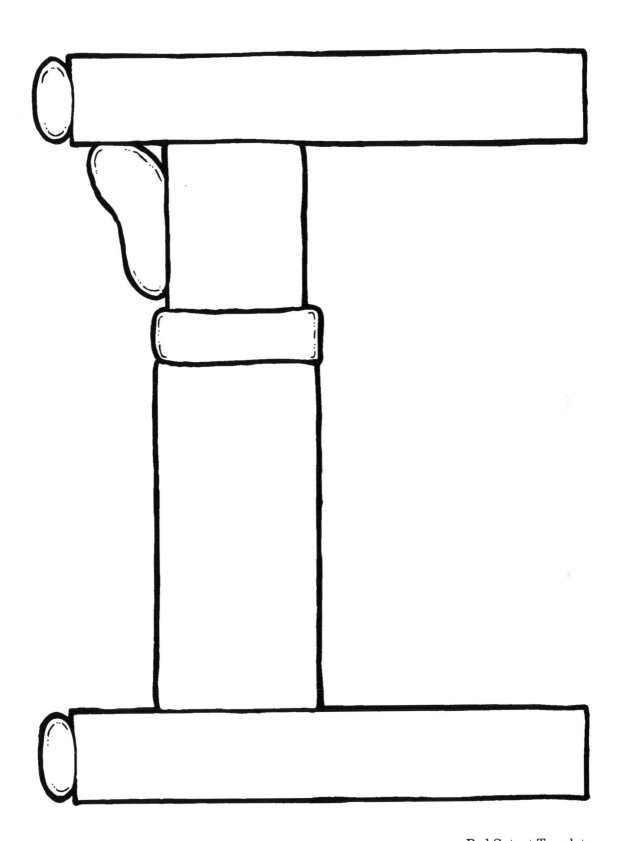

Bed Cutout Template

out some "golden eggs" and attach them to the bulletin board under the beanstalk. If the student can "climb up the beanstalk" by reciting the numerals on the leaves correctly, they sign their name on a golden egg! Vary the activity by having them count from top to bottom, changing the leaves to ordinal numbers, or using simple addition and subtraction problems.

Number Line:

Up and Down the Ladder

Prepare a vertical number line that looks like a ladder. This can be used to introduce or reinforce the concept that addition means advancing up the ladder and subtraction means retreating down. After the initial lesson, provide a stack of 3 x 5 index cards with a simple addition or subtraction fact written on each. Have individuals select a card and use the ladder to solve the problem.

Science & Social Studies

Living Things:

Animals: sea urchin

Undersea/Underground: As part of a study of habitats, have the children make a mural illustrating animals that live under the sea and animals that live under the ground.

Physical Science:

Air: To explain the concept that hot air rises, read *Hot Air Henry* by Mary Calhoun.

Patriotism:

Uncle Sam

Use the computer to look up some background material on the origin and significance of Uncle Sam. Put up a poster that says "I Want You!" Have the children draw a picture of what they think Uncle Sam would want them to do to make this a better country.

Art

Undersea Crayon Resist:

On a large sheet of white construction paper, have each child draw some under-the-sea creatures. Lightly wash over the entire paper with diluted blue tempera. When dry, add some tissue paper seaweed.

Physical Education & Music

Games:

Under the Parachute

Use a large parachute. Have the children squat down and hold the edge of the parachute with both hands. On a signal, have them stand and raise their arms up in front of them. When the parachute rises, the children rush under it.

Movement:

Under and Over: Set up an obstacle course that has the children going under and over a variety of objects.

Music:

The Unfinished Symphony

There are many recordings available of Schubert's Unfinished Symphony. It is not known why Schubert never completed this symphony. It would be fun to have the children listen to it and then tell why they think Schubert did not finish it!

Name:_____

Look at the picture. Circle the objects that are upside-down. Color the objects that are right side-up.

USE YOUR NOODLE: Draw an underwater picture on the back of this page.

Activities for the Letter V

Tactile Introduction of the Letter

Letter Shape: velvet

Alphabet Puzzle: van; vest

Sound Sorting

Valise Sort: (Group Activity)

Gather the children in a circle on the floor. Show the children a suitcase and explain that it can also be called a valise. Discuss its uses and emphasize the sound of the letter *v*. Place the Mystery Box on the floor. Let each child pull one item from the box and tell the class what it is. If it begins with a *v*, then the child places that item in the valise. If it does not begin with a *v*, it is placed back in the box. After each child has had a turn, review each item in the valise with the group.

Room Labels: violet; valentine; vase; video

Oral Language

Sharing: The children can tell about their favorite video.

Cooking and Tasting

Vanilla Pudding: Make the pudding according to package directions.

Other Possible V Foods: vegetables; Velveeta® cheese; vanilla ice cream

Mini Field Trips

vision care center; vegetable stand; video store

Interviews

veterinarian; violinist; school volunteer

Literature & Writing

Authentic Literature & Related Writing Activity:

Read *The Velveteen Rabbit* by Margery Williams. The children can write about their favorite stuffed animal.

Poetry: Read "The Vulture" by Hilaire Belloc.

Additional Writing Activities:

1. Continue the individual *My ABC Book,* "V is for…"
2. See the "V Book List" for further appropriate literature ideas

Sight Vocabulary

- **Pre-primer:** van, vest
- **Primer:** very, visit

Math

Sorting:

Valentines

Prepare a handout with several hearts of varying sizes. Let the children decorate the hearts and then cut them out. Give the children a long sheet of paper on which to arrange the hearts in ascending or descending order by size.

Measurement:

Volume

An early introduction to the concept of volume can be presented by giving the children containers of varying sizes to fill with water. Let them "play" until you can elicit that some containers are bigger and can hold more water than others.

Science & Social Studies

Living Things:

Animals: vulture

Canada Geese: Show the children a picture (or a video) of Canada Geese. Explain how they always fly in a *V* formation.

Patriotism:

Voting

Explain the concept of voting. Take a vote to determine some issue in the classroom (who will be Citizen of the Month, who will be line leader, what time will they go out for recess, what game will they play, etc.).

Art

Native American Vests:

Give each child a large brown grocery bag. Help each child cut a hole for their head in the bottom of the bag and holes for their arms. Cut the vest open in the front. Show some examples of traditional designs by distributing copies of "Native American Symbols." Let the children paint their vests using some of these symbols.

Physical Education & Music

Games:

Vegetable Soup

The game is played in a square. Each of the four corners is designated "home" for a specific vegetable. Four groups are formed. Each group picks the name of a vegetable and moves to its "home" space. You stand in the middle and call out the name of one of the vegetables. Those children run into the center and begin "boiling" by bouncing up and down. When you yell "Soup's burning!" the children scatter and try to run home before being tagged by you. The ones tagged are then your helpers and try to tag the next vegetable group called. The game continues.

Music:

Violin and Viola: Invite a violinist or a violist to come in to give a mini concert. Explain how the strings vibrate to make the sound.

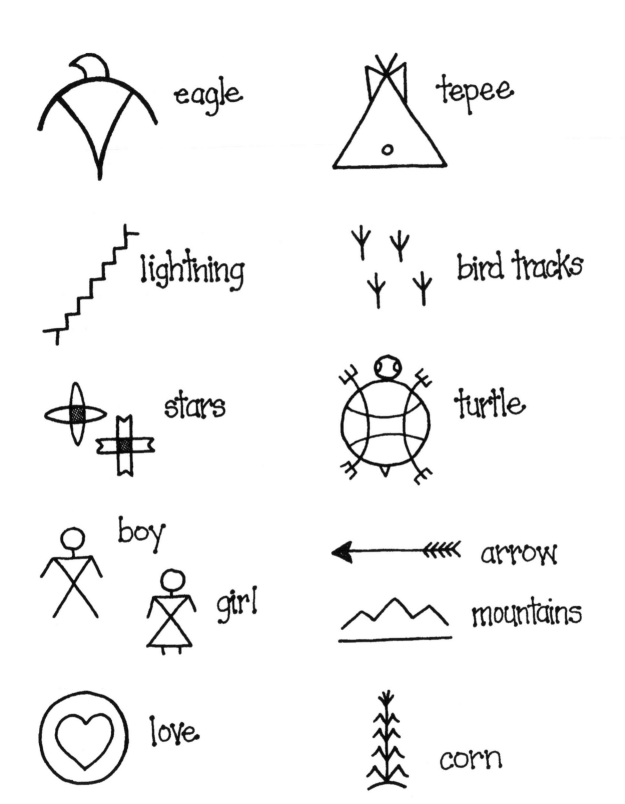

eagle

tepee

lightning

bird tracks

stars

turtle

boy

girl

arrow

mountains

love

corn

Native American Symbols

Name:_____

Say each picture name. Write the beginning
sound. Color each picture.

USE YOUR NOODLE: Draw a vase on the back
of this paper. Put six violets in the vase.

Activities for the Letter W

Tactile Introduction of the Letter

Letter Shape: watermelon seeds; white paint

Alphabet Puzzle: watermelon; worm

Sound Sorting

Wagon Sort: (Group Activity)

Gather the children in a circle on the floor around a wagon. Emphasize the sound of the letter *w*. Place the Mystery Box on the floor. Let each child pull one item from the box and tell the class what it is. If it begins with a *w*, then the child places that item in the wagon. If it does not begin with a *w*, it is placed back in the Mystery Box. After each child has had a turn, review each item in the wagon with the group.

Room Labels: white; window; watch; water

Oral Language

Sharing: The children can bring in something that starts with *w*.

Cooking and Tasting

Wassail:

You need 2 quarts apple juice, 1 pint cranberry juice, 3/4 cup sugar, 2 sticks cinnamon, 1 teaspoon whole allspice, and 1 small orange studded with whole cloves.

Mix all ingredients in a slow cooker and serve warm.

Other Possible W Foods: whipped cream; waffles; walnuts; watermelon

Mini Field Trips

walk to the nurse's office to be *weighed*

Interviews

waiter; waitress; wallpaper hanger

Literature & Writing

Authentic Literature & Related Writing Activity:

Read *Sylvester and the Magic Pebble* by William Steig. Have the children complete the sentence *I will wish for...*

Poetry: Read "There Are Big Waves" by Eleanor Farjeon. (See *Math Anthology: Stories, Poem, and Songs* from the "Mathematics in Action" series published by Macmillan-McGraw-Hill.)

Additional Writing Activities:

1. Continue the individual *My ABC Book,* "W is for..."

2. Read *Where the Wild Things Are* by Maurice Sendak. Trace each child's body on a large sheet of paper. Let the children paint their shape to look like a *wild thing.* Have them write a story about it.

3. See the "W Book List" for further appropriate literature ideas.

Sight Vocabulary

- **Pre-primer:** want; was; went; we; were; what; will; with
- **Primer:** wagon; walk; water; when; where; white; who; window; work

Math

Measurement:

Weight

Have the children walk to the nurse's office to be weighed. Show them how the scale works. Come back to the room and show them a balance scale. Provide lots of small objects to be weighed and balanced.

Telling Time:

Watches: Provide the handout of watches with analog read-outs. Have the children write down the correct time underneath each watch.

Name: _____

_____ _____ _____

_____ _____ _____

Science & Social Studies

Living Things:

Animals: walrus; wolf

Physical Science:

Solid, Liquid, Gas (Water): Discuss the three states of water by heating ice cubes (solid) until they melt (liquid) and finally form steam (gas).

Wind: Make pinwheels and attach them to the end of pencils. Take them outside on a windy day and watch them turn! (See the Appendix for a pinwheel pattern.)

Simple Machines: Wheels

Make a ramp with a plank. Let the children try to push a book down the ramp. Next have them put a pencil under the book and see how much easier it is to move the book. To apply what they have learned about wheels and wind, have the children take small cars and attach a sail. To make the sail, have them cut out a shape and tape it to a straw. Attach the straw to the top of the car with a lump of clay. Have a race where the children move their cars by blowing on the sail.

Seasons:

Winter Weather

Read ***The Winter Noisy Book*** by Margaret Wise Brown. Watch a video on winter and make a classroom story about the season on chart paper. Discuss how to dress appropriately for the cold weather.

Art

Wood Rubbings: Place paper over a variety of samples of wood and—using peeled crayons—the children rub to form neat prints!

Wallpaper Art:

Provide several old wallpaper books for the children to cut out shapes. Let them make attractive collages with the wallpaper. (When outdated, these books are usually given away free to teachers by the wallpaper stores.)

Physical Education & Music

Games:

"Pop Goes the Weasel"

All around the cobbler's bench,

The monkey chased the weasel.

The monkey thought

'Twas all in fun,

Pop! goes the weasel!

This can be played with two or more children. One child bounces the ball in rhythm as the others sing. On "Pop!" the child passes the ball to another child.

Wiggle Relay Race

Divide the class into two teams. Mark start and finish lines. At the "go" signal, the first player in each line flops to his or her stomach, clasps hands behind back, wiggles to the finish line, and then runs back to tag the next player in line. Be sure the children wear old clothes for this race!

Movement:

Walking: Have the children walk to the beat of a variety of songs.

Creative Movement

Have the children move the way they think a witch would move! You might add some scary music! How would they move if they were a washing machine? a windmill? a wooden toy soldier?

Music:

Suggested Songs: "Down by the Bay" by Raffi

Where the Wild Things Are: Watch a video of the opera *Where the Wild Things Are.*

Peter and the Wolf: Watch *Storyteller's Classics: Peter and the Wolf* by Orion Home Videos.

Name:_____

Draw 4 windows on the house.

Draw a worm in the apple.

Draw a wagon to go on the wheels.

Draw a witch to eat the watermelon.

USE YOUR NOODLE: Draw a web on the back of this paper. Draw a spider in the web. Draw what it caught for dinner.

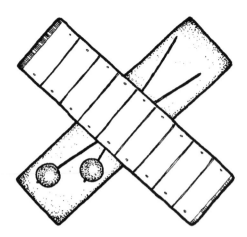

Activities for the Letter X

Tactile Introduction of the Letter

Letter Shape: Trix® cereal

Alphabet Puzzle: the letter *x*

Sound Sorting

X Box Sort: (Group Activity)

Gather the children in a circle around a cardboard box, labeled BOX. Discuss the fact that very few words begin with *x*, but that many words end in *x*. Provide an envelope with pictures, some illustrating words ending in *x (box, fox, ox, as, "sax," six, fix, mix)*. As each picture is drawn out of the envelope let the children decide if they hear the cks sound of *x* at the end of the word. If they do, have a child place that picture in the box. After all the pictures have been used, the teacher reviews each item in the box with the group.

Room Labels: six, box

Oral Language

Sharing:

Have the children share an "x-tra special" friend or toy with their classmates.

Cooking and Tasting

X-tra Special Fudge:

You need 3 cups semisweet chocolate chips, 1 can sweetened condensed milk, dash of salt, 1 cup chopped walnuts, and 1-1/2 tsp. vanilla.

In saucepan, over low heat, melt chips with condensed milk and salt. Remove from heat and stir in walnuts and vanilla. Spread into aluminum foil-lined 8-inch or 9-inch square pan. Chill for 2 hours or until firm. Turn fudge onto cutting board. Peel off foil and cut into squares.

Mini Field Trips

walk to the music room to see a xylophone

Interviews

x-ray technician; percussion player in an orchestra

Literature & Writing

Poetry: Read "X is 'Xcavation" by Phyllis McGinley. (See *Keep a Poem in Your Pocket* by Charlotte Huck, et al.)

Math

Measurement:

X Marks the Spot: Put X's around the room with masking tape and measure the distance from the teacher's desk by pacing it off.

Science & Social Studies

Living Things:

Animals: fox; ox

Physical Science:

X-rays

Invite an x-ray technician to come to the room with an assortment of old x-rays. Have the technician talk about the purposes of x-rays (to check for broken bones, find diseases, look into suitcases at the airport, etc.). Have the children make skeleton pictures. Put a copy of the skeleton on the overhead projector and help the children identify the bones. When this is done, give them a small black piece of paper. Show them how to make skeletons by dipping their thumb in the white paint provided to make a skull and drawing the rest with Q-tips® dipped in white.

Art

Cross-stitch: Have the children cross-stitch a design with yarn on 1-inch graph paper. Show samples of other needlework.

Physical Education & Music

Games:

X Tag: This game is played like regular tag with a chalk *X* as the "safe" spot.

Music:

Suggested Songs: "X Marks the Spot" on Sesame Street Records

Name: _____

TREASURE HUNT!

Look at the treasure map. Find the path that will take you to the X and the treasure!

DANGER!

SHARK PASS

SKULL ISLAND

X

Color your treasure map.

USE YOUR NOODLE: Turn this paper over. Draw 5 things you cannot find in your classroom. After you color the objects, draw a big X over each one!

Activities for the Letter Y

Tactile Introduction of the Letter

Letter Shape: yarn

Alphabet Puzzle: yo-yo

Sound Sorting

Yellow Box Sort: (Group Activity)

Gather the children in a circle on the floor around a box that you have covered with yellow paper. Emphasize the sound of the letter *y*. Place the Mystery Box on the floor. Let each child pull one item from the Mystery Box and tell the class what it is. If it begins with *y*, then the child places that item in the Yellow Box. If it does not begin with *y*, it is placed back in the Mystery Box. After each child has had a turn, review each item in the Yellow Box with the group.

Room Labels: yellow, year, yard (measurement), yo yo

Oral Language

Sharing: The children can bring in something yellow to share. They can measure how many objects in the class are a yard (or more) long or tall.

Cooking and Tasting

Yellow Cake: Prepare the cake according to package directions. Frost with yellow (lemon) canned icing. Prepare on a day when everyone wears at least one yellow thing or piece of clothing.

Other Possible Y Foods: yams; yogurt

Mini Field Trips

school yard

Interviews

yoga instructor; someone from the YMCA or YWCA to explain the available activities

Literature & Writing

Authentic Literature & Related Writing Activity:

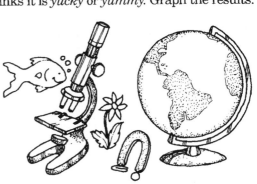

Read *Yertle the Turtle* by Dr. Seuss. Have the children write what they think is the moral of the story.

Poetry: Read "The Yak" by Jack Prelutsky in *Zoo Things.*

Additional Writing Activities:

1. Continue the individual *My ABC Book,* "Y is for…"
2. Have the children complete the sentence *Yesterday I…*
3. See the "Y Book List" for further appropriate literature ideas.

Sight Vocabulary

- **Pre-primer:** yes; you
- **Primer:** yellow; your

Math

Sorting: Provide each child with several short and long strands of various colors of yarn. The children can sort these by color and size.

Graphing:

Yucky–Yummy Yam Graph: Have a yam casserole prepared. Let each child taste the yam casserole and record on a slip of paper if he or she thinks it is *yucky* or *yummy.* Graph the results.

Science & Social Studies

Living Things:

Animals: yak

Yaks: Research yaks on the computer. Make a classroom chart about them.

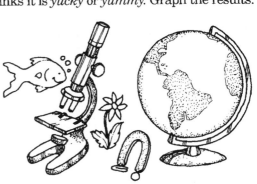

Safety:

Yellow!: Explain that a yellow light means *Caution.* The yellow *Yield* sign means to be careful and let the other car go first.

Art

Yellow Yarn Painting:

Have each child fold a piece of black construction paper in half and open it up. Have flat trays of yellow paint available and pieces of yellow yarn. Dip the yarn in the yellow paint, lay it on the fold of the paper, and shut the paper. While pressing on the top of the black paper, gently pull the string out. Some interesting designs will be formed.

Physical Education & Music

Games:

Yes or No

Each child is given five Popsicle® sticks at the beginning of the game. During the next few minutes, each child tries to get one of the other children to say *yes* or *no*. The children must talk to each other and answer any question they are asked. If they say *yes* or *no*, they must give the other child one Popsicle® stick. The winner is the child with the most Popsicle® sticks at the end of play. This is a great game for a rainy day. It allows children to *talk* and *roam* when no outdoor play is possible!

Movement:

Creative Movement

Have the children pretend to be a yo-yo. They can go up and down, twirl around, swing back and forth, stop abruptly or slowly!

Music:

Suggested Songs: "Yankee Doodle"

Songs by Yani: Many great recordings by Yani are available.

Name: _____

Say each picture name. If it begins with a "Y," color it yellow. If it begins with another letter, color it any color you wish.

USE YOUR NOODLE: Draw 5 things that are yellow on the back of this page.

Activities for the Letter Z

Tactile Introduction of the Letter

Letter Shape: zigzag (rickrack)

Alphabet Puzzle: zebra

Sound Sorting

Ziplock® Bag Sort: (Individual Activity)

Give each child a Ziplock® bag to fill with *z* drawings or pictures cut from magazines.

Oral Language

Sharing: The children can bring in something in a Ziplock® bag to share.

Cooking and Tasting

Zucchini Bread:

You need 3 eggs, 1 cup vegetable oil, 1-1/2 cups sugar, 2 teaspoons vanilla, 2-1/4 cups of grated zucchini (drained), 2 cups all-purpose flour, 1/4 teaspoon baking powder, 2 teaspoons baking soda, 3 teaspoons cinnamon, 1 teaspoon salt, and 1-1/4 cups chopped walnuts and raisins.

Beat eggs lightly in large bowl. Stir in oil, sugar, vanilla, and zucchini. Sift together and stir in dry ingredients; stir in raisins and nuts. Bake in two well-greased bread pans at 375 degrees for one hour.

Other Possible Z Foods: zucchini cake; zucchini stuffing; zucchini stir fry, etc.

Mini Field Trips

petting zoo

Interviews

zookeeper; zoologist

Literature & Writing

Authentic Literature & Related Writing Activity:

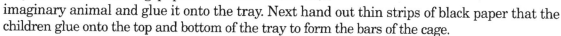

Read *If I Ran the Zoo* by Dr. Seuss. Have the children write about an imaginary animal they would put in the zoo. Give each child a clean Styrofoam meat tray and some drawing paper. Let them draw their imaginary animal and glue it onto the tray. Next hand out thin strips of black paper that the children glue onto the top and bottom of the tray to form the bars of the cage.

Poetry: Read "Zebra Question" by Shel Silverstein. (See *A Light in the Attic*.)

Additional Writing Activities:

1. Complete the individual *My ABC Book*, "Z is for…"
2. See the "Z Book List" for further appropriate literature ideas.

Math

Numbers:

Zero: Introduce or reinforce the concept of zero as a place holder. Illustrate how it works for our number system.

Science & Social Studies

Living Things:

Animals: zebra

Plants: Plant some zinnia seeds in potting soil and watch them grow!

Habitats: Discuss *natural habitats* vs. *zoo habitats*. Show a video of the San Diego Zoo to show the children how this zoo simulates the natural habitat of each animal.

Art

Zoo Mural: Let the class work on a giant zoo mural!

Physical Education & Music

Games:

Zigzag Toss

Arrange the children in two lines facing each other. The first child in one line tosses the beanbag to the first child in the facing line, and so on, until the beanbag gets to the end of the lines.

Music:

Suggested Songs

- "The Zoo" by Peter, Paul and Mary
- "Zippedy Doo Dah"

Name: ______________________

Welcome to the zoo! Draw the animal that is written on the sign at each site. Color your zoo!

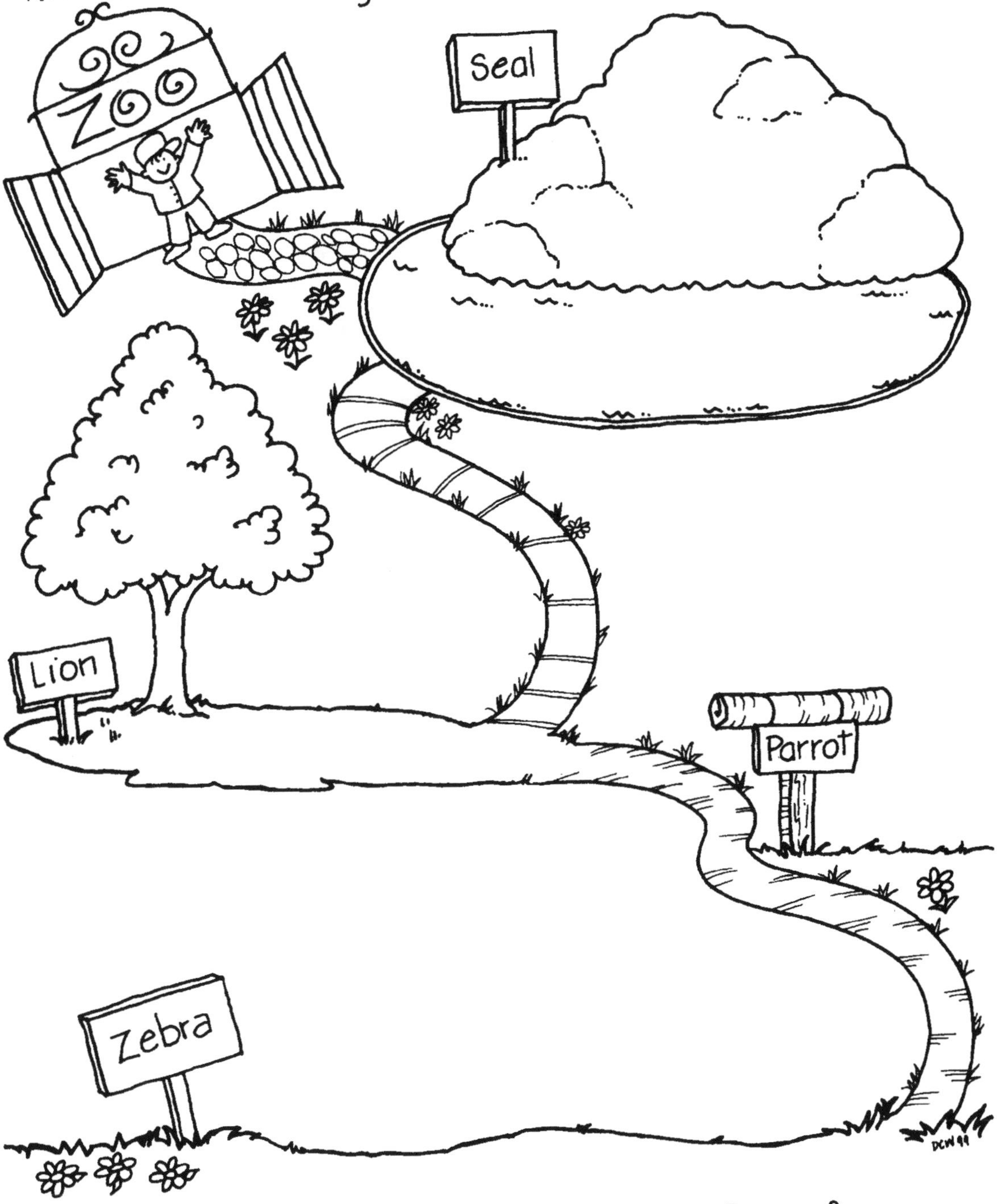

ZOO
Seal
Lion
Parrot
Zebra
DCW 99

USE YOUR NOODLE: Turn this paper over. Draw four zany zoo animals! Think of a name for each one.

Section Two

Hands-on Phonics Activities for Emerging Readers

Grades (1–2)

Emerging readers benefit by the continued teaching of phonics in meaningful contexts. The order of sounds taught should be determined by you and based upon the observed needs of your children. This section provides many innovative ideas to introduce, supplement, and reinforce specific skills. The ideas are brief and simple to implement. Moreover, by utilizing the lists in the last section of the book, almost all of the activities can be adapted to a wide variety of skills.

Sorting and Manipulative Activities:

These activities can be used for individualized instruction, small group work, and for teaching the class as a whole. The necessary materials are generally those found in your classroom.

Puzzles and Games:

Many old, familiar games have been adapted to teach

specific phonics skills. Most of the games are played by small groups and many can be used for whole class instruction. They are simple to make and the children should be able to play most of them independently, after receiving initial instruction.

Independent Activity Cards:

Many ideas are presented for simple task cards that reinforce specific phonics skills. It is suggested that these ideas be printed on index cards and laminated. The beauty of these activities is that they can be done independently. Many of them are self-checking. There are many simple ways to keep these cards organized so that the children can take them, and return them to the proper place when they are finished. Old cardboard pocket charts, cardboard boxes with partitions, and hanging shoebags work well. Label the cards and the storage compartments to match!

Sorting and Manipulative Activities

Visual Discrimination of Upper- and Lower-case Letters:

Make a floor gameboard using an old vinyl table cloth or a shower curtain. On one side, print all the upper-case letters of the alphabet; on the flip side, print the lower-case letters. Provide matching sets of cards. Children can sit on the floor, draw a card from the pile, and match it to the same letter or the corresponding upper- or lower-case letter—depending on which skill you are reinforcing.

Alphabet Fun:

A box of alphabet cereal can provide many activities! Give every child a generous scoop. Children who still are not sure of all the letter names can be asked to simply lay the letters out and identify them. Other activities include putting the letters in alphabetical order, making piles of consonants and vowels, pasting the correct initial letter next to pictures provided, making words and writing them on a piece of paper, and picking out the letters that spell the name of an object the child has drawn and pasting them under the drawing. When the lesson is over, the remaining letters can be eaten for snack!

Sound Train:

This is a game children love to play if you have the room! Line up the chairs to make a *train*. Each child takes a seat on the train. You call on a child and say a word or display a picture or word card. If the child answers correctly (gives the initial consonant sound, final sound, vowel sound, rhyming word, etc.), he or she moves his or her chair to the front of the train. In this way the train *chugs* around the room. This game can also be played outside with the children sitting on the grass.

Magnetic Letters:

Individual Activity:

For individual phonics activities provide metal cookie sheets and a supply of magnetic letters that the children can take to their desks and spell words. If you provide a list of words to sound out and practice, two children can work together. One child calls out the words while the second child spells it on the cookie sheet. The first child can then check to see if it is spelled correctly.

Group Activity:

For a group activity, you can place a container of magnetic letters near the overhead projector. While presenting a particular phonics skill, children can be called up to spell letters on the overhead. This is also a great way to introduce or practice weekly spelling words.

Sand Spelling:

No matter what their age, children love to play in the sand. Provide a shallow box filled with sand for individuals to practice their spelling words. Have the child bring his or her spelling list to the table, say the word, and use his or her finger to write it in the sand.

Feltboard Fun:

Children enjoy playing with feltboards. Cut out an assortment of objects or shapes from felt and prepare simple direction cards that include the number and color words; for example, *two yellow circles, one blue square.* You hold up the card and read what it says, pointing to each word; the child must match what is read by putting the correct felt objects on the board. More advanced students can read the cards themselves.

Letter Circles:

Don't throw away those pizza boards! Paste pictures of objects (old workbooks are a wonderful source!) around the circle and provide matching clip clothespins. The children must clip the clothespin with the corresponding initial sound (or blend or digraph) to the correct picture.

For more advanced students you can write the whole word on the clothespin. If some of the children are ready, this can also be used for antonyms and synonyms.

Store the pins and the circle in the original pizza box!

Letter Clocks:

Prepare some letter clocks as shown here by cutting a 16-inch circle out of posterboard. Letters to be studied are then printed around the clock. Attach the clock hand with a paper fastener. Have the students spin the hand on the clock and give a word that begins or ends with a particular consonant, blend, etc.

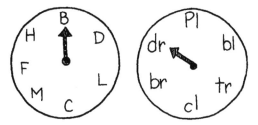

Flip Books:

Make flip books from unlined 3" x 5" index cards. Punch two holes on the left-hand side of the cards and attach with notebook rings. For emergent readers these can be used to teach initial consonants, ending sounds, initial blends and digraphs, as shown.

Reading Rhymes:

Each morning select an appropriate Big Book to read to the class. First read the book from cover to cover for pure reading enjoyment. The second time you read it, place a piece of clear acetate over a page. Encourage students to come up and circle the rhyming words in erasable markers. These rhyming pairs can then be put on a chart to be reviewed again at a later time.

Rhyming Table:

Display mixed-up pairs of rhyming objects on a table in the room; for example: hat, bat, rock, sock. Have the children come to the table and find two objects that rhyme. Change the display frequently. Encourage the students to bring in their own rhyming objects to be added to the table.

Rhyming Flash Cards:

Prepare flash cards with pictures of objects whose names have rhyming possibilities; for example: sock, pen, cat, cake, man, ring, etc. Call on students to think of a word that rhymes with each picture shown.

Sorting Table:

Provide a sorting table that can be changed to meet the objectives in your phonics plans. Many free or relatively inexpensive objects can be used as sorting bins—empty Cool Whip® containers, margarine tubs, fast-food Styrofoam containers, small square plastic baskets available at "dollar stores." Activities will be similar to the ones listed under "Vowel Table" and "Tissue Box Sorts."

Vowel Table:

Display several items on the table to be sorted by vowel sounds; for example: hat, dish, rock, umbrella. At the beginning of the activity, place a large card on the table with the particular vowel you would like to emphasize that day. Ask the children to come up and find an item in which they hear that particular vowel. As a follow-up activity, after introducing *all* the vowels, a card for each can be added and the items on the table may then be sorted by each of the different vowel sounds heard. Change the display frequently. Encourage the students to bring in their own objects to be added to the Vowel Table.

Tissue Box Sorts:

Small square tissue boxes can be used for a variety of phonics sorting activities. To prepare the boxes, carefully remove the plastic insert around the opening. Label each side of the box with a different answer and a different colored sticker. Cut 10-inch strips from posterboard. Depending on your choice of activity, paste a different picture, or write a different vowel, consonant blend, etc. near the top of each strip. On the back of each strip place the colored sticker that corresponds to the correct answer on the tissue box. The child decides which side of the box to use first and turns that side to the front. The strips are then placed face-up on the table. The child decides which strips belong in the box. When the sorting is finished, the child is able to check the answers by removing the strips from the box, turning them over, and seeing if the correct colored sticker is on the back of each one.

Choose from a variety of activities as illustrated on the following page.

Initial Consonant Sounds:

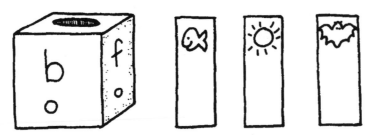

Final Consonant Sounds:

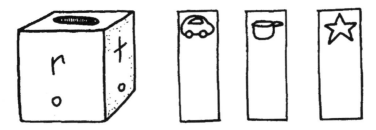

Initial Consonant Blends:

Vowel Sounds:

Vowel Rules:

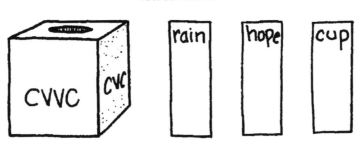

Sorting Boards:

Sorting boards can be made by folding a piece of 22" x 11" tagboard in half so that it makes a stand-up board. Divide the front of the board into five equal squares. In each square place a picture of whatever it is you want the children to sort. It may be initial consonants, final consonants, vowel sounds, blends, digraphs, etc. Provide an envelope of picture or word cards to be sorted as appropriate.

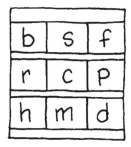

Library Pocket Sorts:

Another way to make a sorting activity is to take a large sheet of posterboard and attach library envelopes to form sorting pockets. Once again, this can be used to sort whatever is appropriate to your phonics lesson.

Pizza Sorts:

Ask parents to send in empty pizza boxes. (If you're lucky your local pizza shop will donate a bunch of unused ones!) For each box make a tagboard pizza by cutting circles 10 inches in diameter. Cut the pizzas into eighths. After deciding on the skill you want to reinforce, write an appropriate word on each slice. For example, if you are studying the long and short vowel sounds, you could label one pizza box *Toppings: Short Vowels* and the other one *Toppings: Long Vowels*. Mix the 16 wedges and let the children sort the slices into the correct boxes until they have a complete pizza in each box!

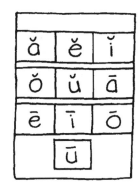

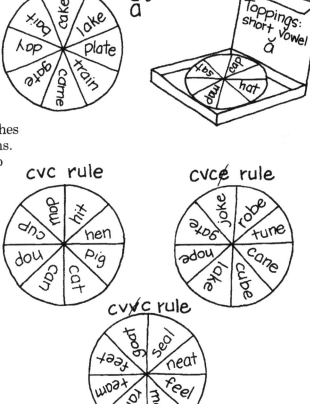

Paper Plate Sorts for Long and Short Vowels:

Give each child one whole paper plate and one cut in half. On the half plate instruct the children to write the vowel they are studying or a particular word that uses the vowel sound you are teaching. Staple the half plate over the whole plate to form a pocket. Provide magazines for the children to look through. Instruct the children to cut out pictures of objects with a matching vowel sound and place it in the paper plate pocket.

Pocket Games:

For the following pocket games, cut manila folders in half. Cut the front flap down to 4 inches. Staple each side of the front flap to the back of the folder to form a pocket.

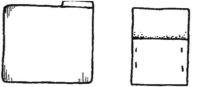

Initial Consonants Pocket Game:

Write the consonants to be studied on the flaps. Provide pictures for children to sort into the correct pockets.

Ending Consonants Pocket Game:

Draw a line and write a consonant to indicate you want the children to find pictures that end with a particular letter. Provide pictures for the children to sort into the correct pockets.

Blends Pocket Game:

Write the blends to be studied on the flaps. Provide pictures for the children to sort into the correct folders.

Individual Chalkboard Activities:

Provide each child with a chalkboard, chalk, and an eraser. Children of all ages love to work with chalkboards. These activities can be adapted to the level and ability of your students.

Beginning Consonant Sounds:

To get the children used to using their chalkboards, start with a simple activity. Pick a child to come to the front of the room and play this adaptation of the game "I Spy." The child thinks of something he or she sees in the room and writes down the first letter of the object. The child then lets the classmates take turns guessing. The child who guesses correctly comes to the front of the room with his or her chalkboard and the game continues.

Ending Consonant Sounds:

The same game can be played as above using the object's *ending* sound.

Beginning and Ending Consonants:

Have each child place a chalkboard on his or her desk. Illustrate on the classroom board how the children are to draw two lines at the bottom of their boards.

When the children are ready, say a word like *bat* and ask them what the word starts with. When someone says *b*, ask them where on the board you should place the *b*. When you have filled in the first line, tell them to put the *b* on their board. Next ask what the word *bat* ends in and where that should go on the board. When you have completed the demonstration and the children have successfully filled in the lines on their boards, have them erase the letters and draw the two lines again. Call out another word and have the children write down the beginning and ending sounds. Have them hold up their boards when they have finished so you can check to see who is having difficulty. After they are adept at this activity, you may increase the difficulty by showing them how to divide their board into four boxes and give them four new words, for example: bank, car, kitten, mother.

This activity can be expanded to include the medial consonant sounds, too! For example, "What sound do you hear at the beginning of the word *mitten?* What sound do you hear in the middle? at the end?"

Phoneme Substitution:

Have the children take out their chalkboards. Discuss a particular word chunk, for example, *at.* In the middle of the board have each child print *at.* Ask the children, "If you want to make the word *cat,* what letter would they need?" When someone says *c,* ask where they would have to put the *c.* After eliciting the correct placement and writing it on the board, check to see if all of the children have the *c* in the proper place on their individual boards. Then ask the children if they can think of a different *at* word to make by changing the *c* to a different letter. Let them erase the *c* and make up a new word. Call on several children to share the word they came up with. See how many different words can be made. (See *Word Ending Combinations* in "Lists for Developing Hands-on Phonics Activities" to help you think of new activities.) As the children's skill level increases, this can be used with blends and digraphs; for example, slat, chat.

Slider Activities:

A good follow-up to the chalkboard activities is the use of sliders. Reproduce one of the sliders provided on the following pages on heavy paper or make your own. The children can cut them out themselves but will need help with the slits. Fit the long strip through the slits cut in the shorter strip. By sliding the long strip up and down, new words appear in the opening. These can be used to study beginning and ending consonant sounds, blends, and word endings. They are a wonderful individual free-time activity and can also serve as a great review. For more advanced students, you can reproduce the blank ones and encourage them to make up their own sliders!

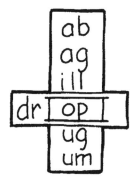

_____ an	_____ ad
b	b
c	d
f	f
m	h
p	l
r	m
t	p
v	s

_____ ag

_____ ap

b
g
l
r
s
t
w

c
g
l
m
n
r
s
t
y

_____ am

_____ ab

d
h
j
r
t
y

c
d
g
j
t

_____ at	_____ ax
_____	_____

b	f
c	l
f	s
h	t
m	w
p	
r	
s	
v	

_____ en

_____

_____ et

_____

d
h
m
p
t
y

b
g
j
l
m
n
p
s
v
w
y

_____ eg

_____ ed

b
k
p

b
f
l
r
w

_____ in

_____ id

b
f
k
p
s
t
w

b
d
h
k
l
m
r

_____ it

_____ ip

b	d
f	h
h	l
k	n
l	qu
p	r
qu	s
s	t
w	z

_____ ig

_____ og

b
d
f
g
j
p
r
w

b
d
f
h
j
l

_____ op

_____ od

b
c
h
m
p
s
t

c
g
m
n
p
r
s

_____ ot	_____ ob

c	b
d	c
g	f
h	g
j	j
l	l
n	m
p	r
r	s
t	

_____ ug

_____ ud

b
d
h
j
l
m
p
r
t

b
c
d
m

_____ up

_____ ut

c
p
s

b
c
g
h
j
n
r

_____ un

_____ um

b
f
g
n
p
r
s

b
g
h
m
r
s

_____ ub	_____ ack

c	b
d	h
h	j
n	l
p	p
r	qu
s	r
t	s
	t

_____ eck	_____ ick
b	k
d	l
n	n
p	p
	qu
	s
	t
	w

_____ ill	_____ ell
b d f g h k m p qu s t w	b d f j qu s t w y

_____ ock

_____ uck

d
h
l
m
r
s

b
d
l
m
p
t
y

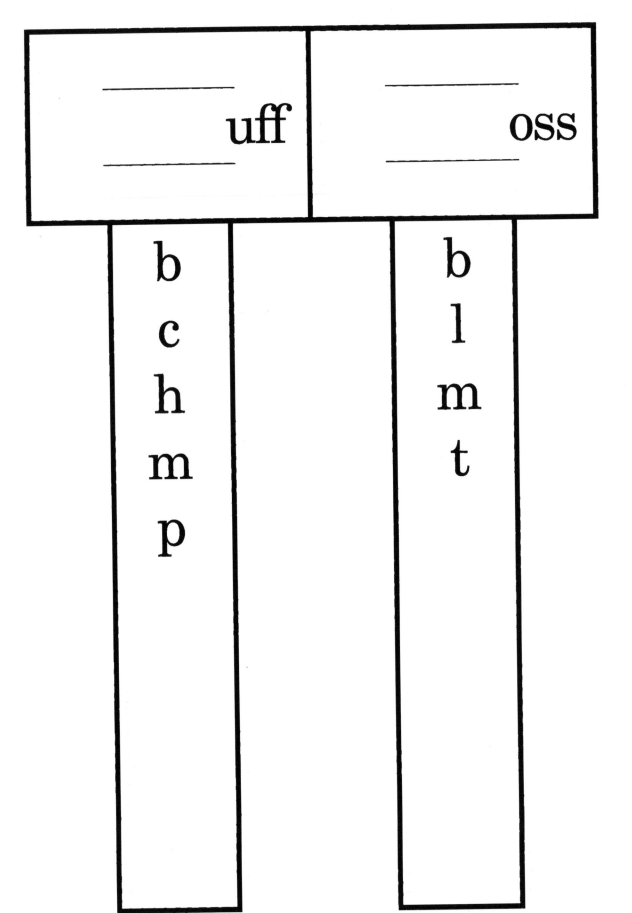

_____ uff

_____ oss

b
c
h
m
p

b
l
m
t

Letter Detectives:

Prepare a set of illustrated word cards omitting the first letter (or last) of each word. Laminate the cards and place in an envelope with an erasable marker. The children can take the cards to their desks and write the correct first letter on the card with the marker. After you check the cards, the student erases them and puts them back in the envelope for the next child. This can be done with initial and final consonants, initial blends, digraphs, etc.

Word Wheels:

Make several word wheels as shown using tagboard circles and a brad. (Punch hole with puncher in the pointer only. Use a pencil to punch a hole in the circle. This will make the spinner work better!) Provide several cards to be used as independent activities with the word wheel. For example:

- Draw a picture for each word you can make on the word wheel.
- Write a sentence for each word you can make on the word wheel.
- Write each word you can make on your paper. Next to it make the plural of the word.
- Write the words on the wheel in ABC order.
- Write an antonym (or synonym) for each word on the word wheel.

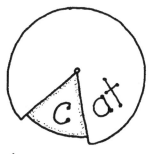 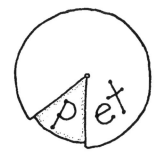

Mini Flash Cards:

Reproduce the blank form provided in the Appendix on light colored construction paper. There are a variety of activities you can do with these minis! When introducing new vocabulary words, give each child a strip and let the children write one new word on each. (For younger children you can write the words on before duplicating.) The strips can be cut apart and saved in an envelope. They can be used as regular flash cards to help the children study the new words at home. You could have the children take out an envelope and put the words in alphabetical order, pick out the words with a particular beginning sound, consonant blend, digraph, vowel sound, etc. The mini cards could be sorted into categories such as *people, places, things.* When the children have enough cards, encourage them to make sentences. When teaching plurals, you can give the children mini cards with a singular noun written on one side and ask them to write the plural on the back.

Word Family Cards:

Write a group of words from the same word family on 3" x 5" index cards. Bind these with a ring binder. As you introduce a particular word family to the students, place the bound cards on the activity table for their use.

Ziploc® Word Building:

The object of this activity is to match word parts to form words. Provide Ziploc® baggies of word cards made from 3" x 5" index cards. Put word endings (such as *art, at, end*) on some of the cards and word beginnings on others (such as *st, br, b*). More advanced students can build words from beginning, medial, and ending parts. To make this a self-correcting exercise, you can print all the possible combinations on a laminated sheet and keep this available for the children to use to check themselves. If you want to keep a record of how well the children do, suggest they write down the words they have built and hand them in to be checked.

| st | art | | tr | end | | br | ake | | pl | an |

Building Words With Word Holders:

Make "word holders" for each child as shown using oaktag. Provide each child with an envelope containing the letters of the alphabet (three of each). (See the Appendix for a reproducible alphabet.) Students can set up their holders on their desks and you can direct an activity to build words. For example, you say:

- "Today we will build the word *bat*."
- "What letter makes the first sound you hear in *bat*?"
- "Put the *b* at the beginning of your holder."
- "What vowel sound do you hear in *bat*?"
- "What is the last sound you hear in *bat*?"

When everyone has the correct letters in the correct position, you might go on to ask, "Who can change one of the letters and make a new word?"

A variation might be to introduce a new vocabulary word by giving clues until the word is spelled out. For example:

- "Our new word starts like the word *duck*."
- "The vowel that comes next is the vowel sound you hear in *hot*."
- "The word ends with the sound you hear at the beginning of *good*."

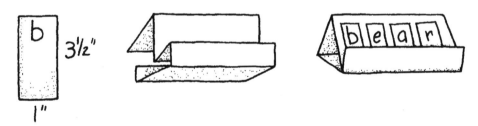

Scrambled Words:

Prepare a set of illustrated cards with scrambled letters for the corresponding word. Number the cards, laminate, and place in an envelope. The children are told to number their paper and to do the cards in numerical order. ("Take card #1, look at the picture, unscramble the word, and write it correctly beside the #1 on your paper.") Provide a numbered answer sheet for the child to self-correct.

Vowel Circle:

Provide a set of vowel cards for each child playing. Children sit in a circle with the vowel cards in their hand. You call out a word with a short vowel sound. Each child is instructed to place the corresponding vowel card face down in front of him or her. When everyone is finished, have the children turn the cards over for a quick check. This game can also be used for initial consonant sounds, final consonants, blends, etc.

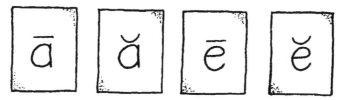

Short Vowel Cards:

Prepare laminated cards as shown. After giving each child a card, elicit what is alike about the three words in each box and what is different. When they realize that each box has words that begin and end alike but have a different short vowel sound, the activity can begin. Give each child an erasable marker and call out one word from each box. This is a great assessment activity and will quickly point out the children who are having difficulty with short vowel sounds.

bat bit bet	cat cut cot	dog dug dig	fan fin fun	get got gut	nut net not
hog hug hag	hot hit hat	bed bad bud	lot let lit	bag big bug	hem hum ham
sit sat set	pot pet pat	lap lop lip	red rid rod	job jib jab	lag lug leg
cad cod cud	rim ram rum	sip sap sup	mad mud mid	led lid lad	pop pup pep

Silent "E" Strips:

Cut 8" x 2" strips of tagboard. Crease the strips about 2 inches from the right end. Write a short vowel word to the left of the crease. Write the *e* to the right of the crease. When the strip is folded, the short vowel word shows. When the *e* is revealed, the letters on the strip spell a word with a long vowel sound. These strips can be used to teach a directed lesson on the silent *e* rule. After the lesson, place the strips in a decorated coffee can for the children to take to their desks and use for practice.

Here are some suggested words:

hop—hope	plan—plane	pin—pine	rat—rate
hat—hate	cap—cape	kit—kite	fat—fate
tap—tape	Tim—time	rid—ride	tub—tube
cub—cube	pal—pale	slid—slide	grip—gripe
man—mane	rip—ripe	fad—fade	fin—fine
slat—slate	scrap—scrape	not—note	mat—mate
cut—cute	dim—dime	mad—made	tam—tame

Coloring Book Word Recognition:

Cut out some pictures of simple objects from old coloring books. Mount these on tagboard and write the name of the object on the back. Laminate. Write each letter of the word on a 1-inch square of tagboard. Put each picture in a separate manila envelope and include a small envelope of the letters to be used to spell the name of the object. The children can take an envelope to their desk and attempt to spell the object correctly. To self-correct, the children simply flip over the picture.

"Take-out" Spell-a-Word:

Fill Styrofoam fast-food containers with macaroni alphabet letters or small magnetic letters. In each one place several little pictures of words to spell. Write the answers on the bottom of the box with a ball-point pen. Children can "take out" a box and try to spell the words. They can then turn the box over to see if they are correct.

Card Sentences:

Once children begin to know some simple sight words, an enjoyable way to instruct them in word functions is to give children cards with one simple word on each. On one side print the word in lower-case letters; on the other, start the word with a capital. For example:

the	jumps
cat	runs
dog	hops
boy	plays
girl	skips

Provide one card with a period.

Ask the child with *the* to come to the front of the room to start the sentence. Make sure to elicit the fact that he or she needs to hold up the side of the card with the capital *T* since this would be the beginning of the sentence. Ask the students who has a word they think could come next in a sentence. Who has a word that could go third? Now what do we need? Once the children have built a complete sentence *(The dog runs.)*, let them continue to substitute nouns and verbs to make a variety of complete sentences.

When the students are doing well at this, add some adjective cards. For example:

black	big
red	fat
tan	little

This activity can be done periodically as the skill level of your students increases. Eventually, you can add a lot more words, question marks, exclamation points, and even quotation marks.

On-a-Roll Vocabulary Practice:

Using posterboard cut out a large square and make two slits as shown. Write the words to be practiced on a roll of adding-machine tape. Insert the end of the tape from the back of the square and through the slit. The children can pair up to do this activity. One child pulls the tape through and reads the word to the other child. When one child completes the roll, the other child becomes the reader.

For a related activity, you can place blank adding machine tape in the carrier and let the children write in words as instructed. For example: "Write down all of the words you can think of that use the *at* chunk. See if your buddy can read your words!"

Puzzles and Games

Greeting Card Puzzles:

Ask the children to bring in old greeting cards. Cut the cards into puzzle pieces and put in envelopes. Children can take an envelope to their desk and sort and assemble the written portion of the card.

Word Family Puzzles:

This is a great activity to reinforce word families. Cut rectangular strips of posterboard. On each card paste a picture of two objects whose names rhyme. Cut each rectangle into two pieces to form a jigsaw puzzle. Keep in an envelope for an individual freetime activity.

For more advanced students paste several rhyming pictures on one piece of posterboard and cut into a jigsaw. Allow them to mix up the puzzle pieces from other envelopes. (If you number the back of each puzzle piece to correspond to the number on the original envelope, the pieces can easily be resorted.) This can also be used with consonant blends, as illustrated.

Use the same idea to prepare reinforcement for homonyms for older children, too.

 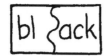  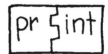

Hopscotch Phonics:

Make a hopscotch board using an old vinyl shower curtain or tablecloth, or construct one on the floor with masking tape, or draw one on the blacktop with chalk, or use an existing painted one on the playground. Place an appropriate card (initial consonants, blends, digraphs, words, synonyms, antonyms, etc.) in each section. There are many variations of this activity. Initially the children can sit around the hopscotch board with markers (bingo chips, bottle caps, etc.). You then call out a child's name followed by a word. That child must then place a chip on the corresponding square that represents the sound in the word. More advanced children may toss a chip into one of the squares and give a word that is appropriate; for example, a word that starts with the blend in the box, an antonym for the word in the box, etc. Later on, as an activity or assessment, you can duplicate boards on paper and ask the children to fill in the board as directed. For example: "In the first square write the final consonant you hear in *cat*." or "Write a word that rhymes with *dish*."

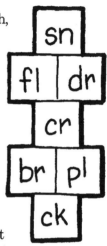

Go Fish:

Prepare decks of "matching" cards according to the skill you are teaching. For example, you might want to teach the matching upper- and lower-case letters. Prepare upper- and lower-case sets of cards and shuffle. Deal an equal number of cards to each child. Children can draw cards in turn. If the cards match, they are placed face down in front of the child. Play continues until all cards have been matched. The children may want to ask for the card they need instead of simply drawing; for example, "Do you have the lower case *d*?"

This game lends itself to opposites, rhyming words, contractions, synonyms, antonyms, etc.

Phonics Tic-Tac-Toe:

See the Appendix for the tic-tac-toe gameboard.

Ending Sound Tic-Tac-Toe:

Prepare tic-tac-toe boards, lettered differently for each child. Laminate these so they can be used frequently. Each child receives a playing board. You say a word (for example, *cat*). The children listen for the ending sound; if that letter appears on their board, they place a marker on the letter. The first child to cover three letters in a row is the winner.

t	r	p
l	g	d
f	s	n

d	l	r
g	p	f
s	n	t

Vowel Tic-Tac-Toe:

Provide a blank tic-tac-toe board on laminated posterboard, X and O markers, and a stack of picture cards whose names have a short vowel sound. Use old workbooks to get the pictures. The cards should have the correct vowel letter written on the back. Put the picture cards in a pile with the picture sides up. The first player picks the top card, says the word, and tells what vowel sound he or she hears. The card is then flipped over to see if the answer is right. If correct, the child puts a marker on a square. The card is then placed on the bottom of the pile and the next player picks the top card. Play continues until one person gets three X's or O's in a line.

Rhyming Tic-Tac-Toe:

This is played as above except you provide picture cards whose name will rhyme with familiar words. As the players draw cards, they must say the word and a word that rhymes with it. If correct, a marker is placed on the board. Play continues as above.

Vocabulary Tic-Tac-Toe:

Prepare tic-tac-toe boards by printing a vocabulary word in each square. Laminate the boards and provide erasable markers and reward chips of two different colors. The child who goes first must choose a square in which to place his or her X or O, but he or she must be able to read the word (or use it in a sentence, or give an antonym or synonym, depending on the skill you are reinforcing) before marking it with the marker.

Phonics Bingo:

Bingo can be used in a variety of ways. Duplicate the Bingo gameboard provided in the Appendix and laminate it on a piece of tagboard to make it reusable. You can then fill in the boxes appropriately with erasable markers, depending on the skill to be taught. Some examples are given here.

Initial Sounds Bingo:

Write an initial consonant, blend, or digraph in each box. Make sure these are written in a different order on each Bingo card. Provide markers for the children. Call out a word (or show a picture of an object) for the students to identify and cover the initial sound they hear. The first student to cover five words in a row (horizontally, vertically, or diagonally) wins the game.

Vocabulary Bingo:

Write the vocabulary words on each card to be used. Make sure they are written in a different order on each Bingo card. Provide markers for the children. Call out the words for the students to identify and cover. The first student to cover five words in a row (horizontally, vertically, or diagonally) wins the game.

Phonics Dominoes:

Initial Consonant Sounds

Prepare domino cards out of posterboard. Choose letters of the alphabet that you would like to emphasize and make cards with these letters on one half of the card and a picture beginning with one of the letters on the other. The letter and the picture on the same card should be different. Remember that the number of pictures must correspond to the number of letters. For instance, if you make five cards with the letter *C*, you must have five pictures beginning with that letter. The game is played by matching the letters and pictures by initial sounds.

Advanced Phonics Dominoes

Prepare a set of 30 3" x 5" index cards by drawing a line with black marker down the middle of each card. Decide on the skill to be taught (visual discrimination of words containing the same initial consonants or blends, rhyming words, opposites, synonyms, etc.). Write the words on each half of the card so it can be matched to another. (This can be done easily if you lay the cards out first.) Make several "Free" cards. To play, deal the cards out to two children. The first child turns up a domino and places it on the table. The other player must match one side of the domino with a card of his or her own. If the child is unable to do this, he or she loses a turn. Play continues until one player is out of cards.

Blender Bender:

Each child receives a magazine or an old workbook and a sheet of manila paper. You show a picture or a word card that contains a specific blend to be reviewed. A kitchen timer is then set for ten minutes and the children must go through the magazines, cut out pictures that start with that particular sound, and paste them on the paper. When the timer rings, the child with the most pictures is the winner.

Blending Buddies Card Game:

Prepare 50 word cards each containing one word beginning with a blend. Cut the word cards in two, separating the blend from the rest of the word. Two or more children may be chosen to play this game. Shuffle the word cards and the blend cards and put each pile face down on the table. The first player picks one card from each stack. If the student thinks he or she forms a word, the child puts them together and says the word. If the child is right, he or she keeps the cards. If the cards do not form a word, the cards are placed on the bottom of each stack. The child with the most cards at the end of the game is the winner.

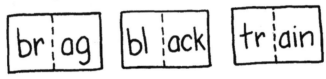

Short Vowel Gameboards:

Make a gameboard for each of the short vowel word families. Provide letter cards (consonants, consonant blends, consonant digraphs) for the children to use to form words. This can be played alone or in partners or teams. The winner is the child who makes the most words.

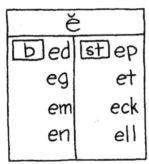 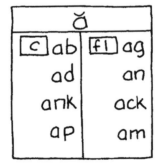

Dial-a-Vowel:

Cut a circle 5 inches in diameter out of heavy posterboard. Divide the circle into five equal segments and write a vowel on each. Make a spinner using a hole punch and brad. (Punch hole with puncher in the pointer only. Use a pencil to punch a hole in the circle. This will make the spinner work better!) Prepare several playing boards with simple words, leaving out the vowel in each. Laminate these. Provide erasable markers.

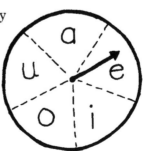 

Two or three students can play. The first player spins and must try to use the vowel the spinner stops on to make a real word on his or her card. If the child can use the vowel, he or she writes it in the blank with the marker. If the vowel cannot be used, the child loses that turn. The person to fill in his or her card first is declared the winner.

Vowel Old Maid:

You can use the same picture cards that you prepared for "Vowel Tic-Tac-Toe." Add one additional card that has a vowel on the back of the card but no picture on the front. This card will be the *Old Maid!* Shuffle the deck and deal out all the cards to the players. Each child picks up his or her cards and matches cards with the same vowel sound. The matches are placed in front of the player. Now the first player takes one card from another player. If it matches one of his or her vowel cards, the child puts that pair down. Play continues until one player is left with the *Old Maid.*

Word Call Card Game:

Prepare a set of 3" x 5" index cards with several sets of identical words. Shuffle the cards and deal to two players. The children turn over the cards simultaneously. When two cards match, the first child to call out the correct word takes both stacks of turned-up cards. The child with more cards at the end of play is declared the winner.

Pick-up Sticks Phonics:

Cover some Crystal Light® or Pringles® cans in self-stick vinyl. Write the words to be studied on Popsicle® sticks. These can be vocabulary sight words, words beginning with particular blends, word families, etc. Store the sticks in the cans. To play, two children take a can and find a quiet place to play. The first player drops all of the sticks. He or she then must pick up one of the sticks—without moving any of the others—and do whatever he or she has been directed to do; for example: read the word, use it in a sentence, give a rhyming word, give a synonym, etc. The child may continue to pick up as long as he or she gives the correct answer and does not move another stick; otherwise, it is the next student's turn. The winner is the person with more sticks at the end of the game.

Phonics 500:

Make your own race track gameboard from posterboard; laminate. (Or, see the Appendix for a gameboard.) You can purchase tiny, inexpensive, plastic cars in a variety of colors (or number the cars in permanent markers). Prepare cards containing letters, sight words, beginning sounds, etc. The cards are placed face down on the table. The child draws a card from the stack. If the child correctly identifies the letter, sound, or word, he or she moves the car one space on the board. The car to reach the checkered flag first is the winner.

Independent Activity Task Cards

Activity Task Cards:

On 3" x 5" index cards, you may want to reproduce the following independent activities.

Beginning Consonants:

Write a word on your paper that begins with each of these letters.

b, c, f, k, l, p, r, s, t, w

Write a word on your paper that begins with each of these letters.

d, g, h, j, m, n, p, s, v, z

Word Families:

Write each of the following tasks on a separate index card:

- Use *c, f, m, p,* and *r* to make words from *an.*
- Use *b, c, f, h, m, p, r,* and *s* to make words from *at.*
- Use *b, f, l, r,* and *w* to make words from *ed.*
- Make a list of words from the *ill* family.
- Make a list of words from the *all* family.
- Make a list of words from the *ing* family.
- Make a list of words from the *ig* family.
- Make a list of words from the *et* family.
- Make a list of words from the *ake* family.
- Make a list of words from the *ound* family.
- Make a list of words from the *ick* family.
- Make a list of words from the *at* family.
- Make a list of words from the *in* family.

Pick the Right Word:

Read the words below. Copy the sentences and put the right word in the blank.

red sun bat ten fed

1. The _____ is hot.
2. The hen is _____ .
3. I hit the ball with the _____ .
4. I _____ the cat.
5. He is _____ .

Vowel Sounds:

Write 10 words that have a short vowel sound.	Write 10 words that have a long vowel sound.

Rhyming Words:

Copy the words on your paper and write a word that rhymes with it.

red	cat	led	fun	play
look	jig	set	cake	ball

Beginning Sounds Cards:

Make cards in which the ending sound of three words on each card are alike, but each has a different beginning sound. Laminate the several sets of cards and put in envelopes with an erasable marker. Let the children take them to their desks and write in the correct letter name. For example:

____an	____en	____ing
____an	____en	____ing
____an	____en	____ing

Ending Sounds Cards:

A similar activity can be used to reinforce ending sounds. For example:

ca____	pi____	ma____
ca____	pi____	ma____
ca____	pi____	ma____

Riddle Activity Task Cards:

Write "phonics" riddles on cards and laminate. Have the children take an envelope of riddles and see who can get the most answers correct. For example:

It rhymes with hat. You use it to hit a ball. What is it?

It rhymes with cot. It is the opposite of cold. What is it?

"Recycled" Activity Task Cards:

Outdated or half-used workbooks or textbooks are a wonderful source of valuable activity task cards. Sometimes you can just laminate a whole page and provide washable markers. Other times, you might want to just pick out a colorful picture, paste it on a task card, and write your own questions! (For example: "Look at the picture. Find three things that begin with the letter *c*. Find four things that begin with the letter *d*. Write them on your paper.")

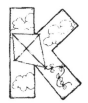

Section Three

Hands-on Phonics Activities for Developing Readers

Grades (2–5)

Developing readers benefit by the continued teaching of phonics in meaningful contexts. The order of sounds taught should be determined by you and based upon the observed needs of your children. This section provides many innovative ideas to introduce, supplement, and reinforce specific skills. The ideas are brief and simple to implement. Moreover, by utilizing the lists in the last section of the book, almost all of the activities can be adapted to a wide variety of skills.

Sorting and Manipulative Activities:

These activities can be used for individualized instruction, small group work, and for teaching the class as a whole. The necessary materials are generally those found in your classroom.

Puzzles and Games:

Many old, familiar games have been adapted to teach specific phonics skills. Most of the games are played by small

groups and many can be used for whole class instruction. They are simple to make and the children should be able to play most of them independently after receiving initial instruction.

Independent Activity Cards:

Many ideas are presented for simple task cards that reinforce specific phonics skills. It is suggested that these ideas be printed on index cards and laminated. The beauty of these activities is that they can be done independently. Many of them are self-checking. There are many simple ways to keep these cards organized so that the children can take them, and return them to the proper place when they are finished. Old cardboard pocket charts, cardboard boxes with partitions, and hanging shoebags work well. Label the cards and the storage compartments to match!

Sorting and Manipulative Activities

Flip Books:

The same flip books used with the emergent readers can be used to teach more advanced skills to older children. At this level they are useful in practicing root words, suffixes, prefixes, antonyms, synonyms, and syllabication, as shown. These books can be made self-checking by placing the answer on the back of each card so the child can give his or her answer and then simply flip to the back side to see if it is correct.

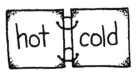 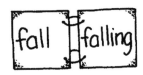

Match the Frame:

Prepare word cards for the words you are teaching. Prepare matching frames of the same words from light colored acetate. Mix up both sets and place in self-closing bags. The student selects a bag and tries to place the correct frame over each word so the printed word shows through.

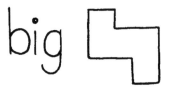 

Slider Activities:

The sliders described in "Hands-on Activities for Emergent Readers" can also be used at this level. They are great for an individual free-time activity. At this level they are used to teach more advanced skills. Reproduce the sliders provided on the following pages.

Digraph and/or Blend Assessment Activity:

This is a great activity to use for assessment. Give the child four 3" x 5" index cards with a different digraph or blend written on each. As you say a word, instruct the child to hold up the card that shows the initial sound. Check off on the Phonics Assessment Profile in the Appendix.

cl _____	pl _____
ad	an
am	ate
an	od
ap	op
ass	ot
ick	uck
iff	ug
ip	um
ock	us
od	
ub	
uck	

bl ___ ___	gl ___ ___
ab	ad
ack	ass
ed	en
ess	oss
iss	um
ob	ut
ock	
ot	
uff	

br ___	gr ___
ad	ab
ag	am
an	ass
ass	een
at	id
ed	ill
ick	im
im	in
	ip
	it
	uff

fl _____	al _____
_____	_____

ab	ab
ack	ack
ag	am
ap	ap
at	at
eck	ed
ed	ick
ick	id
ip	im
ock	ip
op	ot
uff	ug

fr _____	st _____

ee	ab
et	ack
ill	aff
og	ag
om	and
	em
	ep
	ick
	iff
	ill
	ock
	op

sk	sh
_____	_____
_____	_____

id	ack
iff	ad
ill	ag
im	all
in	am
ip	ed
it	ell
	in
	ip
	ock
	ot
	ut

sm ____	sw ____
ack ell ock og ug	ag am ell ig im

sp ___	sn ___

an	ack
at	ap
eck	iff
ed	ip
ell	ob
ill	ub
in	uff
it	ug
ot	
ud	
un	

cr ___ ___	tr ___ ___
ab	ack
ack	ain
aft	ap
am	ash
amp	ay
ank	eat
ash	ee
ib	ick
imp	im
ock	ip
ush	unk
ust	ust

ch _____	th _____

aff	an
ap	at
at	em
eck	en
ess	ick
ick	in
ill	is
in	ud
ip	ug
op	us
ug	
um	

wh ___

___

ack
en
et
iff
im
ip
iz

Vowel Detectives:

Children love to play detective! Laminate some cards that leave out all of the vowels and see if the children can discover which ones are missing. For example:

k _ ng _ r _ _   sk _ l _ t _ n   c _ ns _ n _ nt

Word Chains:

Divide the class into groups and give each group several strips of paper to make chains. Give the class a word that they must start with (perhaps a word from their social studies or science unit) and have one person write the word and form the first link. The children must then think of a word that begins with the last letter of the first word and write it on the next link. A time limit is given. The winning team is the one with the longest chain at the end of play.

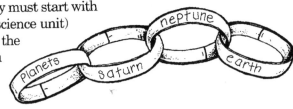

R-controlled Vowels Word Chain:

A variation of the previous activity can be used to teach the r-controlled vowels. Write the r-controlled vowel words on construction paper strips, using a different color for each. Children can sort these strips according to the vowel sound heard and paste together to make chains.

Rhyme-time Erasables:

Prepare several cards with sentences that will rhyme, leaving out the rhyming word; for example: Jack and Jill ran up the _____. Laminate these cards so that they can be written on and later erased. These can be placed in an envelope and taken to the child's desk for a free-time activity.

Rhyming Pairs:

Provide envelopes filled with pairs of cards picturing rhyming objects. The object is for the children to match the pairs. Some envelopes should have pairs of just pictures.

For more advanced students the cards should also include the name of the object.

 hat cat

When the children are ready, provide envelopes with just the words!

cat hat dog log

Rhyme-time Artists:

Divide the class into pairs. Each pair must think of two words that rhyme and whisper them to you. If they are correct, the children are each given a piece of manila paper to illustrate one of the words each. When the class is done, each pair is given an opportunity to show their pictures so that the children may guess the rhyming words.

Rhyme-time Lines:

Have the children fold a piece of lined paper into four columns. At the top of each column, the children write the word chunks you are planning to review. Offer a small prize to the child who comes up with the most words!

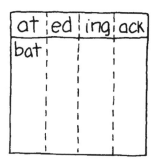

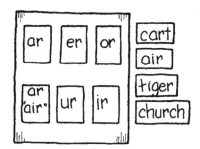

Library Pocket Sorts:

Library pocket sorts can also be used for developing readers. Once again, this can be used to sort whatever is appropriate to your phonics lesson. It is good for r-controlled vowel sounds, antonyms, synonyms, syllabication, contractions, plurals, etc.

Pocket Rule Sorts:

After reviewing specific phonics rules, provide word cards to be sorted by the rule the word follows. You can use the folders as described under *Pocket Games* in "Sorting and Manipulative Activities for Emerging Readers." Write the rule on the fold and have individuals sort the cards you provide.

Rhyming:

For a more challenging rhyming activity, prepare laminated cards such as the ones shown here. The children are asked to circle the one word in the box that does not rhyme. Once again, use washable markers! The children may think this is a snap, but they must be careful—although many of the words have identical endings, they do not rhyme. Sometimes the three words that rhyme have totally different endings.

| word   lord | deer   fear | turn   fern | wood   could |
| bird   third | wear   near | horn   learn | food   should |

bun gone done stun	chief thief leaf deaf	gave have wave save	thread bead bread bed
whom tomb broom from	bait slate eight night	said raid sled head	what flat cat slat
sour four your pour	fright eight hate bait	rush brush crush push	ghost post cost most
night weight plate straight	say key they weigh	toe go know to	roll stole doll bowl
two toe shoe sue	poor boar your tour	show hoe go do	root foot suit hoot

Rhyming Extension:

An extension of this activity is to give the children a list of words and tell them to think of a word that rhymes but is spelled with a different ending. Here is an example:

Read the words on the list. Next to each word write a word that rhymes with that word but has a different ending.

1. please _____
2. laugh _____
3. pane _____
4. plate _____
5. hose _____
6. crawl _____
7. foot _____
8. try _____

9.   gaze _____
10. whale _____
11. suit _____
12. war _____
13. heart _____
14. warn _____
15. fed _____
16. say _____

Define Rhyme:

Give your students several examples of definitions that rhyme, for example:

1. An unhappy father is a _____ (sad dad)

2. A happy Lassie is a _____ (jolly collie)

Divide the class into groups and have each group think of as many funny rhyming definitions as they can. Have each group present their *define rhymes* to the other groups to be solved.

Free-time Three's:

Prepare envelopes of laminated cards for children to use during free time. Provide erasable markers and tissues for cleaning. The child must read the word at the top of the card and write three words that rhyme with it.

Provide some blank cards for your more advanced students to make up their own list of rhyming words.

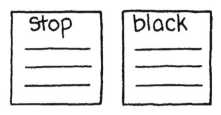

Climb the Ladder:

Ask parents to send in leftover partial rolls of wallpaper. Sometimes wallpaper stores are willing to donate rolls of old patterns or remnants of rolls. Prepare several *ladders* by drawing the rungs on the back of a sheet of wallpaper. These can be easily run through the laminating machine. Depending on the skill to be taught, prepare word or picture cards.

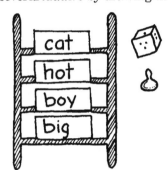

To play, each child places a card on every rung of the ladder. Provide a die and position markers. The first player rolls a die and moves the marker up the ladder the correct number of spaces. If the child can say the word correctly (use it in a sentence, give the correct number of syllables, give a rhyming word, etc.), the card is removed from the rung. Play continues until one player has removed all the cards.

Rule Cards:

After teaching a specific rule, provide laminated cards for the children to see how they can change one word to a totally different word by adding one letter. For example:

fin	tap	quit
___	___	___
grim	hop	twin
___	___	___
rag	rat	plan
___	___	___

Rule Cards Variation #1:

A variation of this activity is to provide cards with just one vowel missing and let the children write in the correct vowel with erasable markers.

f _ ve	c _ ne	fl _ te	b _ ne	b _ gle	r _ ke
p _ e	gl _ be	sl _ de	fl _ me	n _ se	c _ be

rod	pad	best	clam	met
_____	_____	_____	_____	_____
pal	got	pan	ran	fed
_____	_____	_____	_____	_____
net	bet	cot	ten	mad
_____	_____	_____	_____	_____

Rule Cards Variation #2:

Provide cards with just one vowel missing and let the children write in the correct vowel with erasable markers.

l _ af	l _ ap	s _ al	c _ at	m _ at	gr _ en
b _ at	r _ ad	r _ in	t _ en	t _ am	p _ in

Sound Surprises!

Children who appreciate a real challenge might like to have this list of exceptions!

Beware! Every word on this list has a "surprise vowel sound." What you *see* is not necessarily what you *hear*. Sometimes the letters make the sound of a vowel that is not even there. Your assignment, should you choose to accept it, is to pronounce each word silently and write the vowel sound you hear in the underlined portion of the word on the blank provided. Mark the vowel long or short. **This is tricky! Good luck!**

1. b<u>u</u>sy _____	11. r<u>ei</u>gn _____	21. d<u>o</u>ne _____	31. g<u>u</u>y _____
2. ob<u>ey</u> _____	12. s<u>o</u>n _____	22. t<u>ou</u>ch _____	32. h<u>ei</u>ght _____
3. pl<u>ai</u>n _____	13. s<u>o</u>me _____	23. tr<u>ou</u>ble _____	33. br<u>o</u>ther _____
4. pon<u>y</u> _____	14. c<u>o</u>yote _____	24. pl<u>ai</u>d _____	34. ser<u>i</u>al _____
5. w<u>o</u>men _____	15. b<u>oa</u>t _____	25. v<u>ei</u>n _____	35. th<u>ey</u> _____
6. fr<u>ie</u>nd _____	16. pr<u>ey</u> _____	26. n<u>ei</u>ghbor _____	36. y<u>o</u>lk _____
7. pol<u>i</u>ce _____	17. croch<u>et</u> _____	27. d<u>ou</u>gh _____	37. h<u>ei</u>ght _____
8. ph<u>y</u>sical _____	18. tr<u>ea</u>sure _____	28. y<u>ie</u>ld _____	38. h<u>y</u>mn _____
9. w<u>ei</u>ght _____	19. fr<u>ei</u>ght _____	29. k<u>ey</u> _____	39. g<u>ue</u>st _____
10. pr<u>ey</u> _____	20. b<u>uy</u> _____	30. sk<u>i</u> _____	40. br<u>ea</u>d _____

Answer Key for Sound Surprises!

1. busy	ĭ	11. reign	ā	21. done	ŭ	31. guy	ī
2. obey	ā	12. son	ŭ	22. touch	ŭ	32. height	ī
3. plain	ā	13. some	ŭ	23. trouble	ŭ	33. brother	ŭ
4. pony	ē	14. coyote	ī	24. plaid	ă	34. serial	ē
5. women	ĭ	15. boat	ō	25. vein	ā	35. they	ā
6. friend	ĕ	16. prey	ā	26. neighbor	ā	36. yolk	ō
7. police	ē	17. crochet	ā	27. dough	ō	37. height	ī
8. physical	ĭ	18. treasure	ĕ	28. yield	ē	38. hymn	ĭ
9. weight	ā	19. freight	ā	29. key	ē	39. guest	ĕ
10. prey	ā	20. buy	ī	30. ski	ē	40. bread	ĕ

Editing for Vowels:

As the children do more and more writing activities, help them proofread their work by providing editing cards for each child. As rules are taught, reproduce on 3" by 5" index cards and laminate. Provide an "editing envelope" for each child in which to keep the cards. Encourage the children to take out their envelopes and check any writing assignments before handing in. For example:

> Did you use a vowel in each word?
>
> a e i o u

Rule Sorts:

Prepare a chart of rules as follows:

> 1. If a word has one vowel and it appears between two consonants, that vowel is usually short.
> 2. A silent e at the end of a word usually makes the preceding vowel long.
> 3. When two vowels appear side by side, the first vowel is usually long and the second is silent.

Then duplicate material as shown here.

Read the words. Put each word under the correct heading.

cat	rate	slip	hunt	best
fuse	big	pet	goat	sock
drive	cube	side	just	coat
cake	bag	bike	green	dish

Short Vowel Sounds   **Long Vowel Sounds**

1. _____   6. _____   1. _____   6. _____

2. _____   7. _____   2. _____   7. _____

3. _____   8. _____   3. _____   8. _____

4. _____   9. _____   4. _____   9. _____

5. _____   10. _____   5. _____   10. _____

Advanced Rule Sorts:

More advanced students might be given a sheet of words to sort into three groups by the rule. For example:

Read the words. Put each word under the correct heading.

sick	bead	tie	mule	flip
shut	feet	bait	real	mine
boat	made	dock	sand	mule

Rule #1   **Rule #2**   **Rule #3**

1. _____   1. _____   1. _____

2. _____   2. _____   2. _____

3. _____   3. _____   3. _____

4. _____   4. _____   4. _____

5. _____   5. _____   5. _____

For the most advanced students, provide an even more challenging activity by adding a fourth rule, to allow for exceptions, and having the children use diacritical markings and sort by rule.

---

1. If a word has one vowel and it appears between two consonants, that vowel is usually short.

2. A silent e at the end of a word usually makes the preceding vowel long.

3. When two vowels appear side by side, the first vowel is usually long and the second is silent.

4. Some vowel sounds are exceptions and don't follow any of these rules!

Read each word below. For each word mark the vowel with the correct mark for long or short, and cross out any silent vowels. Decide which rule the word follows and write the correct rule number on the line provided. (For example: căt _1_ ; cūbe _2_ ; bōat _3_ ; breăd _4_ .)

1. fine _____   6. tame _____   11. little_____   16. rain _____

2. time _____   7. fold_____   12. friend_____   17. dad _____

3. leaf _____   8. pole _____   13. meal _____   18. cube _____

4. clip _____   9. tax _____   14. grain _____   19. twice _____

5. tread _____   10. sign _____   15. phone _____   20. bread _____

ea Rule Sort:

First teach the rule below. Then prepare a sound sorting activity using the pocket charts.

Rule: When you see "ea" together, try the long "e" sound first. If that doesn't sound right, try the short sound!

ē   ě

clean	breakfast	meadow	threat	leather
beaver	thread	death	cheat	jealous
feature	meant	ideal	dream	dread
deaf	heap	health	heaven	repeat
ream	leave	leaf	feather	reason
ahead	weather	pleasant	ready	season
squeal	cheap	wealth	leash	team

Newspaper Activities:

Phonics Find:

Newspapers can be used for a variety of activities. Have a timed "search." "How many words can you find that begin with *d? cl? br?* How many words can you find that end with *d? ch? es? ing? ed?* How many words can you find that have a short *a?* a long *e?* How many rhyming words can you find? homonyms? homophones?" The children are invited to circle their answers in crayon. The winners are the ones who circle the most correct words.

Alphabetical Order:

Give each child a page from the newspaper and a piece of blank paper. Ask each student to cut out 10 or 15 words from the paper and paste them on the blank paper in alphabetical order. For a more advanced lesson, ask the children to find ten words that start with the same letter so they will have to alphabetize by second or even third letters.

Classifying Words:

Have the children fold a piece of manila paper in half or in quarters. Depending upon the skill to be reviewed, have them label the columns and cut out words from the newspaper to fit in the categories. You might want to do initial consonants, words that represent a theme (such as animals, toys, vehicles, etc.), or a specific category such as verbs, nouns, adjectives, and adverbs.

Silent Letter Cross-out:

Give each child an article from the newspaper. Have them cross out all the silent vowels in red and all the silent consonants in blue.

Alphabetical Fans:

For an independent activity prepare a box of appropriate word cards. Provide manila paper and colored markers. Tell the child to fold the paper into a fan and then flatten it out. Count the number of folds and draw out the same number of cards from the box. Place the cards in alphabetical order on the table and then copy the words onto the fan in the correct order. The child hands the fan in to be checked by you or a peer.

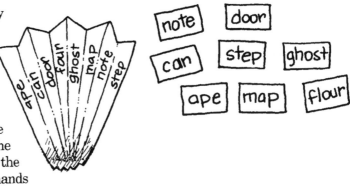

Clothespin Phonics Fun:

Clothespin activities are also fun for developing readers! Try developing ideas for beginning and ending sounds, antonym or synonym matches, contractions, compound words, long and short vowel sounds, rules of syllabication, root words, suffixes and prefixes, and plurals.

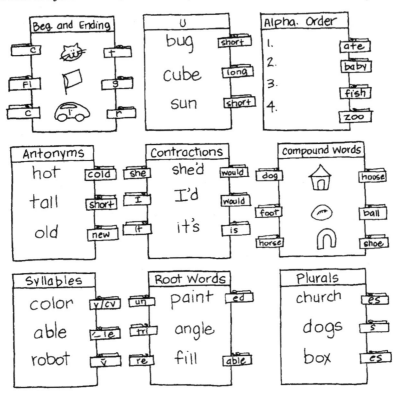

Silly Compound Collage:

Provide old magazines and workbooks. Ask students to find pictures illustrating each part of a compound word. Have them paste both pictures on a strip of paper. After having the students show their endeavor to the group for a guessing game, let them each paste their paper on a classroom collage. This collage can be sent to another classroom to let them identify and write the compound words.

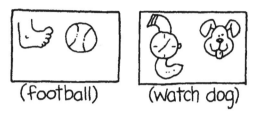

(football)   (watch dog)

Alliterated Animal Sentences:

As a review of the sounds of the alphabet, ask each child to write an animal-related alliterated sentence: *Arthur the aardvark ate apples and artichokes and had an awful ache!* Each student might make a complete book or individuals may choose a letter to add to a classroom book.

Silly Sentences or Silly Stories

Children of all ages enjoy making silly sentences. This activity can be adapted to any level. The children try to make silly sentences using a particular letter, blend, word family, etc. For example:

*S*even *s*illy *s*eals *s*aw *s*ix *s*eesaws.

*Sh*ivering *sh*eep *sh*ut the *sh*utters while *sh*aking.

T*ed* and *Ed* put the r*ed* b*ed* in the sh*ed*.

More advanced students could be encouraged to write stories using particular sounds, homonyms, rhyming words, etc. This activity can be applied to just about any phonics skill being taught or reinforced.

Cooperative Story Chains:

Students can write a cooperative story that emphasizes a particular phonics skill. Divide the class into groups. Give each child a lined index card. Tell the children what phonics skill you want to reinforce; for example, the *ch* digraph. The children then talk among themselves about what type of story they would like to write. One student writes the first sentence on his or her card; for example: *Ch*ildish *ch*impanzees were *ch*ewing *ch*erry *ch*ewing gum. Another student creates the second sentence; for example: The *ch*impanzees *ch*eeks were *ch*anging as they *ch*ewed. Other students continue the story until all the students have contributed to the story. The children can then illustrate their sentences and—using a hole punch and yarn—they can link their index cards in the correct order. The stories should then be shared with the other groups.

Homonyms, Synonyms, Antonyms Sort:

Prepare a set of cards with a word pair on each. The word pairs should be homonyms, synonyms, and antonyms. The child must sort the cards into the correct pile.

Puzzles and Games

Flick-it Phonics Fun:

This activity can be adapted to many skills. If you have a soda machine at school, ask the delivery man to save you the cardboard box bottoms the cans come in. (You can also use shoe box lids.) Cut the lip out of one of the narrow ends. Draw a gameboard, as shown, that is appropriate to the skill you are working on. Provide bottle caps from liter bottles as the "flickers." Two children play this game. The first player puts the bottle cap at the *Start* position and flicks it. The child must figure out what is missing in the box on which the cap lands and say the correct word. Alternate turns. Give one point for each correct answer. This can also be done outside on the blacktop by drawing large boards with chalk and weighting the bottle caps with clay.

Concentration:

When the children are familiar with the cards in the *Rhyming Pairs* activity, these same cards can be used to play the card game Concentration. Instead of looking for matching pairs, the object of the game is to find rhyming pairs!

Rhyming Lotto:

Prepare several different lotto gameboards with nine boxes. (See the Appendix for a lotto gameboard.) Write a word in each box and prepare a playing card with a corresponding word for each. To play, each child receives a gameboard and the playing cards are placed face-down on a table. The children take turns turning over the cards. If the word card rhymes with one of the words on the gameboard, the child covers the word. Play continues until one child has covered all nine boxes. This game can also be prepared for compound words, antonyms, and synonyms.

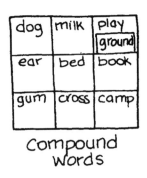

Phonics Bingo:

Bingo can be used in a variety of ways at this level. Duplicate the blank provided in the Appendix and laminate on a piece of tagboard to make reusable. You can then fill in the boxes appropriately with erasable markers, depending on the skill to be taught. Some examples are given here.

Vocabulary Bingo:

Write the vocabulary words on each card to be used. Make sure they are arranged in a different order on each Bingo card. Provide markers for the children. Call out the definition of the words for the students to identify and cover. The first student to cover five words in a row (horizontally, vertically, or diagonally) wins the game.

Final Blends Bingo:

Write final blends on each card to be used. Make sure they are arranged in a different order on each Bingo card. You then call out a list of words containing the final sounds. The students cover the appropriate final sound. The first student to cover five words in a row (horizontally, vertically, or diagonally) wins the game.

Vowel Sounds Bingo:

Write vowel sounds in the boxes. Make sure they are written in a different order on each Bingo card. Provide markers for the children. Pronounce aloud words containing the sounds and have the children cover the sound they hear. The first student to cover five words in a row (horizontally, vertically, or diagonally) wins the game.

Antonym or Synonym Bingo:

The game is played as above with you calling out synonyms or antonyms to match the words written in the boxes.

Phonics Dominoes:

See *Phonics Dominoes* in "Hands-On Activities for Emerging Readers." This game can be adapted for developing readers by including more advanced skills, such as synonyms, antonyms, silent letters, and phonics rules.

Compound Relay:

The class is divided into teams on separate sides of the room. Each team captain has a piece of paper and a pencil. You say a word. (Be sure the words can be used to make compound words.) For example: *ball.* The children in each team quickly think of as many compound words as they can. For example: *football, baseball, snowball.* The captain writes the words on the paper. When you call "time," one point is scored for each correctly spelled compound word.

Slap Jack:

Developing readers may play the game as described in "Puzzles and Games for Emergent Readers." At this time different skills are reinforced, such as synonyms, homonyms, antonyms, etc. It is possible to also look for matching prefixes and suffixes. For example, if the first card turned over is *re,* the student must wait for a card with a root word that goes with it, such as *paint.* As the student slaps the correct card, he or she must say *"repaint."* The same idea can be used with compound words. For example, if the first word turned over is *fire,* the student must be on the lookout for a word to add that would form a compound word, such as *man* for *fireman.*

Card Slap:

As for Slap Jack, prepare cards appropriate to the skill being reinforced. Spread the cards out face up on the floor. Pick several children to play. Call out the word. The first child to slap the card keeps it. The child with the most cards at the end of play is declared the winner.

Go Fish:

See *Go Fish* in "Puzzles & Games for Emergent Readers." This game is easily adapted to more advanced skills such as contractions, synonyms, and homophones.

Letter Combinations Flash Card Challenge:

Prepare flash cards with letter combinations. Hold up cards and let the children write as many words as they can think of that contain that combination. Allow a minute or so for each card. The winner is the child who has the most correct words at the end of play.

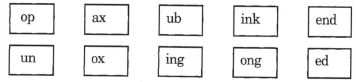

op	ax	ub	ink	end
un	ox	ing	ong	ed

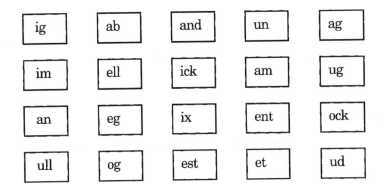

Prefix-Suffix Game:

Prepare three sets of cards—prefixes on one set, root words on another, and suffixes on the third. (If you do each on a different color index card, then the cards can be grouped quickly at the end of the game.) The cards are placed in three piles. The student must sort through them and arrange them to form as many words as possible. The child writes the words on a piece of paper for you to check when time allows.

Independent Activity Cards

On 3" x 5" index cards, you may want to reproduce the following independent activities.

Hard C, Soft C:

> In the word *cat*, you hear the hard *c* sound. In the word *city*, you hear the soft *c* sound. Write the words below on your paper. If the word has a hard *c* sound, draw a line under it. If it has a soft *c* sound, draw a circle around it.
>
> | piece | circle | cavern | pacify | cage |
> |---|---|---|---|---|
> | count | cube | prince | catch | trace |
> | picture | cook | since | price | careful |

Hard G, Soft G:

> In the word *get*, you hear a hard *g* sound. In the word *gem*, you hear a soft *g* sound. Write the words below on your paper. If the word has a hard *g* sound draw a line under it. If it has a soft *g* sound, draw a circle around it.
>
> | gas | gate | stage | giant | magic |
> |---|---|---|---|---|
> | game | again | strange | stingy | sponge |
> | gallop | bag | frog | lunge | snag |

Silent Consonants:

Sometimes consonants are not heard in a word. Write these words on your paper. Draw a line through the silent consonants.

know	wrist	catch	wrap	knife
climb	sign	knot	night	knight
sight	palm	thumb	fudge	rhyme

Alphabetical Order:

Write these words on your paper in alphabetical order

little	better	village	zoo	monitor
pumpkin	computer	never	apple	desk
first	rain	television	elephant	ghost
hospital	kangaroo	igloo	stable	jelly
oven	quilt	under	yellow	vegetable

Proper Names in Alphabetical Order:

Copy these names in alphabetical order by last names.

Cindy Ross	Betty Jasmund	Herb Ziser
Greg Dean	Carol Cimino	Mary Spencer
Trish Hook	Rita Berkey	Monica Knapp
Mandy Apperson	Bob Evans	Kevin Tehan
Anne Livingstone	Glenda Fishman	John Wildgrube

Antonyms:

Copy these words on your paper. Write an antonym for each.

large	kind	open	little	sad
cold	short	over	stand	awake
hot	first	dumb	loud	in

Synonyms:

> Copy these words on your paper. Write a synonym for each.
>
> | big | jolly | mad | little | clever |
> |-----|-------|-----|--------|--------|
> | ill | begin | enjoy | gift | loud |
> | price | real | shout | stop | tale |

Possessives:

> Copy these words on your paper. Make each one a possessive.
> Write a sentence using each of the possessives.
>
> | cat | teacher | boy | Mrs. Smith | man |
> |-----|---------|-----|------------|-----|
> | child | horse | lady | girl | Mr. Brown |
> | baby | turtle | doctor | rabbit | dad |

Plurals, –s:

> Write these words on your paper. Add the suffix –s to each word
> to make it plural. Write a sentence using each new word.
>
> | day | apple | star | hat | car | chair |
> |-----|-------|------|------|-----|-------|
> | girl | number | light | book | dog | paper |

Plurals, –es:

> Write these words on your paper. Add the suffix –es to each word
> to make it plural. Write a sentence using each new word.
>
> | watch | peach | church | glass | witch | sash |
> |-------|----------|--------|-------|-------|-------|
> | fox | princess | box | dress | tax | match |

Plurals, –s or –es:

> Write these words on your paper. Add the –s or –es to make the
> words plural.
>
> | tree | witch | flower | car | chicken |
> |---------|-------|--------|----------|---------|
> | watch | fox | candle | sock | box |
> | tractor | dress | shoe | princess | balloon |

Compound Words:

Copy each compound word onto your paper. Draw a line dividing the compound word into two separate words.

barnyard	football	cowboy	roommate
inside	everyone	sometimes	treetop
fireman	classroom	warehouse	outside
playground	greenhouse	underground	houseboat

Suffix, –ful:

Write these words on your paper. Add the suffix *–ful* to each word. Write a sentence using each new word.

pain	hope	care	play	joy
hand	color	taste	rest	help
arm	bash	cup	delight	truth

Suffix, –est:

Write these words on your paper. Add the suffix *–est* to each word. Change the endings if needed. Write a sentence using each new word.

funny	happy	big	sad	little
mean	loud	soft	red	hot
cold	nice	hard	pretty	warm

Suffix, –er:

Write these words on your paper. Add the suffix *–er* to each word. You may need to change some endings. Write a sentence using each new word.

long	late	thick	big	little
green	heavy	mean	gentle	nice
close	smart	kind	sweet	safe

Suffix, –ed:

Write these words on your paper. Add the suffix –ed to each word. You may need to change some endings. Write a sentence using each new word.

ask	rain	paint	play	sort
count	color	jump	skip	clap
dress	shop	hug	help	stop

Suffix, –ing:

Write these words on your paper. Add the suffix –ing to each word. You may need to change some endings. Write a sentence using each new word.

look	stay	fish	sleep	buy
play	run	skip	see	draw
take	make	cook	sew	laugh

Suffix, –ly:

Write these words on your paper. Add the suffix –ly to each word. Write a sentence using each new word.

quiet	glad	near	neat	soft
late	loud	careful	bright	quick

Suffix, –less:

Write these words on your paper. Add the suffix –less to each word. Write a sentence using each new word.

care	harm	bone	sleep	rest
meat	point	sound	color	weight

Suffix Rules:

If a word contains a short vowel sound and ends with a final consonant, the final consonant is often doubled before adding a suffix such as –ed or –ing. Copy the words below on your paper and add –ed or –ing to the words. You may need to change some endings. Use each new word in a sentence.

drop	sing	wed	nap	hug
smile	stay	saw	fan	clap
chop	plan	color	swing	run

Vowel Digraph oo:

The vowel digraph oo may make the sound of oo in moon or the sound of oo in book. Copy the words on your paper. Circle the oo as in moon in red. Draw a blue line under the oo as in book.

spoon	boot	brook	took	zoo
cool	rooster	spool	tool	soon
zoom	cookie	look	broom	balloon

Number of Vowel Sounds:

Write these words on your paper. Write the number of vowel sounds you actually hear.

broken	little	boat	moon	blame
jail	whale	pound	garage	dime
cake	drove	seed	below	tune

Marking Vowels:

Write these words on your paper. Mark the vowels long or short. Cross out any silent vowels.

little	take	seed	run	jail
drove	cake	queen	dime	wheel
made	maid	bread	find	ghost

Homonyms:

Write these words on your paper. Next to each word write a word that sounds the same but is spelled differently.

ant	our	bare	beat	cell
clothes	dear	eye	find	flea
flour	grate	hair	hall	hoarse
hole	wood	son	sail	plain

Rhyming Words:

Write these words on your paper. Next to each word write a word that rhymes with it.

sleep	play	cat	make	fort
pocket	seed	dish	brain	told
mitten	ball	meet	show	name

List of Activity Card Ideas for Blends and Digraphs:

- Write 15 words that begin with *ch*.
- Write 15 words that end with *ch*.
- Write 15 words that end with *tch*.
- Write 15 words that begin with *bl*.
- Write 15 words that begin with *cl*.
- Write 15 words that begin with *fl*.
- Write 15 words that begin with *gl*.
- Write 15 words that end with *mp*.
- Write 15 words that begin with *pl*.
- Write 15 words that begin with *sc*.
- Write 15 words that begin with *sk*.
- Write 15 words that begin with *sl*.
- Write 15 words that begin with *sm*.
- Write 15 words that begin with *sn*.
- Write 15 words that begin with *sp*.
- Write 15 words that begin with *st*.
- Write 15 words that begin with *sw*.
- Write 15 words that begin with *tw*.
- Write 15 words that begin with *spl*.
- Write 15 words that begin with *br*.
- Write 15 words that begin with *cr*.
- Write 15 words that begin with *dr*.

- Write 15 words that begin with *fr*.
- Write 15 words that begin with *gr*.
- Write 15 words that begin with *pr*.
- Write 15 words that begin with *scr*.
- Write 15 words that begin with *spr*.
- Write 15 words that begin with *str*.
- Write 15 words that begin with *shr*.
- Write 15 words that begin with *thr*.
- Write 15 words that begin with *th*.
- Write 10 words that begin with *qu*.
- Write 15 words that begin with *wh*.
- Write 10 words that begin with *squ*.

Silent e:

The vowel *e* is usually silent when it is at the end of a short word and it causes the preceding vowel to be long. Copy the words below on your paper. Cross out the silent *e* and mark the long vowel.

lake	fade	prize	tape	take	rope
duke	cure	ripe	haste	hope	cute
dome	quake	cake	hive	ape	ate
shame	stroke	joke	blade	cube	kite

Sounds of –ed:

When a word ends in *–ed,* sometimes it has the *d* sound and sometimes it has the *t* sound. Copy the words on your paper. If the word ends in a *d* sound, circle it in red. If the word ends in a *t* sound, underline it in blue.

trailed	skipped	walked	baked	canned
pointed	counted	snapped	hissed	boxed
played	parked	crashed	jumped	rested

ea Digraph:

The vowel digraph *ea* may make the sound of *ea* in *wear,* or the sound of *ea* in *heard,* or the sound of *ea* in *meat,* or the sound of *ea* in *spread.* Copy the words on your paper. Circle the *ea* as in *wear* in red; draw a blue line under the *ea* as in *heard;* circle the *ea* as in *meat* in green; and draw a green line under the *ea* as in *spread.*

wear	breakfast	learn	heaven	bread
treat	heard	tear	earth	pear
deaf	swear	heavy	bear	clear

Double Vowels:

Write three words that each have these double vowels:

ea, ai, oa, ee, oo.

Base Words:

Copy the words. Underline the base word in each.

littlest	named	kinder	sweetly	baked
laughed	cleaning	singing	barked	skipped
running	playing	softly	colorless	tallest

Little-word Find:

Copy the words. Underline a little word in each of these words.

wheat	noon	weak	sheet	treat
boil	friend	pear	kitten	rocket
parent	tall	sweater	catch	stand

Syllables:

Copy the words on your paper. Divide them into syllables.

mitten	today	baseball	basket	princess
dentist	bucket	mailman	happen	rabbit
something	flower	often	climbed	magic

Section Four

Lists for Developing Hands-on Phonics Activities

This Section provides an abundance of useful lists. The book lists provide everything from alphabet books that can be read consistently to pre-readers to help develop their knowledge of the alphabet, to vowel and consonant sound awareness books and poetry anthologies. In addition, there are word lists for initial consonant sounds, final consonant sounds, initial consonant blends, final consonant blends, initial consonant digraphs, final consonant digraphs, variant consonant sounds, silent consonants, short and long vowels, r-controlled vowels, word families, rhyming words, compound words, prefixes, suffixes, homonyms, synonyms, and antonyms. These word lists are a wonderful tool to tailor almost any of the activities in this book to a specific skill!

Alphabet Books

Alexander, Martha	A, You're Adorable
Anno, Mitsumasu	*Anno's Alphabet: An Adventure in Imagination*
Bannatyne–Cugnet, Jo	*A Prairie Alphabet*
Base, Graeme	*Animalia*
Bayer, Jane	*A, My Name Is Alice*
Brown, Marcia	*All Butterflies*
Bruna, Dick	*B, is for Bear*
Carle, Eric	*All About Arthur*
Carter, David	*Alpha Bugs: A Pop-Up Alphabet*
Chess, Victoria	*Alfred's Alphabet Walk*
Dragonwagon, Crescent	*Alligator Arrived With Apples: A Potluck Alphabet Feast*
Duke, Kate	*The Guinea Pig ABC*
Ehlert, Lois	*Eating the Alphabet: Fruits & Vegetables from A to Z*
Eichenberg, Fritz	*Ape in a Cape. An Alphabet of Odd Animals*
Elting, Mary & Folsom, Michael	*Q Is for Duck: An Alphabet Guessing Game*
Emberley, Ed	*Ed Emberley's ABC*
Fain, Kathleen	*Handsigns: A Sign Language Alphabet*
Gág, Wanda	*The ABC Bunny*
Gardner, Beau	*Have You Ever Seen…? An ABC Book*
Geisert, Arthur	*Pigs from A to Z*
Geringer, Laura	*The Cow Is Mooing Anyhow*
Hague, Kathleen	*Alphabears: An ABC Book*
Hoban, Tana	*A, B, See!*
	26 Letters and 99 Cents
————.	
Hyman, Trina S.	*A Little Alphabet*
Isadora, Rachel	*City Seen from A to Z*
Kitchen, Bert	*Animal Alphabet*
LeCourt, Nancy	*Abracadabra to Zigzag*
Lobel, Anita	*Alison's Zinnia*
Lobel, Arnold & Anita	*On Market Street*
MacDonald, Suse	*Alphabatics*
Martin, Bill, Jr, & Archambault, John	*Chicka Chicka Boom Boom*
Neumeier, Marty & Glaser, Byron	*Action Alphabet*
Owens, Mary Beth	*A Caribou Alphabet*
Pallotta, Jerry	*The Bird Alphabet Book*
————.	*The Extinct Alphabet Book*
————.	*The Icky Bug Alphabet Book*
————.	*The Ocean Alphabet Book*
————.	*Peter Rabbit's Alphabet Book*

Sendak, Maurice	*Alligators All Around: An Alphabet*
Seuss, Dr.	*Dr. Seuss's ABC*
Tudor, Tasha	*A is for Annabelle*
Van Allsburg, Chris	*The Z Was Zapped*
Watson, Clyde	*Applebet*
Wildsmith, Brian	*Brian Wildsmith's ABC*
Yolen, Jane	*All in the Woodland Early: An ABC Book*

Vowel Sound Awareness Books

Short A

Anno, Mitsumasa	*Anno's Alphabet: An Adventure in Imagination*
_____.	*Anno's Counting Book*
Arkhurst, Joycy	*The Adventures of Spider*
_____.	*More Adventures of Spider*
Balian, Lorna	*Amelia's Nine Lives*
Barrett, Judi	*Animals Should Definitely Not Act Like People*
_____.	*Animals Should Definitely Not Wear Clothing*
Branley, Franklyn M.	*Air Is All Around You*
Cameron, Polly	*"I Can't," Said the Ant*
Carratello, Patty	*My Cap*
Carrick, Carol	*The Accident*
Cavanah, Frances	*Abe Lincoln Gets His Chance*
Flack, Marjorie	*Angus and the Cat*
_____.	*Ask Mr. Bear*
Fox, Mem	*Arabella the Smallest Girl in the World*
Gag, Wanda	*Millions of Cats*
Gibbons, Gail	*The Seasons of Arnold's Apple Tree*
Ginsburg, Mirra	*Across the Stream*
Griffith, Helen	*Alex and the Cat*
Guilfoile, Elizabeth	*Nobody Listens to Andrew*
Hines, Anna	*All By Myself*
Hughes, Shirley	*All About Alfie*
_____.	*An Evening at Alfie's*
Hurwitz, Johanna	*Aldo Applesauce*
Kent, Jack	*The Fat Cat*
Most, Bernard	*There's an Ant in Anthony*
Nodset, Joan L.	*Who Took the Farmer's Hat?*
Orbach, Ruth	*Apple Pigs*
Robins, Joan	*Addie Meets Max*
Schmidt, Karen L.	*The Gingerbread Man*
Seeger, Pete	*Abiyoyo*

Suess, Dr.	*The Cat in the Hat*
_____.	*The Cat in the Hat Comes Back*
Viorst, Judith	*I'll Fix Anthony*

Long A

Aardema, Verna	*Bringing the Rain to Kapiti Plain*
Bang, Molly	*The Paper Crane*
Burton, Virginia Lee	*Katy and the Big Snow*
Carratello, Patty	*Skate, Kate, Skate!*
Henkes, Kevin	*Sheila Rae, the Brave*
Hines, Anna G.	*Taste the Raindrops*
Howard, Elizabeth	*The Train to Lulu's*
McPhail, David	*The Train*

Long & Short A

| Aliki | *Jack and Jake* |
| Slobodkina, Esphyr | *Caps for Sale* |

Short E

Carratello, Patty	*Brett, My Pet*
Demi	*The Empty Pot*
dePaola, Tomie	*Little Grunt & the Big Egg*
Ets, Marie H.	*Elephant in a Well*
Galdone, Paul	*The Little Red Hen*
Kraus, Robert	*The Happy Egg*
Kroll, Steven	*The Biggest Pumpkin Ever*
McPhail, David	*Emma's Pet*
Ness, Evaline	*Yeck Eck*
Parkes, Brenda	*The Enormous Watermelon*
Shecter, Ben	*Hester the Jester*
Thayer, Jane	*I Don't Believe in Elves*
Tsuchiya, Yukio	*Faithful Elephants*
Vipont, Elfrida	*The Elephant and the Bad Baby*
Wing, Henry Ritchet	*Ten Pennies for Candy*
Wood, Audrey	*Elbert's Bad Word*

Long E

Archambault, John	*Counting Sheep*
Galdone, Pai;	*Little Bo-Peep*
Gordon, Jeffie R.	*Six Sleepy Sheep*
Hughes, Shirley	*An Evening at Alfie's*
Keller, Holly	*Ten Sleepy Sheep*
Martin, Bill	*Brown Bear, Brown Bear, What Do You See?*

Oppenheim, Joanne	*Have You Seen Trees?*
Shaw, Nancy	*Sheep in a Jeep*
————.	*Sheep on a Ship*
Wellington, Monica	*The Sheep Follow*

Long & Short E

Keller, Holly	*Ten Sleepy Sheep*
Soule, Jean Conder	*Never Tease a Weasel*

Short I

Anno, Mitsumasa	*In Shadowland*
Brown, Marc	*The Important Book*
Brown, Ruth	*If At First You Do Not See*
Browne, Anthony	*Willy the Wimp*
Carratello, Patty	*Will Bill?*
Daughtry, Dianne	*What's Inside*
Domanska, Janina	*If All the Seas Were One Sea*
Ets, Marie H.	*Gilberto and the Wind*
Friskey, Margaret	*Indian Two Feet & His Horse*
Gross, Janet & Harste, Jerome	*It Didn't Frighten Me*
Guarino, Deborah	*Is Your Mama a Llama?*
Hoban, Tana	*Is It Red? Is It Yellow? Is It Blue?*
————.	*Is It Rough? Is It Smooth? Is It Shiny?*
Hurd, Edith T.	*I Dance in My Red Pajamas*
Hutchins, Pat	*Titch*
Keats, Ezra Jack	*Whistle for Willie*
Kroll, Steven	*If I Could Be My Grandmother*
Lionni, Leo	*Inch by Inch*
————.	*It's Mine!*
————.	*Swimmy*
Lobel, Arnold	*Small Pig*
Maccarone, Grace	*Itchy, Itchy Chicken Pox*
McPhail, David	*Fix-It*
Numeroff, Laura J.	*If You Give a Moose a Muffin*
————.	*If You Give a Mouse a Cookie*
Shaw, Charles G.	*It Looked Like Spilt Milk*
Small, David	*Imogene's Antlers*
Stevenson, James W.	*If I Owned a Candy Factory*

Long I

Berenstain, Stan & Jan	*The Bike Lesson*
Carratello, Patty	*Mice on Ice*

Carlson, Nancy	*I Like Me*
Cole, Sheila	*When the Tide is Low*
Hazen, Barbars S.	*Tight Times*
Steig, William	*Brave Irene*
Waber, Bernard	*Ira Sleeps Over*

Short O

Benchley, Nathanial	*Oscar Otter*
Carratello, Patty	*Dot's Pot*
Crews, Donald	*Ten Black Dots*
Dunrea, Oliver	*Mogwogs on the March*
Emberley, Barbara	*Drummer Hoff*
Hawkins, Colin & Jacqui	*Tog the Dog*
Martin, Sarah	*Old Mother Hubbard & Her Wonderful Dog*
McKissack, Patricia C.	*Flossie and the Fox*
Peppe, Rodney	*Odd One Out*
Seuss, Dr.	*Fox in Sox*
_____.	*Hop on Pop*

Long O

Carratello, Patty	*My Old Gold Boat*
Cole, Brock	*The Giant's Toe*
Gerstein, Mordicai	*Roll Over!*
Johnston, Tony	*The Adventures of Mole and Troll*
Koontz, Robin M.	*This Old Man: The Counting Song*
Langstaff, John M.	*Oh, A Hunting We Will Go*
Shulevitz, Uri	*One Monday Morning*
Tresselt, Alvin R.	*White Snow, Bright Snow*
Waber, Bernard	*Ira Sleeps Over*
Wadsworth, Olive A.	*Over in the Meadow*

Short U

Abolafia, Yossi	*My Three Uncles*
Anno, Mitsumasa	*Upside-Downers*
Carratello, Patty	*My Truck and My Pup*
Carroll, Ruth	*Where's the Bunny?*
Euvremer, Teryl	*The Sun's Up*
Feczko, Kathy	*Umbrella Parade*
Gibbons, Gail	*Sun Up, Sun Down*
Howe, James	*There's a Monster Under My Bed*
Gill, Madelaine	*Under the Blanket*
Lionni, Leo	*Alexander & the Windup Mouse*
Marshall, James	*The Cut-Ups*

McCloskey, Robert	*Make Way for Ducklings*
Monsell, Mary E.	*Underwear*
Pinkwater, Daniel	*Roger's Umbrella*
Prelutsky, Jack	*The Baby Uggs Are Hatching*
Ryder, Joanne	*Under the Moon*
Seuss, Dr.	*I Am Not Going to Get Up Today!*
Thorne, Jenny	*My Uncle*
Udry, Janice Mae	*Thump and Plunk*
Yashima, Taro	*Umbrella*
Yolen, Jane	*Sleeping Ugly*
Zolotow, Charlotte	*The Unfriendly Book*

Long U

Carratello, Patty	*Duke the Blue Mule*
Coville, Bruce & Katherine	*Sarah's Unicorn*
McCloskey, Robert	*Blueberries for Sal*
Segal, Lore	*Tell Me a Trudy*

B Books

Allen, Pamela	*Bertie and the Bear*
Ancona, George	*It's a Baby!*
Barton, Byron	*Boats*
————.	*Buzz, Buzz, Buzz*
Berenstain, Stan & Jan	*The B Book*
————.	*The Berenstain Bears on the Job*
Berenstain, Stan	*The Bike Lesson*
Brett, Jan	*Goldilocks and the Three Bears*
Brown, Marc	*Benjy's Blanket*
————.	*Big Red Barn*
Cohen, Miriam	*Best Friends*
dePaola, Tomie	*Big Anthony and the Magic Ring*
Freeman, Donald	*Beady Bear*
Gans, Roma	*Bird Talk*
Gibbons, Gail	*Boat Book*
Hoban, Russell	*Bedtime for Frances*
Hutchins, Pat	*Don't Forget the Bacon!*
————.	*Follow That Bus!*
Ipcar, Dahlov Zorach	*The Biggest Fish in the Sea*
Kellogg, Steven	*Jack and the Beanstalk*
Marino, Dorothy	*Buzz Bear Goes South*
Martin, Bill, Jr.	*Brown Bear, Brown Bear, What Do You See?*

Mayer, Mercer	*Bubble Bubble*
McCloskey, Robert	*Blueberries for Sal*
Rice, Eve	*Benny Bakes a Cake*
Wildsmith, Brian	*Bear's Adventure*
Yektai, Niki	*Bears in Pairs*

Bl Book List

Burningham, John	*The Blanket*
Cooney, Nancy	*The Blanket That Had to Go*
Crews, Donald	*Ten Black Dots*
dePaola, Tomie	*Legend of Bluebonnet*
James, Simon	*Dear Mr. Blueberry*
Kraus, Robert	*Leo the Late Bloomer*
_____.	*Mert the Blurt*
Macaulay, David	*Black and White*
MacDonald, Amy	*Rachel Fister's Blister*
McCloskey, Robert	*Blueberries for Sal*
Raskin, Ellen	*Nothing Ever Happens on My Block*
Rice, Eve	*New Blue Shoes*

Br Book List

Bishop, Claire H.	*The Five Chinese Brothers*
Coleridge, Sara	*January Brings the Snow*
Coles, Robert	*The Story of Ruby Bridges*
De Regniers, Beatrice	*May I Bring a Friend?*
Dunrea, Oliver	*Fergus and Bridey*
Gross, Ruth B.	*The Bremen Town Musicians*
Hoban, Tana	*Bread & Jam for Frances*
Klein, Elonore	*Brave Daniel*
Machotka, Hana	*Breath Taking Noses*
Margolis, Richard	*Secrets of a Small Brother*
Martin, Bill, Jr.	*Brown Bear, Brown Bear, What Do You See?*
Steig, William	*Brave Irene*

C Book List

Bridwell, Norman	*Clifford* (series)
Carle, Eric	*Have You Seen My Cat?*
	The Mixed-Up Chameleon
_____.	*Congo Boy: An African Folk Tale*
Clarke, Mollie	*A Pocket for Corduroy*
Freeman, Don	*Millions of Cats*
Gag, Wanda	*Camping Adventures*
Gray, William R.	

Hines, Anna G.	*Come to the Meadow*
Krauss, Ruth	*The Carrot Seed*
Lionni, Leo	*A Color of His Own*
McMillan, Bruck	*Counting Wildflowers*
Numeroff, Laura J.	*If You Give a Mouse a Cookie*
Oxenbury, Helen	*The Car Trip*
Rey, H.A.	*Curious George (series)*
Robart, Rose	*The Cake That Mack Ate*
Seuss, Dr.	*The Cat in the Hat*
Simon, Norma	*Cats Do, Dogs Don't*
Slobodkina, Esphyr	*Caps for Sale*

Ch Book List

Barrett, Judi	*Cloudy With a Chance of Meatballs*
Becvar, Patsy	*Who Was John Chapman*
Ginsburg, Mirra	*The Chick & the Duckling*
_____.	*The Chinese Mirror*
Heller, Ruth	*Chickens Aren't the Only Ones*
Hutchins, Pat	*Changes, Changes*
Keats, Ezra Jack	*Peter's Chair*
Kimmel, Eric A.	*Charlie Drives the Stage*
Little, Lessie	*Children of Long Ago*
Luton, Mildred	*Little Chicks' Mothers & All Others*
Martin, Bill, Jr. & Archambault, John	*Chicka Chicka Boom Boom*
Oakley, Graham	*Magical Changes*
Pomerantz, Charlotte	*The Chalk Doll*
Ryder, Joanne	*Chipmunk Song*
Sendak, Maurice	*Chicken Soup With Rice*
Weiss, Nicki	*Chuckie*
Williams, Vera B.	*A Chair for My Mother*

Cl Book List

Barrett, Judi	*Animals Should Definitely Not Wear Clothing*
_____.	*Cloudy With a Chance of Meatballs*
Calmenson, Stephanie	*The Principal's New Clothes*
dePaola, Tomie	*The Cloud Book*
_____.	*Charlie Needs a Cloak*
Greene, Carol	*Hi, Clouds*
Hutchins, Pat	*Clocks & More Clocks*
Mayer, Mercer	*There's a Nightmare in My Closet*
Miller, Edna	*Mouskin's Close Call*
Oxenbury, Helen	*Clap Hands*

Cr Book List

Bang, Molly	*The Paper Crane*
Carle, Eric	*The Very Quiet Cricket*
Caudill, Rebecca	*A Pocketful of Cricket*
Devlin, Wende & Harry	*Cranberry Thanksgiving*
Isadora, Rachel	*At the Crossroads*
Jorgensen, Gail	*Crocodile Beat*
Lionni, Leo	*Six Crows*
Littledale, Freya	*The Boy Who Cried Wolf*
McDonald, Megan	*Is This a House for Hermit Crab?*
West, Colin	*Have You Seen the Crocodile?*
Yashima, Taro	*Crow Boy*

D Book List

Aliki	*Digging Up Dinosaurs*
Berenstain, Stan & Jan	*The Berenstain Bears Go to the Dentist*
	The Berenstain Bears Go to the Doctor
_____.	
Cohen, Miriam	*Jim's Dog Muffins*
Freeman, Don	*Dandelion*
Freedman, Sally	*Devin's New Bed*
Gibbons, Gail	*Dinosaurs, Dragonflies, & Diamonds*
Hankin, Rebecca	*I Can Be a Doctor*
Hines, Anna G.	*Daddy Makes the Best Spaghetti*
Hoban, Tana	*Dig, Drill, Dump, Fill*
Hoff, Sid	*Danny and the Dinosaur*
Hughes, Shirley	*Dogger*
Hutchins, Pat	*The Doorbell Rang*
Mayer, Mercer	*Just Me and My Dad*
McCloskey, Robert	*Make Way for Ducklings*
Noble, Trinka H.	*The Day Jimmy's Boa Ate the Wash*
Simon, Norma	*Cats Do, Dogs Don't*
Steig, William	*Dr. Desoto*
Wildsmith, Brian	*Daisy*
Zion, Gene	*Harry the Dirty Dog*

Dr Book List

dePaola, Tomie	*The Knight & the Dragon*
Emberley, Ed	*Drummer Hoff*
Estes, Eleanor	*The Hundred Dresses*
Gannett, Ruth S.	*Elmer and the Dragon*
_____.	*My Father's Dragon*

_____.	*The Dragons of Blueland*
James, Betsy	*The Dream Stair*
Kent, Jack	*There's No Such Thing as a Dragon*
Lindgren, Astrid	*The Dragon With Red Eyes*
Stevenson, James	*The Dreadful Day*
Surat, Michele M.	*Angel Child, Dragon Child*
Wildsmith, Brian	*My Dream*

F Book List

Brown, Margaret Wise	*Four Fur Feet*
Cohen, Miriam	*First Grade Takes a Test*
	Starring First Grade
_____.	*Whose Footprints?*
Coxe, Molly	
Eastman, Philip D.	*Sam and the Firefly*
Elkin, Benjamin	*Six Foolish Fishermen*
DeRegniers, Beatrice Scenk & Turkle, Brinton	*Catch a Little Fox*
Fox, Mem	*Hattie and the Fox*
Hutchins, Pat	*Don't Forget the Bacon!*
_____.	*Follow That Bus!*
Ipcar, Dahlov Zorach	*The Biggest Fish in the Sea*
Lionni, Leo	*Fish Is Fish*
McPhail, David	*Farm Morning*
Palmer, Helen	*A Fish Out of Water*
Peet, Bill	*Farewell to Shady Glade*
Pfister, Marcus	*The Rainbow Fish*
Seuss, Dr.	*One Fish, Two Fish*

Fl Book List

Bunting, Eve	*Fly Away Home*
Eastman, Philip D.	*Flap Your Wings*
Gelman, Rita G.	*Why Can't I Fly?*
Heller, Ruth	*The Reason for a Flower*
McKissack, Patricia C.	*Flossie and the Fox*
Peet, Bill	*Merle the High Flying Squirrel*
Pomerantz, Charlotte	*Flap Your Wings and Try*

Fr Book List

Aliki	*We Are Best Friends*
Anglund, Joan W.	*A Friend Is Someone Who Likes You*
Blume, Judy	*Freckle Juice*
Carle, Eric	*Do You Want to Be My Friend?*

Cohen, Miriam	*Will I Have a Friend?*
_____.	*Best Friends*
Crews, Donald	*Freight Train*
Delton, Judy	*Two Good Friends*
De Regniers, Beatrice	*May I Bring a Friend?*
Gross, Janet & Harster, Jerome	*It Didn't Frighten Me*
Heide, Florence & VanClief	*That's What Friends Are For*
Heine, Helme	*Friends*
Hoban, Russell	*Bread and Jam for Frances*
Lionni, Leo	*Frederick*
Lobel, Arnold	*Frog and Toad (series)*
McNaughton, Colin	*Making Friends With Frankenstein*
Oxenbury, Helen	*Friends*

G Book List

Hard G Book List

Burningham, John	*Mr. Grumpy's Motor Car*
Baylor, Byrd	*Guess Who My Favorite Person Is?*
Cohen, Miriam	*No Good in Art*
Delaney, Antoinette	*The Gunnywolf*
Delton, Judy	*Two Good Friends*
Douglas, Barbara	*Good as New!*
Miller, Edna	*Mousekin's Golden House*
Rice, Eve	*Goodnight, Goodnight*
Seuss, Dr.	*I Am Not Going to Get Up Today!*
Showers, Paul	*Where Does the Garbage Go?*
Smith, Judith & Parkes, Brenda	*Gobble Gobble Glup Glup*

Soft G Book List

Arno, Enrico	*The Gingerbread Man*
Berger, Melvin	*Germs Make Me Sick*
Galdone, Paul	*The Gingerbread Boy*
Joyce, William	*George Shrinks*
Keller, Holly	*Geraldine's Blanket*
Lord, John V.	*The Giant Jelly Sandwich*
Marshall, James	*George & Martha One Fine Day*
West, Colin	*"Pardon?" Said the Giraffe*

Gl Book List

Cameron, Ann	*Julian's Glorious Summer*
Peet, Bill	*Farewell to Shady Glade*
Smith, Judith & Parkes, Brenda	*Gobble Gobble Glup Glup*

Gr Book List

Berger, Barbara H.	*Grandfather Twilight*
Buckley, Helen E.	*Grandfather and I*
———.	*Grandmother and I*
Buckley, Richard	*The Greedy Python*
Carle, Eric	*The Grouchy Ladybug*
Cohen, Miriam	*First Grade Takes a Test*
———.	*Starring First Grade*
Cutting, Brian & Jillian	*It Takes Time to Grow*
dePaola, Tomie	*Little Grunt & the Big Egg*
Ehlert, Lois	*Growing Vegetable Soup*
Hoffman, Henrich	*The Green Grass Grows All Around*
Huffman, Mary	*Amazing Grace*
Hutchins, Pat	*You'll Soon Grow Into Them, Titch*
Krauss, Ruth	*Growing Story*
Kroll, Steven	*If I Could Be My Grandmother*
Melser, June	*Grandpa, Grandpa*
Seuss, Dr.	*Green Eggs and Ham*
———.	*How the Grinch Stole Christmas*
Spier, Peter	*Gobble, Growl, Grunt*
Stevens, Carla	*Anna, Grandpa and the Big Storm*

H Book List

Aliki	*My Hands*
Anno, Mitsumasa	*Anno's Hat Tricks*
Asch, Frank	*Happy Birthday, Moon*
Barton, Byron	*Building a House*
Burton, Virginia Lee	*The Little House*
Calhoun, Mary	*Hot Air Henry*
Carle, Eric	*A House for Hermit Crab*
Galdone, Paul	*Henny Penny*
———.	*The Little Red Hen*
Geringer, Laura	*A Three Hat Day*
Geraghty, Paul	*The Hunter*
Fox, Mem	*Hattie and the Fox*
Hoberman, Mary Ann	*A House Is a House for Me*
Hurd, Edith	*Hurry, Hurry*
Johnson, Crockett	*Harold and the Purple Crayon*
Keats, Ezra Jack	*Hi, Cat!*
———.	*Jenny's Hat*
Morris, Ann	*Hats, Hats, Hats*

_____.	*Houses and Homes*
Seuss, Dr.	*Hop on Pop*
_____.	*Horton Hatches the Egg*
_____.	*Horton Hears a Who*
Stow, Jenny	*The House That Jack Built*
Waber, Bernard	*The House on East 88th Street*
Wiesner, David	*Hurricane*
Wood, Audrey	*Heckedy Peg*
Ziefert, Harriet	*Hurry Up, Jessie*
Zion, Gene	*Harry the Dirty Dog*
Zolotow, Charlotte	*The Hating Book*

J Book List

Ahlberg, Janet & Allan	*Jeremiah in the Dark Woods*
_____.	*The Jolly Postman*
Aliki	*Jack and Jake*
Arnold, Tedd	*No Jumping on the Bed*
Berenstain, Stan & Jan	*The Berenstain Bears and Too Much Junk Food*
Briggs, Raymond	*Jim and the Beanstalk*
Carlstrom, Nancy	*Jesse Bear, What Will You Wear?*
Coerr, Eleanor	*The Josefina Story Quilt*
Coleridge, Sara	*January Brings the Snow*
Degen, Bruce	*Jamberry*
Galdone, Paul	*Jack and the Beanstalk*
Hoban, Russell	*Bread and Jam for Frances*
Kalon, Robert	*Jump, Frog, Jump*
Keats, Ezra Jack	*Jenny's Hat*
Lord, John V.	*The Giant Jam Sandwich*
Mayer, Mercer	*Just Grandpa and Me*
Shaw, Nancy	*Sheep in a Jeep*
Tresselt, Alvin	*Johnny Maple Leaf*
Van Allsburg, Chris	*Jumanji*
Walsh, Ellen S.	*Hop Jump*

K Book List

Bridwell, Norman	*Kangaroo Stew*
Chance, E.B.	*Just in Time for the King's Birthday*
dePaola, Tomie	*The Kids' Cat Book*
Keats, Ezra Jack	*Kitten for a Day*
Fox, Mem	*Koala Lou*
Heller, Ruth	*Kites Sail High*

Holl, Adelaide	*One Kitten for Kim*
Mayer, Mercer	*What Do You Do With a Kangaroo*
Patterson, Francine	*Koko's Kitten*
Payne, Emmy	*Katy No-Pocket*
Selsam, Millicent E.	*How Kittens Grow*
Sendak, Maurice	*In the Night Kitchen*
Yashima, Taro	*Momo's Kitten*

L Book List

Beim, Jerrold	*The Boy on Lincoln's Lap*
Burton, Virginia Lee	*The Little House*
Cohen, Miriam	*Liar, Liar, Pants on Fire*
_____.	*Lost in the Museum*
dePaola, Tomie	*The Art Lesson*
Giff, Patricia R.	*Lazy Lions, Lucky Lambs*
Guarino, Deborah	*Is Your Mama a Llama?*
Harshman, Marc	*A Little Excitement*
Hyman, Trina	*Little Red Riding Hood*
Hoban, Tana	*Take Another Look*
Kay, Helen	*One Mitten Lewis*
Keats, Ezra Jack	*A Letter to Amy*
Kraus, Ruth	*Leo the Late Bloomer*
Lionni, Leo	*Little Blue and Little Yellow*
Lobel, Arnold	*Lucille*
Mayer, Mercer	*Liza Lou and the Yeller Belly Swamp*
McCloskey, Robert	*Lentil*
Moncure, Jane B.	*Love*
Piper, Watty	*The Little Engine That Could*
Rice, Eve	*Oh, Lewis!*
Rockwell, Anne	*I Like the Library*
Showers, Paul	*The Listening Walk*
Waber, Bernard	*Loveable Lyle*
_____.	*Lyle, Lyle, Crocodile*

M Book List

Asch, Frank	*Mooncake*
Barrett, Judi	*Cloudy With a Chance of Meatballs*
Bemelmans, Ludwig	*Madeline*
_____.	*Madeline and the Bad Hat*
_____.	*Madeline's Rescue*

Bonsaill, Crosby	*Mine's the Best*
Branley, Francine	*Mickey's Magnet*
Brett, Jan	*The Mitten*
Brown, Margaret Wise	*Goodnight Moon*
_____.	*Wait Till the Moon is Full*
Cohen, Miriam	*Jim's Dog Muffins*
_____.	*Lost in the Museum*
_____.	*The Real-Skin Rubber Monster Mask*
Duncan, Lois	*Birthday Moon*
Eastman, Philip D.	*Are You My Mother?*
Hankin, Rebecca	*I Can Be a Musician*
Hines, Anna	*Come to the Meadow*
Holl, Adelaide	*Moon Mouse*
Kellogg, Steven	*The Mysterious Tadpole*
Langley, Andrew	*The Moon*
Lionni, Leo	*It's Mine!*
Numeroff, Laura J.	*If You Give a Moose a Muffin*
	If You Give a Mouse a Cookie
Simon, Norma	*I Was So Mad!*
Steptoe, John L.	*Mufaro's Beautiful Daughters*
Yolen, Jane	*Owl Moon*

N Book List

Allard, Harry	*Miss Nelson Is Back*
_____.	*Miss Nelson Is Missing*
Arnold, Tedd	*No Jumping on the Bed*
Brown, Margaret Wise	*Noisy Book*
_____.	*The Summer Noisy Book*
_____.	*The Winter Noisy Book*
Cohen, Miriam	*No Good in Art*
dePaola, Tomie	*Now One Foot, Now the Other*
Geraghty, Paul	*Stop that Noise!*
Guilfoile, Elizabeth	*Nobody Listens to Andrew*
Hughes, Shirley	*Noisy*
Kuskin, Karla	*All Sizes of Noise*
Mayer, Mercer	*There's a Nightmare in My Closet*
McGovern, Ann	*Too Much Noise*
Raskin, Ellen	*Nothing Ever Happens on My Block*
Rylant, Cynthia	*Night in the Country*
Wood, Audrey	*The Napping House*
Zion, Gene	*No Roses for Harry*

P Book List

Ahlberg, Janet & Allan	*The Jolly Postman*
Andersen, Hans Christian	*The Princess and the Pea*
Behrens, June	*I Can Be a Pilot*
Bond, Michael	*Paddington* (series)
Carle, Eric	*Pancakes, Pancakes*
Collodi, Carlo	*Pinnochio*
Davies, Andrew & Dianna	*Poonam's Pets*
dePaola, Tomie	*The Popcorn Book*
Ets, Marie H.	*Play With Me*
Freeman, Don	*A Pocket for Corduroy*
Goodall, John S.	*Paddy's New Hat*
Hoban, Tana	*Push Pull Empty Full*
Hurd, Edith T.	*I Dance in My Red Pajamas*
Keats, Ezra Jack	*Peter's Chair*
Leedy, Loreen	*Pingo the Plaid Panda*
Matthias, Catherine	*I Can Be a Police Officer*
Pizer, Abigail	*It's a Perfect Day*
Polacco, Patricia	*Pink and Say*
Potter, Beatrice	*Peter Rabbit*
Steig, William	*Sylvester and the Magic Pebble*
Titherington, Jeanne	*Pumpkin, Pumpkin*
Van Allsburg, Chris	*The Polar Express*
Wood, Audrey	*Little Penguin's Tale*

Pl Book List

Carle, Eric	*Papa, Please Get the Moon for Me*
Kraus, Ruth	*Come Out & Play, Little Mouse*
Leedy, Loreen	*Pingo the Plaid Panda*
Parish, Peggy	*Play Ball, Amelia Bedelia*
Seuss, Dr.	*Marvin K. Mooney Will You Please Go Now!*
Titherington, Jeanne	*A Place for Ben*

Pr Book List

Calmenson, Stephanie	*The Principal's New Clothes*
Campbell, Rod	*My Presents*
dePaola, Tomie	*The Prince of the Dolomites*
Grifalconi, Ann	*Osa's Pride*
Munsch, Robert	*The Paper Bag Princess*
Rand, Gloria	*Prince William*
Rey, Margaret	*Pretzel*
Rylant, Cynthia	*Birthday Presents*

Scieszka, Jon   *The Frog Prince Continued*
Zolotow, Charlotte   *Mr. Rabbit and the Lovely Present*

Q Book List

Brown, Margaret Wise   *The Quiet Noisy Book*
Carle, Eric   *The Very Quiet Cricket*
Causley, Charles   *"Quack" Said the Billy Goat*
Coerr, Eleanor   *The Josefina Story Quilt*
Flournoy, Valerie   *The Patchwork Quilt*
Johnston, Tony   *The Quilt Story*
Jonas, Ann   *The Quilt*
Wood, Audrey   *Quick as a Cricket*
Zolotow, Charlotte   *The Quarreling Book*
_____.   *The Quiet Mother and the Noisy Little Boy*

R Book List

Alborough, Jez   *Running Bear*
Brown, Margaret Wise   *The Runaway Bunny*
Cohen, Miriam   *The Real-Skin Rubber Monster Mask*
Cooney, Barbara   *Miss Rumphius*
Ehlert, Lois   *Planting a Rainbow*
Gregory, Valiska   *Riddle Soup*
Hyman, Trina   *Little Red Riding Hood*
Hutchins, Pat   *Rosie's Walk*
Le Tord, Bijou   *Rabbit Seeds*
Martin, Rafe   *The Rough-Face Girl*
McLean, Anne   *The Bus Ride*
Mclerran, Alice   *Roxaboxen*
Peek, Merle   *Roll Over! A Counting Book*
Pfister, Marcus   *The Rainbow Fish*
Polacco, Patricia   *My Rotten Redheaded Older Brother*
Tafuri, Nancy   *Rabbit's Morning*
Stinson, Kathy   *Red Is Best*
Zion, Gene   *No Roses for Harry*

S Book List

Balian, Lorna   *Sometimes It's Turkey, Sometimes It's Feathers*
Brown, Margaret Wise   *The Summer Noisy Book*
Crews, Donald   *School Bus*
Gibbons, Gail   *The Seasons of Arnold's Apple Tree*

Gregory, Valiska — *Riddle Soup*
Hoban, Lillian — *Silly Tilly & the Easter Bunny*
Hoberman, Mary Ann — *The Seven Silly Eaters*
Le Tord, Bijou — *Rabbit Seeds*
Lionni, Leo — *Six Crows*
———. — *Swimmy*
McGovern, Ann — *Stone Soup*
Morgan, Allan — *Sadie and the Snowman*
Selsam, Millicent E. — *Seeds and More Seeds*
Steig, William — *Sylvester and the Magic Pebble*
Ziefert, Harriet — *Sarah's Questions*
Zolotow, Chalotte — *Something Is Going to Happen*

Sh Book List

Asch, Frank — *Bear's Shadow*
Burton, Virginia Lee — *Mike Mulligan and His Steam Shovel*
Hoban, Tana — *Shapes, Shapes, Shapes*
Kline, Suzy — *SHHHH!*
Parkes, Brenda — *Who's in the Shed*
Peet, Bill — *Farewell to Shady Glade*
Shaw, Nancy — *Sheep in a Jeep*
———. — *Sheep on a Ship*
Tompert, Ann — *Nothing Sticks Like a Shadow*
Wells, Rosemary — *Shy Charles*

Shr Book List

Joyce, Williams — *George Shrinks*

Sk Book List

Cohen, Miriam — *The Real-Skin Rubber Monster Mask*
Gibbons, Gail — *Up Goes the Skyscraper*
Hines, Anna — *Sky All Around*
Kellogg, Steven — *The Island of Skog*
Rose, Gerrald — *The Tiger Skin Rug*

Sl Book List

Dabcovich, Lydia — *Sleepy Bear*
Miller, Eve — *Mousekin's Woodland Sleepers*
Seuss, Dr. — *The Sleep Book*
Waber, Bernard — *Ira Sleeps Over*
Yolen, Jane — *Sleeping Ugly*
Zolotow, Charlotte — *Sleepy Book*

Sm Book List

Cutting, Brian & Jillian	*A Small World*
Fox, Mem	*Arabella the Smallest Girl in the World*
Lobel, Arnold	*Small Pig*
Margolis, Richard	*Secrets of a Small Brother*

Sn Book List

Briggs, Raymond	*The Snowman*
Brown, Ruth	*The Big Sneeze*
Coleridge, Sara	*January Brings the Snow*
Giganti, Paul	*How Many Snails?*
Goffstein, M.B.	*Our Snowman*
Keats, Ezra Jack	*The Snowy Day*
Lobe, Mira	*The Snowman Who Went for a Walk*
McCully, Emily A.	*First Snow*
Morgan, Allan	*Sadie and the Snowman*
Mowaljarlai, David & Lofts, Pamela	*When the Snake Bites the Sun*
Munsch, Robert	*Thomas' Snowsuit*
Rockwell, Anne & Harlow	*The First Snowfall*
Ryder, Joanne	*Snail's Spell*
Tresselt, Alvin	*White Snow, Bright Snow*

Sp Book List

Arkhurst, Joyce	*The Adventures of Spider*
_____.	*More Adventures of Spider*
Carle, Eric	*The Very Busy Spider*
Carter, Jill & Ling, Judy	*Spiders in Space*
Clifton, L.	*The Boy Who Didn't Believe in Spring*
Gelman, R.	*More Spaghetti I Say*
Margolis, Richard	*Big Bear, Spare That Tree*
Moncure, Jane B.	*Spring Is Here*
Pinkney, Jerry	*The Adventures of Spider: A West African Folk Tale*
Raskin, Ellen	*Spectacles*
Rockwell, Anne	*First Comes Spring*
Shaw, Charles G.	*It Looked Like Spilt Milk*

St Book List

Burton, Virginia Lee	*Mike Mulligan and His Steam Shovel*
Cohen, Miriam	*Starring First Grade*
Fisher, Leonard	*Storm at the Jetty*
Lewis, Richard	*In the Night, Still Dark*
McClintock, Mike	*Stop That Ball*
McGovern, Ann	*Stone Soup*

Provensen, Ann	*The Buck Stops Here*
Stevens, Carla	*Anna, Grandpa and the Big Storm*
Stolz, Mary	*Storm in the Night*
Tompert, Ann	*Nothing Sticks Like a Shadow*

Str Book List

Bruchac, Joseph	*First Strawberries: A Cherokee Story*
dePaola, Tomie	*Strega Nona* (series)
Ginsburg, Mirra	*Across the Stream*
Isadora, Rachel	*The Pirates of Bedford Street*
Lobel, Arnold	*On Market Street*
Politi, Leo	*Pedro, the Angel of Olvera Street*
Van Allsburg, Chris	*The Stranger*
Williams, Vera and Williams, Jennifer	*Stringbean's Trip to the Shining Sea*

Sw Book List

Adams, Pam	*There Was an Old Lady Who Swallowed a Fly*
Lionni, Leo	*Swimmy*
Mayer, Mercer	*Liza Lou and the Yeller Belly Swamp*
Politi, Leo	*Song of the Swallows*
Tejima, Keizaburo	*Swan Sky*

T Book List

Baker, Alan	*Two Tiny Mice*
Bang, Molly	*Ten, Nine, Eight*
Bennett, Jill	*Teeny Tiny*
Brett, Jon	*Town Mouse, Country Mouse*
Carle, Eric	*The Tiny Seed*
Cohen, Miriam	*First Grade Takes a Test*
Crews, Donald	*Ten Black Dots*
Gretz, Suzanna	*Teddy Bears 1 to 10*
Hutchins, Pat	*Titch*
Kellogg, Steven	*The Mysterious Tadpole*
Kennedy, Jimmy	*The Teddy Bears' Picnic*
Lester, Helen	*Tacky the Penguin*
Mosel, Arlene	*Tikki Tikki Tembo*
Pomerantz, Charlotte	*How Many Trucks Can a Tow Truck Tow?*
Potter, Beatrice	*The Tale of Peter Rabbit* (series)
Preston, Edna M.	*The Temper Tantrum Book*
Sadler, Marilyn	*Alistair's Time Machine*
Seuling, Barbara	*The Teeny Tiny Woman*

Weiss, Leatie   *My Teacher Sleeps in School*
Zolotow, Charlotte   *A Tiger Called Thomas*

Th Book List

Browne, Anthony   *Things I Like*
Hayes, Sarah   *This is the Bear*
Koontz, Robin   *This Old Man: The Counting Song*
Peet, Bill   *No Such Things*
Perkins, Al   *Hand, Hand, Fingers, Thumb*
Polacco, Patricia   *Thank You Mr. Falker*
————.   *Thunder Cake*
Rockwell, Anne   *Things That Go*
Rylant, Cynthia   *This Year's Garden*
Seuss, Dr.   *Thidwick the Big-hearted Moose*
Slepian, Jan & Siedler, Ann   *The Hungry Thing*
Tashjian, Virginia A.   *Juba This and Juba That*
Terban, Marvin   *I Think I Thought*

Thr Book List

Brustlein, Daniel   *One, Two, Three, Going to Sea*
Appleby, Ellen (illustrator)   *Three Billy-Goats Gruff*
Battaglia, Aurelius (illustrator) *The Three Little Pigs*
Emberley, Rebecca   *Three Cool Kids*
Cauley, Lorinda   *Goldilocks & the Three Bears*
Child, Lydia Maria   *Over the River and Through the Woods*
Galdone, Paul   *The Three Bears*
————.   *The Three Billy Goats Gruff*
————.   *The Three Little Pigs*
Hooks, William   *The Three Little Pigs*
Ivimey, John   *Three Blind Mice*
Parkes, Brenda   *The Three Little Pigs*
Trivizas, Eugene   *The Three Little Wolves and the Big Bad Pig*

Tr Book List

Gackenbach, Dick   *Mighty Tree*
Howard, Elizabeth F.   *The Train to Lulu's*
Isadora, Rachel   *Ben's Trumpet*
Jonas, Ann   *Round Trip*
Keats, Ezra Jack   *The Trip*
Lobel, Arnold   *A Treeful of Pigs*
Margolis, Richard   *Big Bear, Spare That Tree*
Martin, Bill, Jr.   *The Ghost-Eye Tree*
McCord, David   *Every Time I Climb a Tree*

McPhail, David	*The Train*
Miller, Eve	*Mousekin Takes a Trip*
Oxenbury, Helen	*The Car Trip*
Petrie, Catherine	*Joshua James Likes Trucks*
Pomerantz, Charotte	*How Many Trucks Can a Tow Truck Tow?*
Ross, Pat & Joel	*Your First Airplane Trip*
Scieszka, Jon	*The True Story of the Three Little Pigs*
Siebert, Diane	*Truck Song*
Udry, Janice M.	*A Tree is Nice*
Wood, Leslie	*Tom and His Tractor*

V Book List

Andrews, Jan	*Very Last First Time*
Bunting, Eve	*The Valentine Bears*
Carle, Eric	*The Very Busy Spider*
————.	*The Very Hungry Caterpillar*
Cohen, Miriam	*Bee My Valentine*
Ehlert, Lois	*Growing Vegetable Soup*
Viorst, Judith	*Alexander & the Terrible, Horrible, No Good, Very Bad Day*
Williams, Margery	*The Velveteen Rabbit*

W Book List

Aliki	*We Are Best Friends*
Brown, Margaret Wise	*The Winter Noisy Book*
Carle, Eric	*Rooster's Off to See the World*
Carrick, Carol	*Old Mother Witch*
Cristini, Ermanno & Puricelli, Luigi	*In the Woods*
Cohen, Miriam	*Will I Have a Friend?*
Cowley, Joy	*Mrs. Wishy-Washy*
Ets, Marie H.	*Gilberto & the Wind*
Howe, James	*I Wish I Were a Butterfly*
Hutchins, Pat	*Rosie's Walk*
————.	*The Wind Blew*
Kantrowitz, Mildred	*Willy Bear*
Keats, Ezra Jack	*Whistle for Willie*
McMillan, Bruce	*Counting Wildflowers*
Miller, Eve	*Mousekin's Woodland Sleepers*
Parkes, Brenda	*The Enormous Watermelon*
Peet, Bill	*Wump World*
Sendak, Maurice	*Where the Wild Things Are*

| Showers, Paul | *The Listening Walk* |
| Zolotow, Charlotte | *William's Doll* |

Wh Book List

Cohen, Miriam	*So What?*
_______.	*When Will I Read?*
Gackenbach, Dick	*What's Claude Doing?*
Gelman, Rita G.	*Why Can't I Fly*
Gerson, Mary-Joan	*Why the Sky Is Far Away*
Godkin, Celia	*What About Ladybugs*
Hill, Eric	*Where's Spot?*
Jonas, Ann	*Where Can It Be?*
Keats, Ezra Jack	*Whistle for Willie*
Kovalski, Maryann	*The Wheels on the Bus*
Kraus, Ruth	*Whose Mouse Are You?*
Parkes, Brenda	*Who's in the Shed*
Peet, Bill	*Whingdingdilly*
Rockwell, Anne & Harlow	*When I Go Visiting*
Rossetti, Christina	*What Is Pink?*
Sendak, Maurice	*Where the Wild Things Are*
Simon, Norma	*Where Does My Cat Sleep?*
Yabuuchi, Masayuki	*Whose Baby?*
Yoshi	*Who's Hiding Here?*
Zolotow, Charlotte	*When the Wind Stops*

X Book List

Carter, David	*How Many Bugs in a Box?*
Fox, Mem	*Hattie and the Fox*
Hall, Donald	*Ox-Cart Man*

Y Book List

Ehlert, Lois	*Red Leaf, Yellow Leaf*
Félix, Monique	*Yum Yum I'll Be My Own Cook*
Grey, Judith	*Yummy, Yummy*
Hoban, Tana	*Is It Red? Is It Yellow? Is It Blue?*
Johnston, Tony	*Yonder*
Lionni, Leo	*A Busy Year*
_______.	*Little Blue and Little Yellow*
Mayer, Mercer	*Liza Lou and the Yeller Belly Swamp*
Provensen, Alice & Martin	*The Year at Maple Hill Farm*
Ross, Pat & Joel	*Your First Airplane Trip*

Wolff, Ashley   *A Year of Beasts*
————.   *A Year of Birds*

Z Book List

Barton, Byron   *Buzz Buzz Buzz*
Bridges, William   *The Bronx Zoo Book of Wild Animals*
Earle, Ann   *Zipping, Zapping, Zooming Bats*
Ehlert, Lois   *Color Zoo*
Gibbons, Gail   *Zoo*
Hoban, Tana   *A Children's Zoo*
Lopshire, Robert   *Put Me in the Zoo*
McDermott, Gerald   *Zomo the Rabbit*
Peet, Bill   *Zella, Zack, & Zodiac*
Pulver, Robin   *Mrs. Toggle's Zipper*
Seuss, Dr.   *If I Ran the Zoo*
Van Allsburg, Chris   *The Wreck of the Zephyr*
————.   *The Z Was Zapped*

Poetry Books

Adoff, Arnold	*Chocolate Dreams*
Baskwill, Jane	*Pass the Poems Please*
Carle, Eric	*Animals Animals*
De Regniers, Beatrice	*Sing a Song of Popcorn*
Gaber, Susan	*Favorite Poems for Children*
Gander, Father	*Nursery Rhymes*
Hoberman, Maru Ann	*Fathers, Mothers, Sisters, Brothers*
Hopkins, Lee B.	*Side by Side: Poems to Read Together*
Huck, Charlotte	*Keep a Poem in Your Pocket*
_____.	*When Something Happy Happens*
_____.	*The World's So Big*
Lansky, Bruce	*Kids Pick the Funniest Poems*
Lobel, Arnold	*The Random House Book of Mother Goose*
_____.	*Whiskers and Rhymes*
McNaughton, Colin	*Making Friends with Frankenstein*
O'Neill, Mary	*Hailstones and Halibut Bones*
Prelutsky, Jack	*The New Kid on the Block*
_____.	*A Pizza the Size of the Sun*
_____.	*Poems of a Nonny Mouse*
_____.	*The Random House Book of Poetry for Children*
_____.	*Read-Aloud Rhymes for the Very Young*
_____.	*Ride a Purple Pelican*
_____.	*Zoo Doings*
Rogasky, Barbara	*Winter Poems*
Sierra, Judy	*Antarctic Antics*
Silverstein, Shel	*Falling Up*
_____.	*A Light in the Attic*
_____.	*Where the Sidewalk Ends*
Voake, Charlotte	*Over the Moon: A Book of Nursery Rhymes*
Worth, Valerie	*All the Small Poems*

Initial Consonants

b

baby	bear	bone
back	bed	book
bad	bee	boots
bag	beg	bow
bake	bell	box
ball	bib	boy
bank	big	bug
bat	bike	bunny
bath	bird	bus
be	boat	but

g

game	gill	gorilla
garage	girl	got
garden	give	guess
gas	go	guitar
gate	goat	gull
gave	gold	gulp
geese	golf	gum
get	gone	gun
ghost	good	guy
gift	goose	guest

c

cab	cane	coin
cabin	cap	cold
cage	cape	color
calf	car	colt
cake	card	come
call	carrot	cook
camel	cat	cookie
camp	cave	cow
can	coat	cup
candy	cob	

h

hand	hid	hop
happy	high	hope
hat	hill	horn
he	him	horse
heart	hip	hose
heat	his	hot
hello	hit	house
help	hold	hug
hen	home	hum
here	hook	hunt

d

dad	desk	doctor
dance	dew	doe
dark	dig	does
date	dim	dog
day	dime	doll
deep	dirt	don't
deer	dish	door
dent	dive	down
dentist	do	dozen
desert	dock	duck

j

jacket	jeep	joy
jacks	jelly	judge
jail	jet	jug
jam	jewel	juice
January	job	July
jar	join	jump
jaw	joke	June
jay	jolly	just

f

face	fat	finger
fact	father	fire
fair	feather	first
fairy	feel	fish
fall	feet	fit
family	fell	five
fan	fence	foot
far	fill	for
farm	fin	four
fast	fine	fun

k

kangaroo	kettle	king
keep	key	kiss
keg	kick	kit
kennel	kid	kitchen
kept	kill	kite
ketchup	kind	kitten

l

ladder	leaf	lock
lady	leg	log
lake	lemon	long
lamb	light	look
lamp	like	lost
land	line	lot
last	lion	loud
late	lip	love
laugh	list	luck
lazy	live	lunch

m

made	men	mop
mail	met	more
make	mice	most
man	middle	mother
many	milk	mouse
map	miss	move
March	mitten	much
mat	money	mud
match	month	must
may	moon	my

n

nail	net	none
name	new	noon
nap	news	north
near	next	nose
neat	nice	not
neck	nickel	nothing
need	night	now
needle	nine	number
neighbor	no	nurse
nest	noise	nut

p

pack	pass	pink
page	paste	pipe
pail	path	pond
paint	pen	pony
pair	penny	pop
pal	people	pot
pan	pet	pull
paper	pick	pump
parade	pie	pup
park	pig	push
part	pin	puzzle

r

rabbit	ribbon	roof
race	rich	room
rag	riddle	rope
rain	ride	rose
rake	ring	round
ran	rip	row
rat	road	rub
rattle	rob	rug
read	robin	rule
red	rock	ruler
rest	rocket	run
rib	roll	rut

s

said	seed	sit
sail	seem	six
sale	sell	size
salt	send	so
same	sent	socks
sand	set	soft
sang	seven	sold
sank	sew	some
sat	sick	son
save	side	song
saw	sift	soon
say	sight	soup
sea	silly	suit
seal	sing	sun
seat	sink	sunk
see	sip	sunny

t

table	tell	ton
tail	ten	too
take	tent	took
talk	test	tools
tall	tie	tooth
tap	tiger	top
tape	time	toss
tax	tin	town
taxi	tiny	toy
tea	tip	tub
teacher	tire	tug
team	to	tune
teeth	today	turkey
telephone	toe	twin
television	told	

V

vacation	veil	violet
vacuum	vent	violin
vain	verb	visit
valentine	verse	voice
valley	very	volcano
van	vest	volume
vase	view	vote
vegetable	vine	vulture

W

wag	web	wind
wake	wedding	window
walk	weed	wine
wall	week	wire
want	well	wise
war	went	wish
warm	were	witch
was	west	with
wash	wet	wolf
watch	wide	woman
water	wife	wood
wave	wig	word
wax	wild	work
way	will	world
we	willow	worm
wear	win	would

X

ax	fox	xylophone
box	mix	x-ray
fix	wax	

Y

yak	yell	yolk
yank	yellow	yo-yo
yap	yelp	you
yard	yes	young
yarn	yesterday	your
yawn	yet	yours
year	yield	youth

Z

zebra	zinc	zipper
zero	zing	zone
zest	zinnia	zoo
zigzag	zip	zoom

Final Consonants

b

cab	dab	rub
club	globe	scrub
cob	grab	snob
cobweb	jab	sob
corncob	job	stab
crab	knob	stub
crib	mob	tab
cub	rib	tub
cube	rob	web

d

afraid	lid	read
bad	loud	red
bed	mad	rid
bread	maid	road
feed	mud	rod
glad	nod	sad
good	odd	seed
had	pad	shed
head	paid	skid
hid	pod	sled
hood	proud	stood
kid	raid	wood

f

beef	hoof	sheriff
brief	if	sniff
calf	leaf	staff
chef	life	stiff
chief	loaf	stuff
cliff	myself	surf
cuff	off	thief
deaf	oneself	wharf
elf	puff	whiff
half	roof	wife
herself	self	wolf
himself	shelf	yourself

g

bag	fog	plug
beg	frog	rag
bog	gag	rug
bug	hug	sag
chug	jug	shrug
clog	lag	snag
dig	leg	snug
dog	log	tag
dug	mug	tug
egg	nag	wag
fig	peg	wig
flag	pig	zigzag

k

back	park	skunk
book	pink	smoke
chick	quack	snack
cook	rack	snake
desk	rake	stick
duck	rock	tank
ink	sack	think
joke	shake	track
lake	shark	trick
mask	shrink	walk
neck	sick	wick
pack	sink	work

l

animal	pail	smile
ball	peel	snail
bell	pencil	spell
doll	pool	steal
girl	purple	stool
grill	puzzle	tall
heel	sail	toll
hotel	school	turtle
kill	seal	wall
nail	shell	well
nickel	small	whale
owl	smell	wheel

m

am	hem	slam
arm	jam	some
broom	rhyme	stem
clam	rim	stream
dime	roam	sum
dream	room	team
drum	same	them
from	seam	time
game	seem	trim
gum	shame	warm
gym	skim	zoom

n

afternoon	lion	ran
an	men	run
balloon	mitten	seven
barn	noon	skin
bean	ocean	son
brown	open	spin
can	oven	spoon
corn	pan	ten
fan	pen	thin
green	plane	train
gun	queen	van
kitten	rain	yarn

p

ape	help	shop
bump	hip	skip
camp	hop	slap
cape	Jeep	sleep
champ	jump	soap
chip	lamp	stamp
clap	map	step
clip	mop	stop
cup	nap	sweep
damp	pup	trap
drop	rip	trip
flap	ship	wrap

r

after	fear	stir
another	fire	store
answer	for	sugar
bear	hear	summer
car	hour	supper
chair	letter	sure
collar	our	tear
color	pair	tire
deer	paper	water
doctor	snore	where
fair	sour	winter
far	star	year

s

across	glass	paints
boots	goose	pants
chess	grass	plus
circus	guess	press
close	horse	promise
cross	house	purse
dress	kiss	sense
else	less	tennis
gas	mess	us
geese	nurse	yes

t

about	eat	kite
ant	eight	meat
aunt	fat	nest
bat	fight	pet
boat	foot	pocket
but	fruit	rat
cat	gift	skate
coat	goat	state
cost	hat	street
count	heart	sweet
cut	hot	test
east	jet	wet

v

above	glove	prove
alive	grave	remove
brave	grove	serve
carve	have	shave
curve	hive	slave
dive	leave	sleeve
dove	live	solve
drove	move	starve
eve	native	stove
forgive	nerve	twelve
give	olive	wave

z

amaze	fuzz	seize
breeze	gauze	size
bronze	jazz	sneeze
buzz	maze	snooze
daze	ooze	squeeze
freeze	prize	trapeze
froze	quiz	whiz

Two-letter Initial Consonant Blends

bl

black	bled	blood
blackboard	bleed	bloom
blade	blend	blossom
bland	bless	blot
blank	blest	blouse
blanket	blew	blow
blare	blimp	blue
blast	blind	bluff
blaze	blindfold	blunt
bleach	blink	blur
bleak	block	blush

br

brace	breathe	brisk
bracelet	bred	brittle
brag	breed	broad
braid	breeze	broccoli
brain	breezy	broil
brake	bribe	broke
branch	brick	bronze
brand	bride	brook
brass	bridge	broom
brave	brief	brother
bread	bright	brought
break	brim	brown
breath	bring	brush

cl

claim	clean	close
clam	clear	closet
clamp	clerk	clot
clang	clue	cloth
clank	click	clothes
clap	cliff	cloud
clarinet	climate	clover
clash	climber	club
class	cling	cluck
classroom	clinic	clump
claw	clip	clumsy
clay	clock	clutter

cr

crab	crazy	crime
crack	cream	crisp
cracker	crease	crooked
cradle	create	crop
craft	creature	cross
cramp	credit	crow
crane	creek	crowd
crank	creepy	crown
crash	crescent	crumb
crate	crest	crunch
crater	crew	crush
crawl	crib	cry

dr

draft	dreary	drive
drag	drench	driver
dragon	dress	drizzle
drain	dresser	drool
drama	dressing	drop
drank	drier	drown
drape	drift	drowsy
draw	driftwood	drug
drawer	drill	drugstore
drawing	drink	drum
dream	drip	dry

fl

flag	flesh	flop
flake	flew	florist
flame	flexible	flour
flannel	flight	flow
flap	flip	flower
flash	flirt	fluid
flashlight	float	flush
flat	flock	flute
flavor	flood	flutter
flea	floor	fly

fr

fraction	freeze	frog
fracture	freight	from
fragile	frequent	front
fragrance	fresh	frontier
frail	friction	frost
frame	friend	frosting
freak	frighten	frown
freckle	frill	froze
free	fringe	fruit
freedom	frisky	fry

gl

glacier	gleam	glory
glad	glee	gloss
glade	glide	glossary
glance	glimpse	glove
glare	glitter	glow
glass	globe	glue
glaze	gloomy	glum

gr

grab	grasshopper	grill
grade	gravel	grim
graduate	gravity	grin
grain	gravy	grip
grand	gray	grizzly
grandfather	grease	groan
grandmother	great	grocery
grant	greedy	groom
grape	green	grouch
grapefruit	greet	ground
graph	greeting	group
grasp	grew	grow
grass	grief	growl

pl

place	platform	pliers
plaid	platter	plot
plain	play	plow
plan	playful	pluck
plane	playground	plug
planet	playhouse	plum
plank	plead	plumber
plant	pleasant	plumbing
planter	pleasure	plume
plastic	pledge	plump
plate	plenty	plus

pr

practice	pressure	private
praise	pretend	prize
pray	pretty	problem
preach	pretzel	produce
precious	prevent	product
predict	price	profit
prefer	pride	program
prepaid	prince	progress
prepare	princess	project
present	print	promise
president	printing	prompt

sc

scab	scarf	scold
scale	scatter	scoop
scalp	scene	scooter
scan	scenery	scorch
scar	scent	score
scarce	science	scout
scare	scientist	sculpture
scarecrow	scissors	scum

sk

skate	skillet	skull
skeleton	skim	skunk
sketch	skin	sky
ski	skinny	skyline
skid	skip	skyscraper
skill	skirt	

sl

slam	sleigh	sliver
slang	slender	slogan
slant	slept	slope
slap	slice	sloppy
slate	slid	slot
slave	slide	slouch
slavery	slight	slow
sled	slim	slug
sleek	sling	slum
sleep	slip	slumber
sleepy	slipper	slump
sleet	slippery	slur
sleeve	slit	sly

sm

smack	smell	smooth
small	smile	smother
smart	smirk	smudge
smash	smock	smug
smear	smoke	smuggle

sn

snack	sniff	snow
snag	sniffle	snowball
snail	snip	snowdrift
snake	snob	snowfall
snap	snoop	snowflake
snare	snooze	snowplow
snatch	snore	snowy
sneak	snort	snug
sneeze	snout	snuggle

sp

space	speck	spirit
spaceship	speech	spit
spade	speed	spite
spaghetti	spell	spoil
spank	spelling	spoke
spanking	spend	spoken
spare	spent	sponge
spark	sphere	spook
sparkle	spice	spool
sparrow	spider	spoon
splatter	spike	sport
speak	spill	spot
speaker	spin	spotlight
spear	spinach	spout
special	spine	spy

st

stable	stay	stone
stack	steak	stood
staff	steal	stool
stage	steam	stop
stain	steel	store
stair	steep	storm
stall	stem	story

st (continued)

stamp	step	stove
stand	stick	stuck
staple	still	student
star	sting	studio
start	stir	study
starve	stitch	stuffing
state	stock	stump
station	stocking	stupid
statue	stomach	style

sw

swallow	sweat	swift
swam	sweater	swim
swamp	sweep	swing
swan	sweet	swirl
swarm	sweetheart	switch
swat	swell	sword
swear	swept	swung

tr

trace	trash	trim
track	travel	trimming
tractor	tray	trip
trade	treasure	triple
tradition	treat	troop
traffic	treatment	trot
tragic	tree	trouble
trail	tremble	trout
trailer	trembling	truck
train	trench	true
training	trial	truly
tramp	triangle	trunk
trample	tribe	trust
transfer	trick	truth
trap	tricky	truthful
trapeze	tried	try

tw

tweed	twice	twinkle
tweet	twig	twirl
tweezers	twilight	twist
twelve	twin	twister
twenty	twine	

Three-letter Initial Consonant Blends

scr

scram	scratch	screw
scramble	scrawl	scribble
scrap	scream	script
scrapbook	screech	scroll
scrape	screen	scrub

squ

squabble	squaw	squid
squad	squawk	squint
square	squeak	squirm
squash	squeal	squirrel
squat	squeeze	squirt

shr

shrank	shrill	shrivel
shred	shrimp	shrub
shrew	shrine	shrubbery
shrewd	shrink	shrug
shriek	shrinkage	shrunk

str

straight	strap	stretcher
strainer	straw	strike
strand	strawberry	string
strange	stream	stripe
stranger	streamer	strong
strangle	street	struggle

spl

splash	splendor	split
splatter	splice	splotch
spleen	splint	splurge
splendid	splinter	

thr

thrash	thrift	throne
thread	thrifty	through
threat	thrill	throughout
threaten	thrive	throw
three	throat	thrown
thresh	throb	thrust

spr

sprain	spree	sprite
sprang	sprig	sprout
sprawl	spring	spruce
spray	springy	sprung
spread	sprinkle	

Final Consonant Blends

ct

collect	fact	project
connect	impact	react
correct	inject	reflect
duct	inspect	reject
effect	instruct	select
elect	perfect	subject
exact	predict	suspect

ft

cleft	heft	sift
craft	left	soft
deft	lift	swift
draft	loft	theft
drift	raft	thrift
gift	shaft	tuft
graft	shift	waft

ld

bald	gold	sold
bold	held	told
build	hold	weld
child	mild	wield
cold	mold	wild
field	old	yield
fold	rebuild	
gild	scald	

lf

elf	himself	shelf
golf	myself	wolf
gulf	self	yourself
herself		

lk

bulk	hulk	talk
caulk	milk	walk
chalk	silk	
elk	sulk	

lm

balm	elm	helm
calm	film	realm

lp

gulp	kelp	scalp
help	pulp	yelp

lt

adult	halt	occult
belt	insult	pelt
bolt	jolt	quilt
colt	kilt	result
dealt	knelt	salt
fault	lilt	silt
felt	malt	smelt
guilt	melt	spilt

mp

blimp	dump	ramp
bump	jump	shrimp
camp	lamp	slump
champ	limp	stamp
clamp	lump	stump
cramp	plump	swamp
damp	pump	tramp

nce

advance	fence	prance
announce	finance	prince
bounce	glance	pronounce
chance	lance	romance
convince	once	since
dance	ounce	trance
dunce	pounce	wince

nch

bench	drench	pinch
branch	French	punch
brunch	hunch	quench
bunch	inch	ranch
cinch	launch	scrunch
clench	lunch	trench
crunch	munch	wrench

nd

band	ground	sand
bend	hand	send
blend	hound	sound
bound	land	spend
found	mend	stand
friend	pound	tend
grand	round	wind

nk

bank	honk	skunk
blank	ink	spank
blink	junk	tank
bunk	link	thank
crank	pink	think
drink	sank	trunk
frank	shrink	wink

nt

ant	haunt	rent
bent	hunt	scent
cement	lint	sent
cent	mint	spent
dent	paint	squint
faint	plant	tent
front	print	vent

pt

abrupt	corrupt	intercept
accept	crept	interrupt
adapt	crypt	kept
adept	disrupt	opt
adopt	Egypt	script
apt	erupt	swept
concept	except	wept

rb

absorb	disturb	perturb
adverb	garb	superb
barb	harbor	turban
blurb	herb	urban
curb	orb	verb

rg (rge)

barge	gargle	merge
burg	George	splurge
dirge	gorge	submerge
emerge	iceberg	surge
enlarge	immerge	urge
forge	large	verge

rk

bark	lark	shark
clerk	mark	shirk
cork	park	spark
dark	perk	stark
fork	pork	stork

rl

curl	girl	snarl
earl	gnarl	swirl
early	hurl	twirl
furl	pearl	whirl

rm

arm	harm	swarm
charm	inform	term
dorm	norm	uniform
farm	perform	warm
firm	reform	worm
germ	storm	

rn

adorn	earn	scorn
barn	fern	stern
born	horn	thorn
burn	intern	torn
churn	learn	turn
corn	morn	worn
darn	return	yarn

rp

burp	harp	tarp
carp	sharp	usurp
chirp	slurp	warp

rse

coarse	immerse	sparse
converse	inverse	submerse
course	nurse	terse
curse	purse	universe
disperse	rehearse	verse
endorse	reverse	worse

Initial Consonant Digraphs

ch

chain	checkerboard	chime
chair	cheek	chimney
chalk	cheep	chimpanzee
champ	cheerful	chin
chance	cheese	chip
chapter	chess	chirp
charcoal	chest	chocolate
charge	chew	choke
charm	chewing	choose
chart	chick	chop
chase	chicken	chopsticks
chat	chief	chore
cheap	child	chubby
cheat	children	chuckle
check	chilly	church

ph (f)

phantom	philosophy	photographer
Pharaoh	phobia	photographic
pharmacist	phoenix	photography
pharmacy	phone	phrase
pharynx	phoneme	physical
phase	phonetics	physician
pheasant	photo	physics
phenomenon	photogenic	physique

qu

quack	quart	quick
quadrangle	quarter	quicken
quadruplet	quartet	quicksand
quail	quartz	quiet
quaint	queasy	quill
quake	queen	quilt
qualification	quell	quintet
qualify	quench	quit
quality	query	quite
quantity	quest	quiver
quarantine	question	quiz
quarrel	questionnaire	quota
quarrelsome	quibble	quote

sh

shark	shin	show
sharp	shine	shower
sharpen	shiny	shown
shave	ship	shudder
shawl	shirt	shut
she	shoe	shutter
shed	shoot	shy

th (voiced)

than	them	they
that	themselves	this
the	then	those
their	there	though
theirs	these	thus

th (unvoiced)

thank	thick	thirteen
thankful	thicken	thirty
Thanksgiving	thief	thorn
thaw	thimble	thought
theater	thin	thousand
theft	thing	thumb
theme	think	thunder
thermometer	third	Thursday
Thermos®	thirst	

wh

whack	whenever	whirl
whale	where	whirlwind
wharf	wherever	whisk
what	whether	whisker
whatever	which	whisper
wheat	whiff	whistle
wheel	while	white
wheelbarrow	whimper	whiz
wheeze	whine	whopper
when	whip	why

Final Consonant Digraphs

ch

beach	each	quench
bench	inch	ranch
branch	leech	rich
bunch	lunch	such
church	much	teach
couch	perch	torch
crunch	pinch	touch
ditch	punch	which

ck (k)

back	knock	shamrock
black	lick	shock
block	lipstick	sick
brick	lock	smack
broomstick	luck	smock
candlestick	neck	smokestack
check	pack	snack
chick	pancake	sock
clock	peacock	stick
cluck	pick	tack
crack	quack	thick
dock	quick	tick
drumstick	rack	toothpick
duck	rock	track
jack	sack	truck
kick	shack	wreck

gh (f)

cough	laugh	tough
enough	rough	trough

ng

awning	hang	spring
bang	king	sting
bring	long	string
ceiling	lung	strong
clang	ring	swing
cling	sang	thing
duckling	sing	wing
evening	sling	wrong
gang	song	young

ph (f)

autograph	Joseph	telegraph
epitaph	phonograph	triumph
graph	photograph	

sh

bash	flash	sash
brush	fresh	splash
cash	hush	stash
crash	mash	swish
dash	posh	trash
dish	push	wash
fish	rash	wish

tch

batch	hitch	sketch
catch	latch	snatch
clutch	match	stretch
crutch	patch	switch
ditch	pitch	witch

th

bath	fifth	seventh
both	fourth	sixth
breath	growth	south
cloth	math	stealth
death	mouth	tooth
earth	ninth	wealth
eighth	path	wrath

Variant Consonant Sounds

c (s)

cedar	ceremony	fence
ceiling	certain	ice
celery	certificate	juice
cell	cider	lace
cellophane	cigar	mice
cemetery	cinnamon	nice
cent	citizen	niece
center	city	piece
centimeter	cylinder	place
centipede	cymbal	race
central	cypress	twice
century	dice	voice
cereal	face	

s (z)

adds	dreams	jobs
as	drives	leaves
bears	ears	miles
blames	elves	names
boys	ends	oars
brings	eyes	planes
bugs	fairies	please
chains	families	rains
chairs	frogs	smiles
cheese	girls	tails
cookies	has	tease
daisies	his	trees
dogs	homes	wars

g (j)

gelatin	genie	gigantic
gem	genius	gin
gene	gentle	ginger
general	gentleman	gingerbread
generalization	genuine	gingersnap
generalize	geography	giraffe
generally	geometry	gym
generate	George	gymnasium
generation	Georgia	gymnastics
generator	geranium	gyp
generosity	German	gypsy
generous	gesture	gyrate
genial	giant	gyroscope

Silent Consonants

ck

block	cricket	luck
brick	deck	neck
bucket	duck	nick
buckle	fleck	nickel
check	flick	package
chick	freckle	pick
click	jacket	pickle
clock	kick	quack
cluck	knock	
crack	lock	

gn

align	feign	lasagne
assign	foreign	malign
benign	gnarl	realign
campaign	gnash	reign
champagne	gnat	resign
consign	gnaw	sign
design	gnome	
designer	gnu	

h

aghast	honest	rhetoric
ghastly	honor	rhinestone
gherkin	honorable	rhinoceros
ghetto	hour	rhubarb
ghost	hourly	rhyme
ghoul	oh	rhythm
homage	pharaoh	thyme

igh

bright	light	sigh
delight	lighter	sleigh
eight	lightning	slight
fight	might	straight
freight	neigh	thigh
fright	neighbor	tight
high	nigh	tighten
height	night	weigh
highway	right	

kn

knack	knew	knoll
knapsack	knife	knot
knave	knight	know
knead	knit	knowledge
knee	knob	known
kneel	knock	knuckle
knelt	knocker	

l

alm	caulk	qualm
almond	chalk	stalk
balk	folk	talk
balm	half	walk
calf	palm	yolk
calm	psalm	

mb

bomb	dumb	plumber
climb	lamb	plumbing
comb	limb	thumb
crumb	numb	tomb

mn

autumn	condemn	solemn
column	hymn	

p

psalm	psyche	psychic
pseudo	psychiatrist	psychology
pseudonym	psychiatry	

s

aisle	debris	isle
corps	island	

tch

batch	latch	stitch
blotch	match	stretch
catch	notch	stretcher
catcher	patch	swatch
ditch	pitch	switch
etch	pitcher	twitch
fetch	scratch	watch
hatch	sketch	witch
hitch	snatch	wretch
itch	snitch	
ketchup	splotch	

wr

wrack	wren	writer
wrangle	wrench	writhe
wrangler	wrestle	writing
wrap	wretch	written
wrapper	wriggle	wrong
wrath	wring	wrote
wreath	wringer	wrought
wreck	wrinkle	wrung
wreckage	wrist	wry
wrecker	write	

Short Vowels (vc)

ă

add	glass	pat
ant	half	patch
ax	ham	quack
back	jacks	raft
bad	jam	ran
bag	lad	rap
band	lamb	rat
bat	lap	sack
bath	lash	sad
black	lass	sag
calf	latch	scab
cat	mad	scratch
catch	man	spank
crab	mat	splash
crack	math	stab
dad	map	tack
fan	nap	tag
fat	pad	tap
flag	pan	van
gas	pass	wag

ĭ

bib	is	sift
big	itch	sink
bit	kick	slip
brick	king	spilt
brim	kit	spit
chick	knit	sprint
chin	lick	sting
chip	list	swim
clip	milk	swing
crib	mitt	switch
did	mix	thin
dig	nick	twig
din	pick	twins
dish	pig	whip
drink	pink	wick
fin	pit	wig
fish	quit	win
in	rich	witch
inch	rip	zip
ink	shift	
inn	ship	

ĕ

bed	elf	send
beg	help	set
bell	hem	shelf
belt	hen	shell
bench	jet	sled
bend	left	smell
bent	leg	stem
bet	lend	step
cell	let	stretch
cent	melt	ten
check	men	twelve
chef	mend	twenty
chess	neck	vest
chest	nest	web
den	net	well
dent	peg	went
desk	pest	west
dress	pet	wet
Ed	red	yell
egg	sell	

ŏ

blob	flop	plot
block	fox	pod
blond	got	pond
Bob	hog	pot
bog	hop	rob
bomb	job	rock
bond	jot	rod
box	knob	rot
chop	knot	shock
clock	lock	shop
cob	log	shot
cop	loll	sob
cot	lot	sock
crop	mob	sod
dock	mod	spot
dog	moss	stock
doll	nod	stop
dot	not	top
drop	notch	toss
flock	odd	trot

Ŭ

brush	fuzz	plum
bud	gull	puff
bug	gulp	punch
bump	gum	pup
bun	gun	rub
bus	hub	rug
but	hug	run
buzz	hut	scrub
club	jug	shrub
crumb	jump	shrug
crust	lump	shut
cub	mud	such
cuff	muff	suds
cup	mug	sum
drum	muss	sun
dull	must	sup
dust	mutt	thumb
fun	nun	truck
fur	nut	tub
fuss	plug	tug

Long Vowels (cv)

ā	ē	ī	ō	ū
a	be	hi	fro	flu
	he	pi	go	gnu
	me		ho	
	she		no	
	we		pro	
			so	
			yo-yo	

Long Vowels

āi

afraid	frail	rain
aid	gain	raise
ail	hail	regain
aim	jail	retail
bail	laid	sail
bait	lain	snail
braid	maid	sprain
brain	mail	stain
chain	main	straight
claim	nail	strait
contain	paid	tail
drain	pain	trail
explain	plain	vain
fail	raid	wail
faith	rail	wait

āy

away	highway	relay
bay	hurray	say
betray	inlay	slay
clay	jay	spray
day	lay	stay
decay	may	stray
delay	mislay	subway
dismay	Monday	sway
Friday	okay	Thursday
gay	pay	today
gray	play	tray
halfway	portray	Tuesday
hallway	pray	way
hay	ray	Wednesday

ēa

beach	flea	seal
beak	freak	seat
beam	gleam	sneak
bean	grease	speak
beat	heal	squeak
bleach	heap	steal
bleat	heat	steam
cheap	jean	streak
cheat	leak	stream
clean	leap	tea
creak	meal	teacher
cream	meat	team
crease	neat	treat

ēa (continued)

dream	pea	wheat
east	peach	wreath
eat	pleat	
feast	scream	

ēe

bee	greed	sheet
beef	green	sleep
beet	greet	sleeve
bleed	greeting	sneeze
cheek	heel	speed
cheese	Jeep	squeeze
creek	knee	street
creep	kneel	sweep
deep	meet	sweet
eighteen	parakeet	teeth
feed	peek	three
fourteen	queen	tree
free	screen	weed
freeze	see	week
geese	seed	wheel

ēi

ceiling	leisure	receive
conceive	neither	seize
deceive	perceive	seizure
either	protein	sheik

ēy

alley	journey	pokey
barley	key	pulley
donkey	kidney	trolley
galley	medley	turkey
gallery	money	valley
hockey	monkey	volley
honey	motley	
jockey	parsley	

ī¢

applied	died	pried
complied	fried	tie
cried	implied	tied
defied	lie	tried
denied	lied	vie
die	pie	

ōą

approach	foam	oath
bloat	gloat	poach
boast	goat	roach
boat	groan	road
charcoal	load	roam
cloak	loaf	roast
coach	loan	soak
coal	moan	soap
coast	moat	throat
coat	oaf	toad
croak	oak	toast
float	oat	

ō¢

doe	hoe	toe
floe	mistletoe	woe
foe	poem	
goes	roe	

ōʋ

boulder	doughy	soul
dough	poultice	thorough
doughnut	poultry	

ūɨ

bruise	juice	recruit
cruise	juicy	sluice
fruit	nuisance	suit
fruitful	pursuit	suitor

ū¢

avenue	flue	residue
barbecue	glue	revenue
blue	hue	subdue
cue	overdue	sue
due	pursue	true

Long Vowels (vce)

ā_e

age	frame	same
bake	game	scale
base	gate	scrape
brake	grape	shade
cage	hate	shave
cake	lace	skate
cane	lake	snake
case	make	space
cave	name	stage
chase	page	tape
crane	pale	vane
date	place	vase
drape	plane	wake
face	plate	wave
flake	race	whale
flame	rake	

ē_e

athlete	gene	scene
cede	impede	scheme
Chinese	intervene	secrete
compete	Japanese	serene
concede	kerosene	stampede
concrete	obese	supreme
convene	obscene	theme
eve	precede	these
excrete	recede	trapeze
extreme	replete	

ī_e

bike	mice	smile
bride	mile	spice
dice	mine	strike
dime	nine	tide
dive	pile	tile
file	pine	time
fine	pipe	tribe
fire	pride	twice
five	prize	vine
hide	rice	white
hike	ride	wide
ice	ripe	wife
kite	rise	wipe
knife	shine	wise
like	side	write
lime	slice	
line	slide	

ō_e

awoke	hose	slope
bone	joke	smoke
broke	mole	sole
choke	nose	spoke
close	note	stole
Coke®	phone	stone
cone	poke	stroke
dome	pole	throne
doze	promote	tone
drove	quote	vote
explode	robe	whole
froze	rode	woke
globe	role	yoke
hole	rope	zone
home	rose	
hope	shone	

ū_e

abuse	flute	reduce
altitude	fume	refuge
assume	fuse	rude
chute	huge	rule
consume	include	salute
costume	introduce	seclude
crude	intrude	solitude
cube	June	spruce
cute	minute	substitute
duke	molecule	tube
dune	mule	tune
exclude	mute	use
excuse	parachute	
execute	produce	

Short and Long Vowel Changes
(Useful examples for explaining rules)

ў̆c	to	v̄cé		v̆c	to	v̄ÿ
at		ate		am		aim
bit		bite		bet		beat
can		cane		bet		beet
cub		cube		bled		bleed
cut		cute		bran		brain
dim		dime		bred		breed
fad		fade		can		cain
fin		fine		clam		claim
glob		globe		cot		coat
hat		hate		den		dean
hid		hide		got		goat
hop		hope		lid		lied
hug		huge		mad		maid
kit		kite		man		main
mad		made		met		meat
man		mane		met		meet
met		mete		pad		paid
not		note		pal		pail
pal		pale		pan		pain
pan		pane		pet		peat
pet		Pete		plan		plain
pin		pine		ran		rain
plan		plane		rod		road
rip		ripe		run		ruin
rod		rode		set		seat
shin		shine		sop		soap
sit		site		stem		steam
slid		slide		ten		teen
slop		slope		van		vain
tap		tape				
them		theme				
Tim		time				
tub		tube				
us		use				
win		wine				

R-controlled Vowels

ar

alarm	dark	mark
arch	dart	park
argue	farm	parsley
arm	garage	partner
armor	garbage	shark
artist	garden	smart
army	gargle	spark
barber	guard	sparkle
bark	harbor	star
barn	hard	starch
car	harm	target
card	harp	varnish
carpet	jar	yard
cart	large	yarn
cartoon	marble	war
charm	march	warn
chart	margin	

ar(air)

air	flair	scarce
aware	flare	scare
bare	glare	share
beware	hair	snare
blare	hare	spare
compare	impair	square
care	lair	stair
dare	pair	stare
declare	pare	ware
eclair	prepare	welfare
fair	rare	
fare	repair	

er

alert	her	person
amber	herd	prefer
anger	iceberg	reverse
baker	insert	scatter
banner	jerk	serve
butter	jeweler	swerve
beaver	kerchief	term
camper	kernel	Thermos®
chapter	merge	tiger
clerk	murder	transfer
cracker	nerve	verb
dessert	northern	verse
expert	number	whisper
fern	perch	worker
germ	perk	zipper

ir

affirm	firm	squirt
aspirin	first	stir
birch	flirt	stirrup
bird	girdle	swirl
birth	girl	third
birthday	irk	thirst
chirp	quirk	thirsty
circle	shirk	thirteen
circuit	shirt	thirty
circus	sir	twirl
confirm	skirt	whirl
dirt	smirk	
fir	squirm	

or

afford	fork	pork
airport	form	port
before	fort	resort
born	forth	score
chlorine	glory	shore
chore	horn	short
chorus	horse	snore
cord	lord	sore
core	meteor	sort
corn	morn	sport
door	morning	store
dorm	normal	stork
explore	north	storm
floral	oral	story
for	ore	support
force	perform	sword
ford	porch	

ur

blur	flurry	purse
burglar	fur	return
burn	furnace	scurry
burp	furniture	sturdy
burr	gurgle	suburb
burro	hurl	surf
burst	hurry	surface
church	hurt	surgeon
churn	hurtle	turban
curb	murder	turkey
curdle	nurse	turn
current	occur	turtle
curse	perturb	urban
curtain	purchase	urge
curve	purple	urgent
disturb	purr	urn

Other Vowel Sounds

al

all	balk	malt
almost	ball	recall
already	call	salt
also	enthrall	scald
altar	exalt	small
alter	fall	stall
altogether	false	squall
always	hall	wall
bald	halt	waltz

au

applaud	clause	haunt
applause	default	jaunty
assault	defraud	launch
astronaut	distraught	laundry
audit	exhaust	naughty
August	fraught	pause
auto	fault	taught
because	flaunt	vault
caught	fraud	
cause	haul	

aw

awe	fawn	saw
awful	flaw	scrawl
awning	gnaw	scrawny
bawl	hawk	seesaw
brawl	jaw	shawl
claw	law	sprawl
coleslaw	lawn	straw
crawl	outlaw	yawn
dawdle	pawn	
dawn	raw	

ĕa

bread	heaven	pleasure
breath	instead	read
dead	jealous	ready
deaf	lead	spread
death	leather	sweat
dread	leaven	thread
feather	meant	threat
head	measure	zealous
health	peasant	
heather	pheasant	

ēa

break	great	steak

ei (ā)

beige	neigh	veil
eight	reign	vein
feign	rein	weigh
feint	skein	weight
freight	sleigh	

ew

blew	jewel	shrew
brew	knew	slew
chew	new	stew
crew	newt	steward
dew	pew	strewn
few	renew	threw
flew	review	yew
grew	screw	

iē

achieve	field	relieve
apiece	grief	retrieve
babies	grieve	siege
belief	hygiene	shield
believe	niece	shriek
brief	piece	spiel
chief	priest	wield
cities	rabies	yield

oi

appoint	exploit	point
asteroid	foil	poise
avoid	hoist	poison
boil	join	rejoice
broil	joint	soil
coil	loiter	spoil
coin	moist	toil
disappoint	noise	voice
doily	oil	void
embroider	oink	

o͞o

balloon	kangaroo	shoot
bloom	loom	smooth
boot	loop	snooze
broom	loose	soon
doom	moon	spook
choose	moose	spool
cocoon	noon	spoon
cool	pool	tattoo
cuckoo	raccoon	too
food	rooster	tooth
goose	school	troop
groom	scoop	zoo
hoof	scooter	
igloo	shampoo	

o͝o

book	good	stood
booklet	hood	took
brook	hook	wood
cook	look	wooden
crook	plywood	woof
firewood	rookie	wool
fishhook	shook	
foot	soot	

ou

bayou	pouf	you
coup	rouge	youth
couth	through	
ghoul	wound	

ough

cough	rough	trough
enough	tough	

ow

allow	drowsy	powder
anyhow	eyebrow	power
bow	flower	prowl
brow	fowl	prowler
brown	frown	shower
chowder	gown	towel
clown	how	tower
cow	howl	town
crowd	now	vow
crown	owl	vowel
down	plow	wow
drown	pow	yowl

ōw

below	know	sorrow
bellow	low	sow
billow	marshmallow	sparrow
blow	meadow	stow
borrow	minnow	swallow
bow	mow	throw
bungalow	narrow	tomorrow
crow	pillow	tow
elbow	rainbow	wallow
fellow	row	willow
flow	shadow	window
follow	shallow	yellow
glow	show	
grow	slow	

oy

alloy	destroy	oyster
annoy	employ	ploy
boy	employee	royal
convoy	enjoy	soy
corduroy	foyer	toy
cowboy	joy	voyage
coy	joyful	
decoy	loyal	

y (ī)

apply	hydrant	shy
by	hydrogen	sly
cry	hyper	spy
cycle	hyphen	sty
cyclist	July	style
cyclone	lye	Styrofoam®
cypress	my	supply
dry	nylon	terrify
dynamite	paralyze	try
eye	pry	typist
fly	python	why
fry	rhyme	
hybrid	rye	

y (ē)

angry	fairy	navy
army	funny	penny
battery	fuzzy	pony
beauty	galaxy	pretty
berry	gravy	puppy
bunny	happy	rusty
canary	heavy	shady
candy	hungry	shiny
carry	icy	sleepy
cherry	ivy	snowy
city	jelly	tardy
cloudy	jewelry	thirsty
dirty	juicy	tiny
dizzy	lady	ugly
dusty	lucky	wavy
easy	marry	windy
factory	muddy	

Word Ending Combinations
(Word Families or Word Chunks)

Two-Letter Chunks:

-ab

cab	gab	stab
dab	nab	tab

-ad

add	fad	pad
bad	glad	sad
cad	had	
dad	mad	

-ag

bag	gag	rag
brag	hag	sag
drag	lag	tag
flag	nag	wag

-am

am	ham	slam
clam	jam	swam
dam	ram	yam

-an

ban	man	ran
can	pan	tan
fan	plan	van

-ap

cap	map	trap
clap	nap	wrap
flap	snap	zap
lap	tap	

-at

at	gap	rat
bat	hat	sat
fat	mat	vat
flat	pat	

-ax

fax	max	wax
lax	tax	

-ay

bay	lay	stay
clay	may	stray
day	pay	tray
gay	play	way
hay	ray	
jay	say	

-ed

bed	led	wed
fed	red	
fled	sled	

-eg

beg	keg	peg
dreg	leg	

-em

gem	stem
hem	them

-en

den	pen	when
hen	ten	wren
men	then	

-ep

pep	step

-et

bet	met	wet
get	net	yet
jet	pet	
let	set	

-ex

flex	sex	vex
hex		

-ib

bib	jib	rib
fib		

-id

bid	kid	skid
did	lid	slid
hid	rid	

-ig

big	jig	twig
dig	pig	wig
fig	sprig	

-im

dim	skim	trim
him	slim	
rim	swim	

-in

chin	pin	thin
fin	sin	twin
in	skin	win
kin	spin	

-ip

dip	rip	strip
drip	sip	tip
flip	skip	trip
lip	slip	zip

-it

bit	knit	spit
fit	lit	split
flit	pit	wit
hit	quit	
kit	sit	

-ix

fix	mix	six

-ob

blob	knob	slob
cob	lob	snob
gob	mob	sob
job	rob	throb

-od

cod	rod	sod
pod		

-og

bog	frog	log
dog	hog	smog
fog	jog	

-om

mom	prom	tom-tom

-on

bonbon	con	don

-op

cop	hop	stop
chop	mop	top
drop	pop	
flop	shop	

-ot

blot	hot	pot
cot	knot	rot
dot	lot	tot
got	not	

-ox

box	lox	sox
fox	pox	

-ub

club	scrub	sub
cub	shrub	tub
hub	snub	rub
rub	stub	

-ud		
bud	dud	thud
cud	mud	

-ug		
bug	jug	shrug
chug	lug	tug
dug	mug	
hug	rug	

-um		
bum	hum	sum
drum	plum	
gum	rum	

-un		
bun	gun	stun
dun	pun	sun
fun	run	

-up		
cup	pup	sup

-ut		
but	hut	rut
cut	jut	shut
gut	nut	

-ux		
crux	flux	tux

Three-letter Chunks:

-ack

back	jack	sack
black	pack	snack
crack	quack	tack
hack	rack	track

-aft

craft	draft	shaft
daft	raft	

-ald

bald	scald

-all

all	fall	tall
ball	hall	wall
call	small	

-amp

camp	damp	stamp
champ	lamp	tamp
clamp	ramp	tramp

-and

and	grand	sand
band	hand	stand
brand	land	

-ang

bang	hang	slang
clang	rang	
gang	sang	

-ank

bank	hank	tank
blank	rank	thank
clank	sank	yank
crank	spank	

-ant

ant	plant	rant
pant		

-ash

ash	flash	sash
bash	gash	smash
cash	lash	splash
crash	mash	trash
dash	rash	

-ask

bask	mask	task
cask		

-ast

cast	last	past
fast	mast	

-ave

brave	gave	shave
cave	pave	slave
crave	save	wave

-eck

check	neck	wreck
deck	peck	
fleck	speck	

-eft

cleft	heft	theft
deft	left	

-eld

held	meld	weld

-ell

bell	shell	tell
fell	smell	well
sell	spell	yell

-end

bend	lend	spend
blend	mend	tend
end	send	

-ent

bent	lent	vent
cent	sent	went
dent	tent	

-esh

flesh	mesh	thresh
fresh		

-est

best	nest	test
chest	pest	west
guest	quest	
lest	rest	

-ice

dice	nice	slice
ice	price	spice
mice	rice	twice

-ick

brick	pick	tick
chick	quick	trick
kick	sick	wick
lick	thick	

-ift

gift	lift	sift

-ill

bill	ill	spill
chill	kill	still
fill	mill	will
hill	pill	

-ilt

built	quilt	wilt
guilt	spilt	
kilt	tilt	

-imp

blimp	crimp	skimp
chimp	limp	

-ing

bring	ring	thing
cling	sing	wing
fling	spring	
king	string	

-ink

blink	link	think
clink	pink	wink
drink	shrink	
ink	sink	

-int

flint	lint	splint
glint	mint	squint
hint	print	tint

-ish

dish	squish	wish
fish	swish	

-isk

brisk	frisk	whisk
disk	risk	

-ist

fist	list	twist
gist	mist	wrist

-ine

dine	nine	vine
fine	pine	wine
line	shine	
mine	spine	

-ind

bind	grind	wind
blind	kind	
find	mind	

-ock

block	flock	rock
clock	knock	sock
dock	lock	

-oft

loft	soft	

-oil

boil	foil	spoil
broil	oil	toil
coil	soil	

-old

bold	hold	sold
cold	mold	told
fold	old	
gold	scold	

-oll

doll	loll	

-omp

chomp	romp	tromp
clomp	stomp	

-ond

blond	fond	pond

-ong

bong	gong	pong
dong	long	song

-orn

born	scorn	torn
corn	shorn	worn
horn	thorn	

-ost

cost	frost	lost

-uck

buck	luck	suck
cluck	pluck	truck
duck	stuck	tuck

-ull

bull	full	pull

-ump

bump	jump	pump
dump	lump	stump
hump	plump	

-ung

clung	lung	sung
flung	sprung	
hung	strung	

-unk

bunk	flunk	sunk
chunk	hunk	trunk
dunk	skunk	

-unt

blunt	hunt	runt
bunt	punt	

-ush

blush	gush	rush
brush	hush	slush
crush	lush	thrush
flush	mush	

-usk

dusk	husk	tusk

-ust

bust	gust	must
dust	just	rust

Four-letter Chunks:

-atch

| batch | hatch | match |
| catch | latch | patch |

-etch

| fetch | sketch | vetch |
| retch | stretch | wretch |

-ight

| bright | might | sight |
| light | right | tight |

-itch

| ditch | itch | stitch |
| hitch | pitch | witch |

-otch

| blotch | crotch | notch |
| botch | | |

-ouch

couch	ouch	vouch
crouch	pouch	
grouch	slouch	

-ound

bound	hound	round
found	mound	sound
ground	pound	wound

-utch

| clutch | Dutch | hutch |
| crutch | | |

Rhyming Words

ād

aid	laid	shade
braid	made	trade
fade	paid	
grade	raid	

āj

age	page	stage
cage	rage	
gauge	sage	

āk

ache	lake	steak
bake	make	take
break	rake	
cake	snake	

āl

fail	pale	tail
jail	sale	whale
mail	scale	
nail	snail	

al

all	hall	tall
ball	mall	wall
crawl	shawl	
fall	small	

ām

aim	fame	same
blame	flame	shame
came	game	

ān

brain	gain	plane
chain	lane	rain
crane	main	train
drain	pain	

āp

ape	grape	tape
cape	scrape	
crepe	shape	

ar

air	fair	share
bear	hair	square
care	pear	there
chair	scare	wear

ās

base	lace	trace
brace	place	vase
chase	race	
face	space	

āt

date	hate	straight
eight	late	wait
gate	plate	
great	skate	

āz

blaze	haze	praise
glaze	phase	raise
graze	phrase	

ăs

bass	gas	lass
brass	glass	mass
class	grass	pass

ē

bee	knee	tea
fee	me	we
he	sea	
key	she	

ēd

bead	lead	read
bleed	need	seed
feed	plead	weed

ēf

beef	grief	thief
brief	leaf	
chief	reef	

ēl

deal	meal	steal
feel	peel	wheel
heel	seal	
kneel	squeal	

ēm

beam	scheme	team
cream	scream	teem
dream	seem	theme
gleam	steam	

ēp

cheap	Jeep	sheep
creep	keep	sweep
deep	leap	weep

ēr

cheer	fear	tear
clear	here	year
dear	near	
ear	spear	

ēs

cease	grease	peace
crease	lease	piece
geese	niece	

ēt

beat	greet	sheet
cheat	heat	street
eat	meat	sweet
feet	neat	

ēz

breeze	seize	these
cheese	sneeze	wheeze
freeze	squeeze	
please	tease	

ĕd

bed	head	sled
bread	led	spread
fed	red	thread
fled	said	wed

ī

buy	guy	pie
cry	high	sky
die	lie	try
dye	my	why

īd

bride	pride	tied
cried	ride	vied
hide	side	wide
lied	tide	

īl

aisle	pile	tile
file	smile	while
mile	style	

īm

climb	grime	rhyme
crime	I'm	time
dime	lime	

īt

bite	light	sight
fight	might	white
kite	night	write

ĭm

dim	limb	slim
gym	rim	swim
him	skim	trim

ĭn

been	in	spin
chin	pin	thin
fin	skin	twin

ĭst

fist	list	twist
hissed	missed	wrist
kissed	mist	

ō

crow	mow	sow
dough	no	throw
flow	oh	toe
go	row	woe
low	so	

ōd

code	road	snowed
crowed	rowed	strode
load	slowed	toad

ōk

broke	joke	soak
choke	poke	stroke
croak	smoke	woke

ōl

bowl	mole	roll
coal	pole	troll
goal	role	whole

ōm

chrome	foam	roam
comb	gnome	
dome	home	

ōn

cone	hone	moan
flown	loan	own
groan	lone	phone

ōp

cope	Pope	slope
dope	rope	soap
nope	scope	

or

core	more	score
door	oar	snore
floor	pour	store
four	roar	

ōst

boast	ghost	post
coast	host	roast
dosed	most	toast

ōt

boat	note	throat
coat	oat	vote
goat	quote	wrote

ōz

chose	goes	rows
clothes	hose	those
doze	nose	toes

ou

bough	chow	how
brow	cow	now

oun

brown	down	gown
clown	drown	noun
crown	frown	town

ū

blue	glue	too
chew	new	who
do	shoe	you

ūl

cool	pool	spool
drool	rule	tool
fool	school	yule

ūm

boom	loom	tomb
broom	plume	zoom
gloom	room	

ūn

dune	noon	spoon
June	prune	tune
moon	soon	

ūp

coop	scoop	troupe
hoop	snoop	
loop	soup	

ūs

goose	loose	spruce
juice	moose	truce

ūt

boot	hoot	shoot
chute	loot	toot
flute	root	

ūz

bruise	news	whose
choose	ooze	zoos
cruise	shoes	
lose	snooze	

ŭch

clutch	hutch	touch
crutch	much	
Dutch	such	

ŭf

bluff	muff	stuff
cuff	puff	tough
fluff	rough	
huff	scuff	

ŭm

bum	dumb	some
come	gum	thumb
crumb	hum	
drum	plum	

ŭng

clung	rung	sung
flung	sprung	tongue
hung	strung	young

ur

blur	purr	stir
fur	sir	were
her	slur	

urs

curse	purse	worse
hearse	terse	
nurse	verse	

Compound Words

afternoon	beefsteak	buttermilk	drugstore
aircraft	beehive	buttonhole	drumstick
airplane	beeline	campfire	earache
airport	beeswax	candlelight	eardrum
anteater	billboard	cardboard	earphone
anybody	birdbath	carload	earthquake
anyhow	birthday	chairman	evergreen
anyone	birthplace	checkerboard	everybody
anything	blackberry	chopsticks	everyone
anywhere	blackbird	classmate	eyeball
archway	blackboard	classroom	eyebrow
armchair	blackout	collarbone	eyelash
backbone	blacksmith	cornbread	eyelid
backfield	blindfold	clothespin	eyesight
backfire	bloodhound	corncob	farmhouse
background	blueberry	corncrib	firecracker
backhand	bluebird	cornfield	firefly
backstroke	blueprint	courthouse	fireman
backward	boathouse	courtyard	fireplace
bagpipe	bombshell	cowboy	firewood
bareback	bookcase	crossword	fisherman
barnyard	bookkeeper	daydream	flashlight
baseball	bookmark	daylight	football
baseboard	bookworm	daytime	footprint
basketball	boxcar	doghouse	footstep
bathrobe	breakdown	doorstep	goldfish
bathroom	bridegroom	doorway	grandmother
battlefield	bridesmaid	doughnut	grapefruit
bedclothes	broadcast	downfall	grapevine
bedrock	broomstick	downhill	grownup
bedroom	buckwheat	downstairs	gumdrop
bedside	bulldog	downtown	hairpin
bedspread	bullfight	dragonfly	handcuff
bedtime	butterfly	driveway	handkerchief

headache	overcoat	schoolteacher	sweetheart
headlight	overhand	schoolyard	taxicab
headline	overlook	seashore	teacup
highway	overnight	seaweed	teakettle
homemade	overtime	shopkeeper	teaspoon
homesick	overweight	sidewalk	textbook
honeybee	pancake	skyline	thunderstorm
honeymoon	patrolman	skyscraper	tightrope
horseback	pickpocket	smokestack	toothache
horseshoe	pillowcase	snapshot	toothbrush
houseboat	pitchfork	snowball	toothpaste
housewife	playground	snowfall	toothpick
housework	pocketbook	snowflake	tugboat
jackknife	pocketknife	snowplow	undershirt
jellyfish	policeman	snowshoe	underwear
keyboard	popcorn	somebody	upstairs
keyhole	postman	someone	wallpaper
landscape	rainbow	something	watchdog
lifetime	raindrop	spaceship	watchman
lighthouse	rainfall	springtime	waterfall
lookout	roadside	staircase	watermelon
milkman	roommate	starfish	weekday
moonlight	rosebud	steamboat	wildcat
motorboat	rosebush	stepladder	wildlife
motorcycle	rowboat	storeroom	windmill
mousetrap	runaway	storybook	windowpane
necktie	salesman	strawberry	wishbone
newspaper	sandpaper	sunburn	wintertime
nightgown	saucepan	Sunday	withdrawn
notebook	sawdust	sunflower	without
outdoor	scarecrow	sunglasses	workday
outfield	schoolbook	sunlight	workman
outside	schoolroom	sunshine	wristwatch

Prefixes

Prefix	Meaning	Examples
a–, ab–	away from	apart, absent, abstract
a–, ad–, ap–, at–	to, toward	advance, adhere, appoint, attach
amphi–, ambi	around	amphibian, ambidextrous
ante–	before	antecedent
anti–	against	antifreeze, antitrust
be–	by	beside, beneath
bi–	two	bicycle, bifocal
circum–	around	circumference
co–, com–, cor–	with	cooperate, combine, correct
con–, col–	together	conflict, collect
contra–	against	contradict
de–	away, against	decay, deform
dia–	around	diameter, diagram
dis–, di–	apart, not	disagree, divide
en–, em–	into	enforce, embark
epi–	upon	epidermis
e–, ex–	out of	emit, exhale
hetero–	different	heterogeneous
homo–	same	homonym
in–, im–	into	incision, implant
in–, im–	not	inappropriate, immortal
il–, ir–	not	illegal, irregular
inter–	between	intermission
intra–, intro	inside	intravenous, introduce
mis–	wrong	misled, misspell
mono–	one	monotone, monopoly
non–	not	nonsense
ob–, of–, op–	against	object, offense, opposite
pan–	whole	panorama
per–	fully	persist
peri–	around	perimeter
post–	behind	postwar
pre–	before	prevent
pro–	in front of	project
re–	again	repaint
semi–	half	semiprivate
sub–	under	submarine
super–	over	supervise
syn–	together	synonym
trans–	across	transcend
tri–	three	tricycle
ultra–	beyond	ultrasound
un–	not	unbelievable

Suffixes

Suffix	Meaning	Example
–able, –ible, –ile	able to be	portable, sensible, docile
–acy	act	literacy
–age	act of	courage
–al	related	maternal
–an, –ian	one who	artisan, comedian
–ance, –ence	doing	significance, independence
–ancy, –ency	doing	constancy, emergency
–ant	quality	immigrant
–ar	one who	beggar
–ary	like	tributary
–ate	quality of	imitate
–dom	state of	kingdom
–en	to make	harden
–ent	one who	president
–er, –eur, –eer	one who	teacher, amateur, engineer
–et, –ette, –let	small	cabinet, dinette, booklet
–ful	full of	joyful
–fy, –ify	to make	satisfy, clarify
–hood	state of	fatherhood
–ic, –iac	made of	heroic, maniac
–cle, –cule	little	article, molecule
–ier, –ist	one who	skier, dentist
–id	state of	vivid
–ism	being	organism
–ize	to make	organize
–ive	able to	narrative
–ity, –ty	state of	nobility, fidgety
–less	without	careless
–ly	quality	fondly
–ment	state of	excitement
–ness	state of	neatness
–or	one who	actor
–ory	place	factory
–ous, –ious	full of	dangerous, amphibious
–some	full of	wholesome
–tion, –ion	action	vacation, division
–tude	state	attitude
–ty	state of	beauty
–ward	toward	forward

Homonyms

ant—aunt
ate—eight
bare—bear
bass—base
beat—beet
bee—be
blew—blue
board—bored
by—bye—buy
cell—sell
cent—sent—scent
chord—cord
close—clothes
creak—creek
dear—deer
dew—do—due
doe—dough
die—dye
eye—I
fair—fare
find—fined
fir—fur
flea—flee
flour—flower
for—four
foul—fowl
gait—gate

grate—great
guessed—guest
hall—haul
hay—hey
him—hymn
ho—hoe
hoarse—horse
hole—whole
idol—idle
I'll—isle—aisle
inn—in
knead—need
knight—night
knot—not
know—no
lie—lye
loan—lone
made—maid
mail—male
meddle—medal
moan—mown
new—knew
none—nun
oh—owe
one—won
pail—pale
pain—pane

pair—pear
paws—pause
peace—piece
plain—plane
praise—prays—preys
rain—rein
read—reed
right—write
sail—sale
sew—so
sole—soul
some—sum
son—sun
steal—steel
tail—tale
their—there
toe—tow
to—too—two
vain—vein
wail—whale
wait—weight
weak—week
wear—ware
which—witch
wood—would

Synonyms

absent—away
act—behave
afraid—fearful
aid—help
always—forever
ask—question
bad—evil
begin—start
big—large
chief—leader
close—near
desire—wish
earth—world
enjoy—like
fact—truth
firm—solid

gift—present
guide—lead
hard—firm
house—shelter
huge—gigantic
idea—thought
ill—sick
keep—hold
little—small
loud—noisy
make—build
odd—strange
odor—smell
plan—plot
price—cost
problem—puzzle

quiz—test
real—true
rear—back
reply—answer
shape—form
shout—yell
steal—rob
stop—end
street—road
sum—total
tale—story
thief—robber
town—city
train—teach
wealthy—rich

Antonyms

always—never	happy—sad	queen—king
bad—good	hard—soft	rich—poor
before—after	here—there	right—wrong
begin—end	him—her	run—walk
boy—girl	in—out	sell—buy
city—country	last—first	sick—healthy
dark—light	laugh—cry	sit—stand
day—night	little—big	start—stop
dirty—clean	lost—found	stay—go
dry—wet	morning—night	take—give
easy—hard	mother—father	under—over
empty—full	near—far	up—down
forget—remember	now—then	white—black
found—lost	off—on	whole—part
front—back	old—young	work—play
gave—took	open—close	yes—no
go—stop	push—pull	

Section Five

Appendix

This section provides reproducible pages which help you prepare many of the materials needed for the hands-on activities described in this book. These include a field-trip form, upper- and lower-case alphabet cards, and mini-flash cards. In addition, several game boards are provided as well as sample puzzles and patterns. The alphabet pictures included at the end of the appendix may be used to produce a wall chart, individual student alphabet booklets, or coloring sheets for incentive awards as the children learn their letter sounds. Most importantly, a simple *Phonics Assessment Profile* is provided to help you with record keeping as you track each student's progress with letters and their sounds.

Name _____

Field Trip Fun

Date _____

Place _____

Things I Saw

_____

_____

_____

Words I Learned

_____

_____

_____

The best part of the trip was _____

_____

_____

_____

_____

Draw a picture of your field trip!

Phonics Rules

Studies have shown that the knowledge of certain consistent phonics rules provide a valuable decoding tool for elementary children. These rules are provided below.

1. When there are two vowels side by side, the first vowel is usually long and the second silent. *(rail, real, boat, suit)*

2. When a vowel is in the middle of a one-syllable word, the vowel is usually short. *(hat, dress)*

3. When there is one *e* in a word that ends with a consonant, the *e* is usually short. *(leg, neck, technical)*

4. If the only vowel is at the end of a word it is usually long. *(me, go)*

5. When there are two vowels, one of which is final *e*, the first vowel is long and the *e* is silent. *(cake, pine)*

6. An *r* gives the preceding vowel a sound that is neither long nor short. *(barn, turn)*

7. Words that have a double *e* usually have the long *e* sound. *(green, seen)*

8. In *ay* the *y* is silent and gives *a* its long sound. *(day, stay)*

9. When *y* is the final letter in a word, it usually has a long vowel sound. *(try, empty)*

10. When the letter *i* is followed by the letters *gh,* the *i* usually stands for its long sound and the *gh* is silent. *(high, night)*

11. When *a* is followed by *r* and the final *e,* we usually hear the sound heard in *care.* *(dare, glare)*

12. When *c* and *h* are next to each other, they make one sound, usually pronounced as in *child. (chair, reach)*

13. When *c* is followed by *e* or *i,* the sound of *s* is usually heard. *(cent, city)*

14. When *c* is followed by *o, u,* or *a,* the sound of *k* is usually heard. *(comb, cart)*

15. When *ght* is in a word, *gh* is silent. *(weight, night)*

16. When two of the same consonants are side by side, only one sound is heard. *(berry, follow)*

17. When a word ends in *ck,* the sound of *k* is heard. The preceding vowel is short. *(duck, chick)*

18. If the last syllable of a word ends in *le,* the consonant preceding the *le* usually begins the last syllable. *(stumble, table)*

19. When the first vowel in a word is followed by *ch, sh,* or *th,* these letter combinations are not split when the word is divided into syllables and may go with either the first or second syllable. *(wishes. lather)*

20. In two-syllable words that end in a consonant followed by *y,* the first syllable is usually accented and the last is unaccented. *(baby, carry)*

A	B	C
D	E	F
G	H	I
J	K	L
M	N	O
P	Q	R
S	T	U
V	W	X
Y	Z	

Mini Flash Cards—Upper Case Letters

a	b	c
d	e	f
g	h	i
j	k	l
m	n	o
p	q	r
s	t	u
v	w	x
y	z	

Mini Flash Cards—Lower Case Letters

Mini Flash Cards

Template

TIC-TAC-TOE

BINGO

		FREE!		

LOTTO

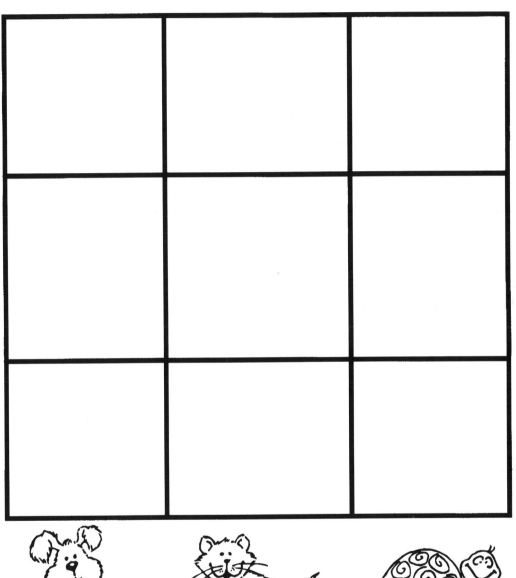

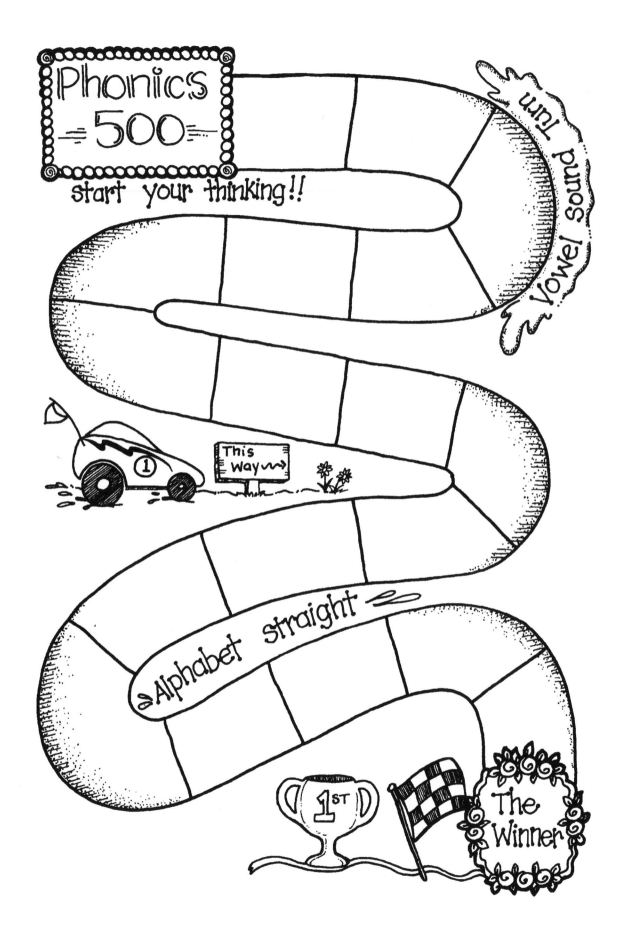

Phonics 500
start your thinking!!

Vowel Sound Turn

This Way →

Alphabet straight

1ST

The Winner

Pinwheel Pattern

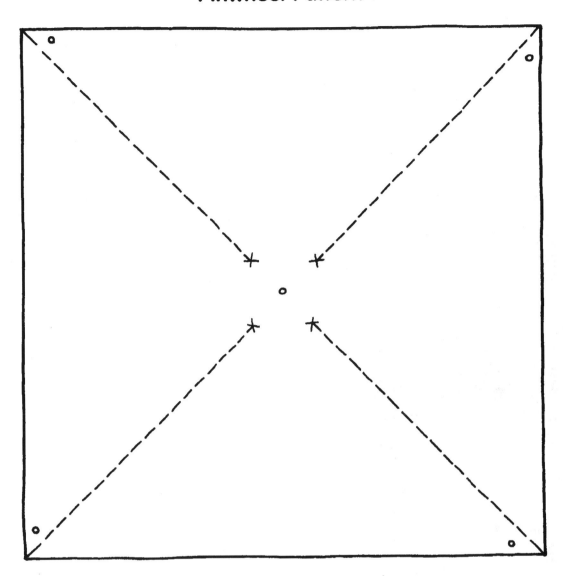

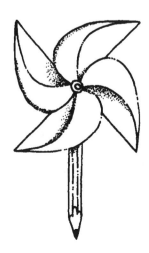

Color the pinwheel square.

Carefully cut out the square.

Cut along the dotted lines to the "x".

Fold each corner, marked with a "o", to the center. Secure ends with a push pin.

Attach pinwheel to a pencil-top eraser. (See illustration.)

Alphabet Puzzle Examples

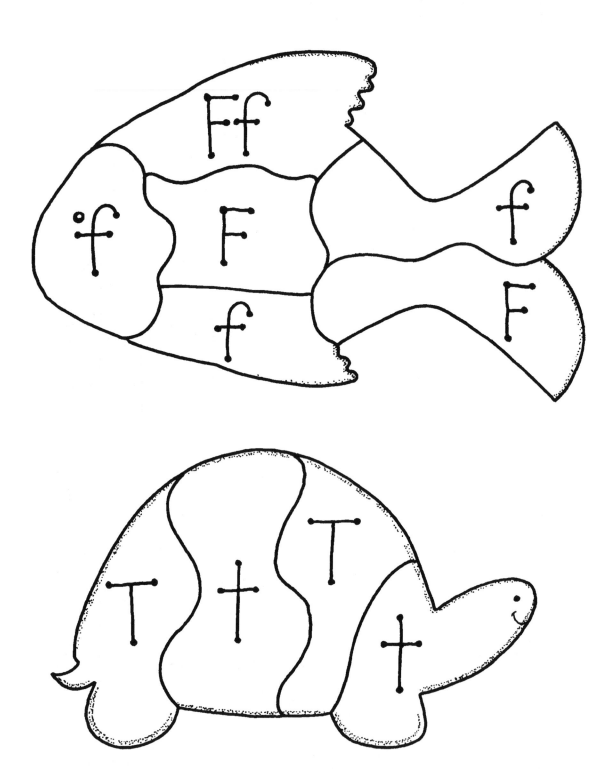

Phonics Assessment Profile

Name _____

0 = Mastery

Consonants	bat (b)	cat (c)	dog (d)	fish (f)	goat (g)	house (h)	jump (j)	kite (k)	look (l)	milk (m)	nest (n)	pig (p)	queen (qu)
Consonants	rat (r)	see (s)	turtle (t)	vase (v)	wig (w)	box (x)	yellow (y)	zoo (z)	city (c=s)	gem (g=j)	bugs (s=z)		
Initial Consonant Blends	blue (bl)	broom (br)	clam (cl)	crab (cr)	drum (dr)	flower (fl)	frog (fr)	glue (gl)	play (pl)	present (pr)	scale (sc)	skate (sk)	sleep (sl)
Initial Consonant Blends	smile (sm)	snake (sn)	spoon (sp)	stop (st)	sweep (sw)	tree (tr)	twin (tw)	scream (scr)	shrimp (shr)	splash (spl)	spray (spr)	straw (str)	three (thr)
Final Consonant Blends	fact (ct)	left (ft)	child (ld)	elf (lf)	milk (lk)	calm (lm)	colt (lt)	help (lp)	bump (mp)	once (nce)	inch (nch)	band (nd)	bank (nk)
Final Consonant Blends	ant (nt)	kept (pt)	verb (rb)	large (rg(e))	bark (rk)	girl (rl)	arm (rm)	barn (rn)	harp (rp)	horse (rse)			
Initial Consonant Digraphs	chair (ch)	ship (sh)	than (th) (voiced)	thing (th) (unvoiced)	whale (wh)	photo (ph=f)	quack (qu)						
Final Consonant Digraphs	search (ch)	chick (ck=k)	cough (gh=f)	song (ng)	dish (sh)	graph (ph=f)	path (th)	patch (tch)					
Vowel Sounds	apple (ă)	egg (ĕ)	indian (ĭ)	octopus (ŏ)	umbrella (ŭ)	ape (ā)	eagle (ē)	ice (ī)	oval (ō)	unicorn (ū)	by (y=ī)	baby (y=ē)	
Vowel Combinations	pain (ai)	car (ar)	August (au)	raw (aw)	day (ay)	eat (ea)	bread (ea)	great (ea)	green (ee)	vein (ei)	ceiling (ei)	her (er)	blew (ew)
Vowel Combinations	key (ey)	chief (ie)	stir (ir)	boat (oa)	toe (oe)	oil (oi)	good (oo)	zoo (oo)	corn (or)	ouch (ou)	soup (ou)	cow (ow)	snow (ow)
Vowel Combinations	boy (oy)	blue (ue)	suit (ui)	burn (ur)	eight (eigh)	light (igh)	through (ough)						

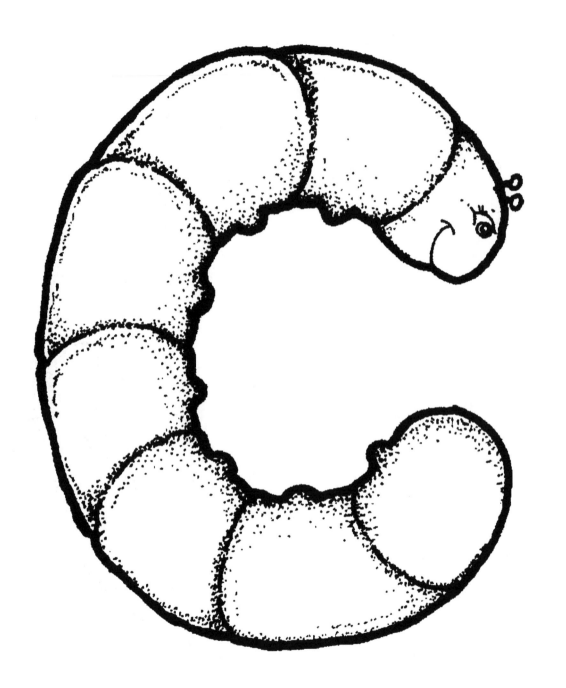

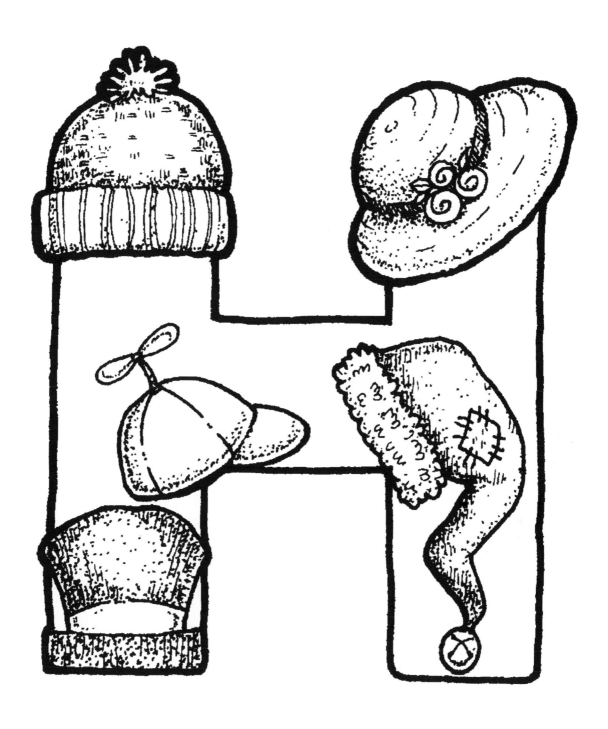

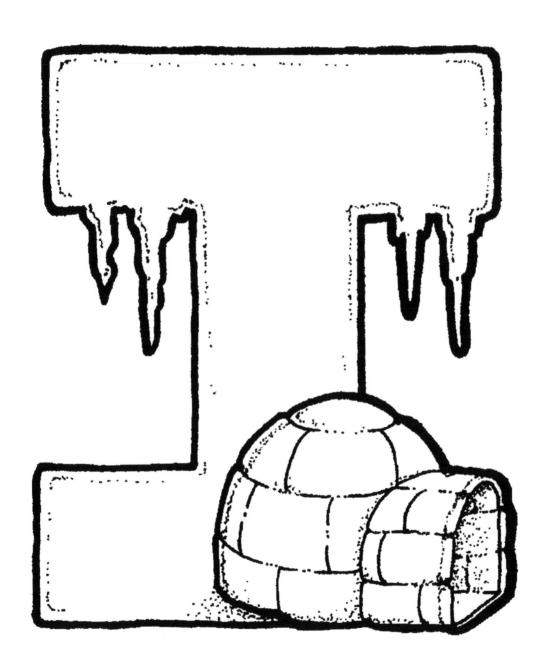

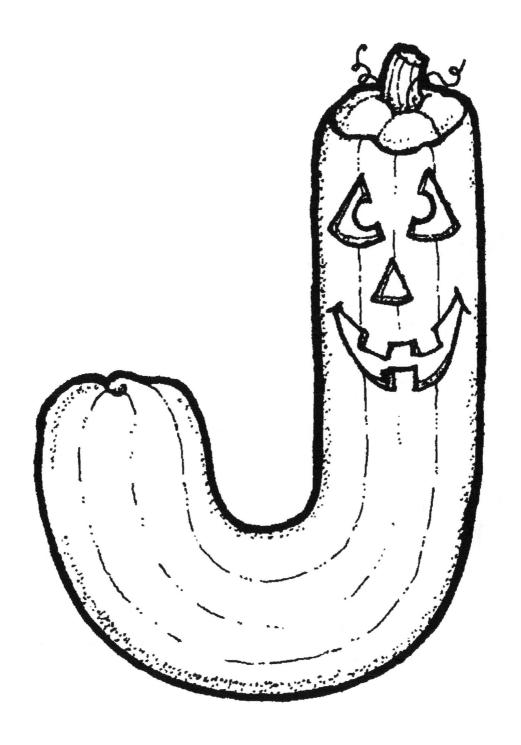

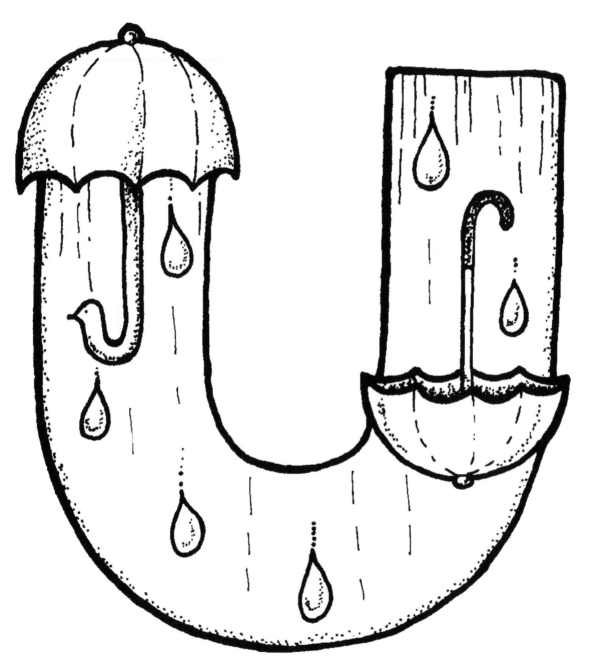

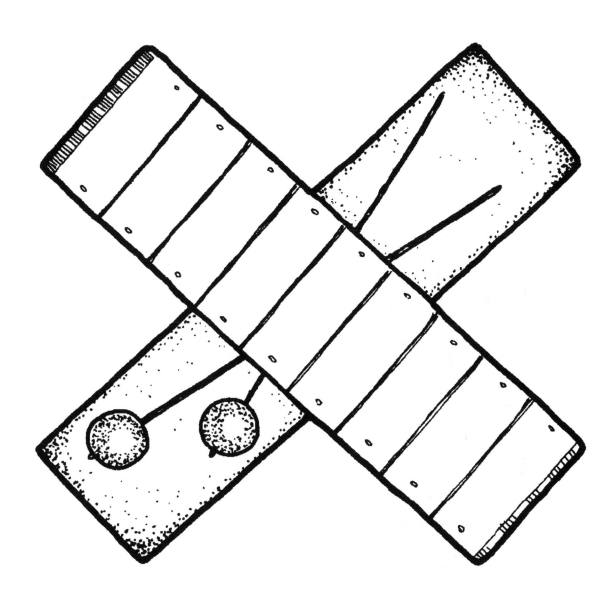

Teacher Notes

Teacher Notes

Teacher Notes

Teacher Notes

Teacher Notes

Teacher Notes

Teacher Notes

Made in the USA
Lexington, KY
06 March 2011